PRAYER QUOTES
inspiration to draw you closer to God

Kevin W. Shorter

Copyright 2018 Kevin Shorter

This publication is protected under the US Copyright Act of 1976 and all other applicable international, federal, state and local laws, and all rights are reserved, including resale rights: You are not allowed to give or sell this ebook to anyone else.

Please note that much of this ebook are quotes from others. Although the author has made every reasonable attempt to achieve complete accuracy of the quotes in this book through books, sermons, and online, he assumes no responsibility for errors or omissions. Also, you should use this information as you see fit, and at your own risk. Your particular situation may not be exactly suited to the examples illustrated here; in fact, it's likely that they won't be the same, and you should adjust your use of the information and recommendations accordingly.

No part of this book may be reproduced in any form without permission in writing from the author, except in the case of brief quotations where the author of the quote is cited. We'd appreciate a mention that you found the quote from this book.

Any trademarks, service marks, product names or named features are assumed to be the property of their respective owners, and are used only for reference. There is no implied endorsement if we use one of these terms.

Scripture quotations are taken from the Holy Bible, New International Version®, NIV® Copyright © 1973, 1978, 1984, 2011 by Biblica, Inc.® Used by permission. All rights reserved worldwide.

https://JosiahsCovenant.com
https://Prayer-Coach.com

Table of Contents

Introduction

1. Definition of Prayer — 7
Prayer Is... — 7
Prayer Is Not... — 14

2. Focus of Prayer — 21
Communication with God — 21
Entering God's Presence — 27
Fix Your Eyes on Him — 35
To Know God — 37

3. The Role of the Father — 41
God Our Father — 41
If God is For You... — 44
God's Desire in Prayer — 46
What God is Like — 51

4. The Role of the Son — 57
Jesus' Role in Prayer — 57
Fix Your Eyes On Jesus — 64

5. The Role of the Holy Spirit — 67
What the Holy Spirit Does — 67
Participating with the Holy Spirit — 71

6. Our Responsibility in Prayer — 77
The Role of Holiness — 77
The Role of Belief — 82
The Role of Faith — 89
The Role of Listening — 98
The Role of Obedience — 112
The Role of Thanksgiving — 118
The Role of Worship — 121
The Role of Forgiveness — 126
A Heart for God — 130

The Role of Perseverance	136
The Role of Passion	140
The Role of Poverty	147
The Role of Perspective	155
How to Pray	161
The Role of God's Word	168
The Role of the Secret Place	173

7. The Benefits of Prayer — 179

General Benefits	179
The Answers of Prayer	192
The Prayer of Intercession	201
Learning to Pray by Praying	212
The Importance of Praying Big	216
The Importance of Praying with Power	221

8. Why We Should Pray — 225

Personal Reasons	225
External Motivation	232
Obligation	239
Prayer Meetings	252
Spiritual Warfare	255
Revival	263

9. Additional Resources From Prayer Coach — 271

7 Tips to a Better Prayer Life	271
5 Ways to Find God	274
4 Ways to Effectively Pray for Others	276
2 Truths to Revolutionize Your Prayers	278

10. Prayer Lists — 281

10 Things to Pray for Your Husband	281
10 Things to Pray for Your Wife	282
10 Things to Pray for Your Marriage	283
10 Things to Pray for Your Kids	284
10 Things to Pray for Your Pastor	285

11. About Prayer Coach — 287

INTRODUCTION

In 2009 I started the Prayer Coach blog to help remove the burden off of prayer. Surveys of people in the church show that the number one area they would like to see improvement is in this area. It is the most vital aspect of our Christian walk, yet it is also the place we often feel we don't do enough.

Prayer is not hard; it's a conversation. People of every culture and of every age group can do this. We make it harder with misunderstandings of what God wants, who He is, and how He views us. The desire of this book is to gather nuggets of wisdom from people who have explored the depths of prayer and have left us nuggets of wisdom to take us farther in our journey. These quotes are intended to inspire us to continue pressing in and fanning the flame of passion to spend time with God.

This book has been categorized by topics to help the ease of use. However, as this is an electronic file, you can use the search function to find quotes by author or specific words. I understand there are differing views on prayer, so I did my best to include it all without filtering out my personal disagreements. You may also come across some with which you disagree - keep reading, with over 3,500 quotes you will find plenty that you will love and want to highlight.

At the back I have included a few articles from the Prayer Coach blog that I believe add to the goal of this book. The blog contains much more information with over 600 posts all designed to add life to your prayers. Please check us out on any of our online communities: prayer-coach.com, facebook.com/PrayerCoachBlog, or twitter.com/Prayer-Coach.

Thank you and enjoy.
Kevin Shorter

1

DEFINITION OF PRAYER

Prayer Is...

A prayer in its simplest definition is merely a wish turned Godward.
Phillip Brooks

Prayer is seeking the will of God and following it. Prayer is the way of getting God's will done on earth.
Adrian Rogers

Prayer is about knowing God - not manipulating Him.
Tom Blackaby

Prayer is us entering the communication of heaven. If we don't listen, we are butting in (Romans 8:26-28).
Kevin Shorter

Prayer is the greatest of all forces, because it honors God and brings him into active aid.
E.M. Bounds

Prayer is one of the easiest subjects to talk upon, but one of the hardest to practice.
Henrietta Mears

Prayer is God's business to which men can attend.
E.M. Bounds

Prayer is the link between finite man and the infinite purposes of God.
Pat Robertson

Prayer is where the action is.
John Wesley

And all true prayer promotes its own progress and increases our power to pray.
P.T. Forsyth

Prayer becomes the means by which the purposes of God are accomplished, so that in this way prayer changes things.
Matt Chandler

Prayer should not be merely an act, but an attitude of life.
Billy Graham

Prayer is essentially the expression of our heart longing for love.
Jeffrey Imbach

True prayer is an approach of the soul by the Spirit of God to the throne of God.
C.H. Spurgeon

We think of prayer as a preparation for work, or a calm after having done work, whereas prayer is the essential work. It is the supreme activity of everything that is noblest in our personality.
      Oswald Chambers

Prayer is how God gives us so many of the unimaginable things He has for us.
      Tim Keller

Prayer is the union of the believer's thought with the will of God.
      Watchman Nee

Prayer is essentially a partnership of the redeemed child of God working hand in hand with God toward the realization of His redemptive purposes on earth.
      Jack Hayford

Prayer completes the circuit of God's action in the world.
      Ben Jennings

Prayer is a shield to the soul.
      John Bunyan

Prayer is a sincere, sensible, affectionate pouring out of the heart and soul to God, through Christ, with the strength and assistance of the Holy Spirit, for such things as God has promised, or according to the Word, for the good of the church, with submission, in faith, to the will of God.
      John Bunyon

To pray, I think, does not mean to think about God in contrast to thinking about other things, or to spend time with God instead of spending time with other people. Rather, it means to think and live in the presence of God.
      Henri Nouwen

Prayer is no fitful, short-lived thing. It is no voice crying unheard and unheeded in the silence. It is a voice which goes into God's ear, and it lives as long as God's ear is open to holy pleas, as long as God's heart is alive to holy things.
      E.M. Bounds

Prayer is my chief work, and it is by means of it that I carry on the rest.
      Thomas Hooker

Prayer is the opening of the heart so we can receive all these good things that God has for us every day.
      Jim Cymbala

Prayer is about finding out what God wants to do and then asking Him to do it.
      Graham Cooke

Prayer is the wing on which the soul flies to heaven.
      Ambrose Bierce

Prayer is the nearest approach to God and the highest enjoyment of Him that we are capable of in this life.
      William Law

Without prayer religion in the soul would die, as without respiration temporal death would ensue. Prayer is the breath of the soul.
J.B. Johnson

When you pray you step into the operation of the Trinity.
Ben Jennings

Prayer is the central avenue God uses to transform us.
Richard Foster

Prayer is a moment of incarnation - God with us. God involved in the details of my life.
Paul Miller

To pray the Lord's Prayer is to participate in heaven's invasion of earth.
Darrell Johnson

Prayer is giving input for the outcome.
Bill Johnson

Prayer is a confession of creature weakness, yes, of helplessness. Prayer is the acknowledgment of our need and the spreading of it before God.
A.W. Pink

Prayer is God's appointed means for appropriating the blessings that are ours in Christ Jesus.
D.A. Carson

Prayer moves the hand that moves the world.
Henrietta Mears

True prayer is a lonely business.
Samuel Chadwick

Prayer is the exercise of drawing on the grace of God.
Oswald Chambers

Prayer is partnership with God in His planet-sized purposes, and includes the all things beside, as an important detail of the whole.
S.D. Gordon

Prayer is the conduit through which power from heaven is brought to earth.
O. Hallesby

Through prayer God gives humankind the dignity of limited causality.
Blaise Pascal

Prayer is the supreme instance of the hidden character of the Christian life.
Dietrich Bonhoeffer

True prayer is not asking God for what we want but for what He wants.
Unknown

Prayer is my response to His invitation to come boldly into a throne room and there to have discourse that alters the course of world history.
Bill Johnson

Prayer can do anything that God can do.
E.M. Bounds

Definitions of prayer are like definitions of a sunset; they don't capture the reality, dynamic, and beauty of the subject itself.
Stephen Olford

Prayer is the soul's breathing itself into the bosom of its heavenly Father.
Thomas Watson

The attributes of prayer must be: love of God, sincerity, and simplicity.
John of Kronstadt

To pray is to grasp heaven in one's arms, to embrace the Deity within one's soul, and to feel one's body made a temple of the Holy Spirit.
C.H. Spurgeon

Prayer is my declaration of dependence on God.
John Maxwell

Prayer honors God, acknowledges His being, exalts His power, adores His providence, secures His aid.
E.M. Bounds

Prayer is to religion what original research is to science.
P.T. Forsyth

Prayer is the vital breath of the Christian; not the thing that makes him alive, but the evidence that he is alive.
Oswald Chambers

Prayer is the core of the day. Take prayer out, and the day would collapse ...
Amy Carmichael

Prayer is the native movement of the spiritual life that receives its meaning and its soul only in Eternity, that works in the style and scale of Eternity, owns its principles, and speaks its speech.
P.T. Forsyth

Prayer is the atmosphere of revelation, in the strict and central sense of that word. It is the climate in which God's manifestation bursts open into inspiration.
P.T. Forsyth

Truly he who prays puts, not God, but his own spiritual life to the test!
The Kneeling Christian

Prayer is an exchange. We leave our burdens, worries and sin in the hands of God. We come away with oil of joy and the garment of praise.
F.B. Meyer

Prayer is God's plan to supply man's great and continuous need with God's great and continuous abundance.
E.M. Bounds

Prayer is knowing the heart of God and engaging Him on that level.
Kevin Shorter

Prayer is the place where we find the plot lines for our lives.
Stephen Roach

Prayer, like everything else in the Christian life, is for God's glory and for our benefit, in that order.
R.C. Sproul

Prayer is the net by which we catch the thoughts and ideas of God.
Kevin Shorter

In the morning, prayer is the key that opens to us the treasures of God's mercies and blessings; in the evening, it is the key that shuts us up under His protection and safeguard.
Billy Graham

Prayer is a process of recognizing God's power and plan for our lives.
Daniel McCasland

Prayer and theology both deal with God, but from different perspectives. Theology, like a telescope, views the distant stars of His qualities. Prayer, like a space vehicle, moves us among His qualities. Theology studies God and prayer engages Him. Both are adventuresome. Both necessary.
Ben Jennings

Prayer, in one phase of its operation, is a disinfectant and a preventive. It purifies the air; it destroys the contagion of evil.
E.M. Bounds

At its deepest level, prayer is fellowship with God: enjoying His company, waiting upon His will, thanking Him for His mercies… listening in the silence for what He has to say to us.
Billy Graham

Prayer is first of all listening to God. It's openness. God is always speaking; he's always doing something.
Henri Nouwen

Prayer at its best is living with mind and heart utterly open to God.
Albert D. Belden

Prayer is simple, as simple as a child making known its wants to its parents.
Oswald Chambers

Prayer is an honest exchange between people who are doing things together. God and I are working together.
Dallas Willard

Prayer is a rising up and a drawing near to God in mind and in heart, and in spirit.
Alexander Whyte

Prayer is more than something you do; it is something God does through you.
Ben Jennings

Prayer is like time exposure of the soul to God, in which process the image of God is formed on the soul.
Unknown

Prayer is an end to isolation. It is living our daily life with someone; with Him who alone can deliver us from solitude.
Georges Lefevre

Prayer is designed to adjust you to God's will, not to adjust God to your will.
Henry Blackaby

Prayer is the slender nerve that moveth the muscle of Omnipotence.
C.H. Spurgeon

Prayer is simply asking God to do for us what He has promised us He will do if we ask Him.
Gerhard Tersteegen

Prayer is a coming to God, telling Him my need, committing my way unto the Lord, and leaving Him to deal with it as seemeth Him best.
A.W. Pink

Prayer is our lifeline to God.
Billy Graham

Prayer is an investment. The time you dedicate to prayer isn't lost; it will return dividends far greater than what a few moments spent on a task ever could.
Charles Swindoll

Prayer is the rope that pulls God and man together. But, it doesn't pull God down to us: It pulls us up to Him.
Billy Graham

Prayer is thinking deeply about something in the presence of God.
Wayne Cordeiro

Prayer is the expression of human dependence on God.
Henrietta Mears

Prayer is a great weapon, a rich treasure, a wealth that is never exhausted, an undisturbed refuge.
John Chrysostom

The purpose of all prayer is to find God's will and to make that will our prayer.
Catherine Marshall

The Bible is a letter God has sent to us; prayer is a letter we send to Him.
Matthew Henry

Prayer is the link that connects us with God.
A.B. Simpson

To pray means to stop expecting from God the same small-mindedness, which you discover in yourself. To pray is to walk in the full light of God and to simply say, without holding back, "I am human and you are God."
Henri Nouwen

PRAY, v. To ask that the laws of the universe be annulled in behalf of a single petitioner confessedly unworthy.
Ambrose Bierce

The best and sweetest flowers of paradise God gives to His people when they are upon their knees. Prayer is the gate of heaven.
      Thomas Brooks

Prayer is a spiritual law which cooperates with the mind of God. It has more in it than merely petition. It clothes itself in reality and power, with the force of God Himself. It is an attitude of spirit and mind. Language is secondary in true prayer.
      John Gossner

Our prayer is an act of faith - a requirement of our God. Such a mystery - since before a word is on our tongue He knows it.
      Lori Sedlak

Prayer, like faith, obtains promises, enlarges their operation, and adds to the measure of their results.
      E.M. Bounds

Prayer is the hand that takes to ourselves the blessings that God has already provided in His Son.
      R.A. Torrey

Prayer is finding out what the Father wants, then standing in Christ before Him and asking Him to do it by the power of the Holy Spirit.
      Graham Cooke

A godly man is a praying man. As soon as grace is poured in, prayer is poured out. Prayer is the soul's traffic with Heaven; God comes down to us by His Spirit, and we go up to Him by prayer.
      Thomas Watson

What is prayer? It is a sign of spiritual life.
      The Kneeling Christian

Prayer is exhaling the spirit of man and inhaling the spirit of God.
      Edwin Keith

Prayers are prophesies. The transcript of your prayers becomes the script of your life.
      Mark Batterson

Prayer is indeed a continuous violent action of the spirit as it is lifted up to God. This is comparable to that of a ship going against the stream.
      Martin Luther

Prayer is the pulse of the renewed soul; and the constancy of its beat is the test and measure of the spiritual life.
      Octavius Winslow

Prayer is as vast and mighty as God, because He has committed Himself to answer it. All that God is, and all that God has, is at the disposal of prayer!
      Etienne Piek

Prayer serves as an edge and border to preserve the web of life from unraveling.
      Robert Hall

Prayer is sitting calmly in God's lap and placing our hands in his steering wheel. He handles the speed and ensures safe arrival.
Max Lucado

Prayer is the child's approach, the child's plea, the child's right.
E.M. Bounds

All that true prayer seeks is God Himself, for with Him we get all we need.
The Kneeling Christian

Prayer is the rope up in the belfry: we pull it, and it rings the bell up in heaven.
Christmas Evans

Prayer is nothing but the breathing that out before the Lord, that was first breathed into us by the Spirit of the Lord.
Thomas Brooks

Prayer is the breath of the new creature.
Richard Baxter

For prayer is nothing else than being on terms of friendship with God.
Mother Teresa

Prayer is the way we work our way out of the comfortable but cramped world of self and into the spacious world of God.
Eugene Peterson

True prayer is an awareness of our helpless need and an acknowledgment of divine adequacy.
Ray Stedman

Prayer is the easiest and hardest of all things; the simplest and the sublimest; the weakest and the most powerful; its results lie outside the range of human possibilities; they are limited only by the omnipotence of God.
E.M. Bounds

Prayer Is Not…

Prayer is not to inform "poor, misinformed God" about how bad your situation is!
Andrew Wommack

Prayer is not everything, but everything is by prayer.
Armin Gesswein

Prayer isn't convincing God to do our will but aligning ourselves with His will, which requires overcoming evil with good.
Rick Warren

Prayer is not conquering God's reluctance, but taking hold of God's willingness.
Phillip Brooks

Prayer is not a fruitless exercise that God asked us to perform to determine whether or not we're faithful. Prayer is the vehicle that releases God to move in the earth!
Joseph Cameneti

God is not a piñata, and prayer is not a stick.
Mark Driscoll

Prayer is not an exercise, it is the life.
Oswald Chambers

Prayer is not a mystical experience of a few special people, but an aggressive act in the face of impossibility an act that may be performed by anyone who will accept the challenge.
Jack Hayford

Prayer is not monologue, but dialogue; God's voice is its most essential part.
Andrew Murray

It is not, of course, that prayer changes God, or awakens in Him purposes of love and compassion which He has not already felt.
Hannah Hurnard

Prayer is not logical, it is a mysterious moral working of the Holy Spirit.
Oswald Chambers

Prayer is not designed to inform God, but to give man a sight of his misery; to humble his heart, to excite his desire, to inflame his faith, to animate his hope, to raise his soul from earth to heaven.
Adam Clarke

Prayer is not mere wishing. It is asking—with a will. Our will goes into it. It is energy.
P.T. Forsyth

Prayer is not the FOUNDATION of your work. Foundations are stationary. Real prayer MOVES you. It is the ENGINE.
Steven Furtick

Prayer is not so much an act as it is an attitude—an attitude of dependency, dependency upon God.
A.W. Pink

Prayer is not a natural activity. It has been well said that prayer is stupid when viewed in the purely human realm.
David Jeremiah

Prayer is not flight; prayer is power. Prayer does not deliver a man from some terrible situation; prayer enables a man to face and to master the situation.
William Barclay

Prayer is not only asking, but an attitude of mind which produces the atmosphere in which asking is perfectly natural. 'Ask and it shall be given you.'
Oswald Chambers

Prayer is not our using of God; it more often puts us in the position where God can use us.

Billy Graham

Jesus had to reveal what prayer was not, before He taught what it is.

Andrew Wommack

Prayer is not to get the goods. It is to enjoy the one who is good.

Jon Courson

The essence of prayer does not consist in asking God for something but in opening our hearts to God, in speaking with Him, and living with Him in perpetual communion. Prayer is continual abandonment to God. Prayer does not mean asking God for all kinds of things we want; it is rather the desire for God Himself, the only Giver of Life, Prayer is not asking, but union with God. Prayer is not a painful effort to gain from God help in the varying needs of our lives. Prayer is the desire to possess God Himself, the Source of all life. The true spirit of prayer does not consist in asking for blessings, but in receiving Him who is the giver of all blessings, and in living a life of fellowship with Him.

Sadhu Sundar Singh

Prayer is not a preparation for the battle; it is the battle!

Leonard Ravenhill

Prayer is not given us as a burden to be borne, or an irksome duty to fulfill, but to be a joy and power to which there is no limit.

The Kneeling Christian

Prayer, if it be done as a task, is not prayer.

John Mason

Prayer is the most abused part of the Christian life today. Misguided understandings about prayer mess more people up spiritually than anything else out there!

Andrew Wommack

Prayer is not overcoming God's reluctance; it is laying hold of God's willingness.

George Müller

Prayer is not eloquence, but earnestness; not the definition of helplessness, but the feeling of it; not figures of speech, but earnestness of soul.

Hannah More

A prayer is not holy chewing gum and you don't have to see how far you can stretch it.

Lionel Blue

Prayer is not made so that God can find out what we need... God wants us to pray because prayer expresses our trust in God and is a means whereby our trust in him can increase.

Wayne Grudem

If some people couldn't complain they won't have a prayer life.

Kris Vallotton

Prayer is not like a good recipe: simply follow a set of mechanical directions and everything turns out right in the end.
D.A. Carson

Prayer is not monologue, but dialogue. God's voice in response to mine is its most essential part.
Andrew Murray

Nowadays Christians appear to treat prayer as a means to accomplish their aims and ideas. If they possessed just a little deeper understanding, they would recognize that prayer is but man uttering to God what is God's will.
Watchman Nee

Prayer isn't designed to get God to do our will; prayer is designed so that we can stand in His presence and know what His will is, and submit to it.
Henry Blackaby

Prayer is not earning God's favor; it enters you into the favor He already has for you.
Kevin Shorter

Prayer is not overcoming God's reluctance; it is adjusting to God's willingness.
Ivan French

Poor self-esteem will transform our prayers from conversations to plea bargains.
Kevin Shorter

Prayer is not the cunning art of using God, subjecting Him to one's selfish ends in an effort to get out of Him what you want.
F.J. Huegel

Prayer is often conceived to be little more than a technique for self-advancement, a heavenly method for achieving earthly success.
A.W. Tozer

Prayer is not something we do at a specific time, but something we do all the time.
Richard Owen Roberts

Prayer is not asking for what you think you want, but asking to be changed in ways you can't imagine.
Kathleen Norris

Prayer is not the least we can do; it is the most.
John Blanchard

Our biggest mistake is to think that a time of prayer is different from any other time. It is all one.
Brother Lawrence

Prayer is not a question of altering things externally, but of working wonders in a man's disposition.
Oswald Chambers

Prayer is not a painful effort to gain from God help in the varying needs of life. Prayer is the desire to possess God Himself.
Sundar Singh

The purpose of prayer is not to notify God but to express our trust, our faith, our expectation, and our heart desire.
Watchman Nee

Prayer is not an escape from responsibility; it is our response to God's ability.
Warren Wiersbe

Prayer is not what is done by us, but rather what is done by the Holy Spirit in us.
Henri Nouwen

Prayer is not about getting what you want, it's about getting what God wants for you.
Ed Young

When we become too glib in prayer we are most surely talking to ourselves.
A.W. Tozer

The value of persistence in prayer is not that God will hear us, but that we will finally hear God.
William McGill

Prayer shouldn't be casual or sporadic, dictated only by the needs of the moment. Prayer should be as much a part of our lives as breathing.
Billy Graham

Prayer is not just asking. It is listening for God's orders. Nothing will drive us to our knees quicker than trouble.
Billy Graham

Prayer does not fit us for the greater work; prayer is the greater work.
Oswald Chambers

Prayer is not getting things from God, that is the most initial stage; prayer is getting into perfect communion with God; I tell Him what I know He knows in order that I may get to know it as He does.
Oswald Chambers

God cannot be persuaded to alter His Word nor talked into answering selfish prayer.
A.W. Tozer

Prayer is not a hard requirement-it is the natural duty of a creature to its creator, the simplest homage that human need can pay to divine liberality.
C.H. Spurgeon

Is the Son of God praying in me, or am I dictating to Him?....Prayer is not simply getting things from God, that is a most initial form of prayer; prayer is getting into perfect communion with God. If the Son of God is formed in us by regeneration, He will press forward in front of our common sense and change our attitude to the things about which we pray.
Oswald Chambers

Prayer is not a collection of balanced phrases; it is the pouring out of the soul.
Samuel Chadwick

Prayer is something you do instead of worry; it's not something we do with worry.
Joyce Meyer

Our Lord did not say it was wrong to pray in the corners of the street, but He did say it was wrong to have the motive to be seen of men.
Oswald Chambers

Prayer is not overcoming God's reluctance, but laying hold of His willingness.
Martin Luther

Prayer is not a way of making use of God; prayer is a way of offering ourselves to God in order that He should be able to make use of us.
William Barclay

Prayer is not you trying to win back God's favor; it is you participating in the favor He has for you.
Kevin Shorter

2

FOCUS OF PRAYER

Communication with God

Just like we read the Bible or have fellowship with other believers, walking in creativity can be one more way you develop friendship and connection with God.
Allison Shorter

If prayer stands as the place where God and human beings meet, then I must learn about prayer. Most of my struggles in the Christian life circle around the same two themes: why God doesn't act the way we want God to, and why I don't act the way God wants me to. Prayer is the precise point where those themes converge.
Phillip Yancey

God wants to take what you discern and talk to Him about it.
Shawn Bolz

In prayer, speak like God is there because He is!
Jay Harris

Pray not to be seen of men but to be heard of God.
John Mason

God communicates himself to us in proportion as we are prepared to receive him.
Madame Guyon

Start today by practicing constant conversation with God and continual mediation on his Word. Prayer lets you speak to God; mediation lets God speak to you.
Rick Warren

The point of prayer is not to get answers from God, but to have perfect and complete oneness with Him.
Oswald Chambers

Prayer to God is like a child's conversation with his father. It is natural for a child to ask his father for the things he needs.
Billy Graham

Prayer does not mean simply to pour out one's heart. It means rather to find the way to God and to speak with Him, whether the heart is full or empty.
Dietrich Bonhoeffer

You are going to go somewhere so how much better to have a direction that has been set by communion with the divine Center.
Richard Foster

How can you keep your mind from wandering when you pray? Remember what you are doing: talking to God. If you had the opportunity to talk with the president, I doubt if your mind would wander. [We] have the privilege of talking to someone far greater: the King of kings!
Billy Graham

In place of reading the news this morning, couldn't you get just a few thoughts of God while eating your grapefruit?
A.W. Tozer

You have permission to be your true self! God relates to your true self not who you think you are!
Kevin Shorter

Talk to Him in prayer of all your wants, your troubles, even of the weariness you feel in serving Him. You cannot speak too freely, too trustfully to Him.
François Fénelon

The purpose of prayer is the maintenance of fitness in an ideal relationship with God amid conditions which ought not to be merely ideal but really actual. ...by prayer we lay hold on God and He unites us into His consciousness.
Oswald Chambers

The greatest use of your words is prayer. Talk to God about EVERYTHING, all the time. Maintain a running conversation.
Rick Warren

Faith engages the person and promises of God and rests upon them with perfect assurance.
A.W. Tozer

Because God wants us to have a strong identity, He talks through His nature more than He does through direct words.
Shawn Bolz

Prayer is keeping company with God.
Clement of Alexandria

It is no use to ask God with factitious earnestness for A when our whole mind is in reality filled with the desire for B. We must lay before him what is in us, not what ought to be in us.
C.S. Lewis

To despise the world is the way to enjoy heaven; and blessed are they who delight to converse with God by prayer.
John Bunyon

Saul was always a praying man. Paul connected with God. Do we know the difference?
Kevin Shorter

Prayer is talking with God and telling Him you love Him, conversing with God about all the things that are important in life, both large and small, and being assured that He is listening.
C. Neil Strait

God wants us to talk to him as to a friend or father—authentically, reverently, personally, earnestly.
Bill Hybels

Whenever the insistence is on the point that God answers prayer, we are off the track. The meaning of prayer is that we get hold of God, not of the answer.
Oswald Chambers

If you're a Christian and you're bored, then you might want to check the distance between yourself and the Master.
Bill Johnson

My longings are best met when, in prayer, I simply let my heart beat in time with the Lord's.
Joni Eareckson Tada

Prayer pulls the rope down below and the great bell rings above in the ears of God. He who communicates with heaven is the man who grasps the rope boldly and pulls continuously with all his might.
C.H. Spurgeon

Prayer keeps us in constant communion with God, which is the goal of our entire believing lives. Without a doubt, prayerless lives are powerless lives, and prayerful lives are powerful lives; but, believe it or not, the ultimate goal God has for us is not power but personal intimacy with Him.
Beth Moore

Without this intimate relationship there can be no real power.
Morris Cerrulo

No man can expect to make progress in holiness who is not often and long alone with God.
Andrew Murray

The right way to pray, then, is any way that allows us to communicate with God.
Colleen Townsend Evans

Asking God what He wants you to pray about is the first step to a powerful prayer life.
Kevin Shorter

To have power with God through prayer, you must live in unbroken fellowship with God.
Morris Cerrulo

So if God says pray without ceasing, then He's willing to communicate without ceasing.
John Bevere

The activities we do for God are secondary. Above all else, God is looking for people who long for communication with Him.
Erwin Lutzer

Prayer invites me to lower defenses and present the self that no other

person fully knows to a God who already knows.
Phillip Yancey

When men only talk about God instead of with God they are manifesting a deteriorated faith, for the purpose of all faith is to bring us into direct, personal, vital touch with God.
Ray Stedman

God loves the sound of your voice. He doesn't hide when you call. He hears your prayers.
Max Lucado

He is God, He holds the key and that's just the deal. Sometimes, He is more interested in the conversation than in giving the solution.
Misty Edwards

There is not in the world a kind of life more sweet and delightful than that of a continual conversation with God.
Brother Lawrence

Prayer ushers us into perpetual communion with the Father.
Richard Foster

True prayer is neither a mere mental exercise nor a vocal performance. It is a spiritual commerce with the Creator of heaven and earth.
C.H. Spurgeon

Remember that you can pray any time, anywhere. Washing dishes, digging ditches, working in the office, in the shop, on the athletic field, even in prison - you can pray and know God hears!
Billy Graham

I can tell you that God is alive because I talked with him this morning.
Billy Graham

Real prayer is communion with God, not just praying words.
John G. Lake

God will not forces us into a conversation, but if we talk to Him, He will talk back.
IHOP

You can't go in faith where you haven't gone in intimacy.
Bill Johnson

Many souls who are called to the enjoyment of God himself and not merely to the gifts of God, spend all their lives in pursuing and in feeding on little consolations.
Madame Guyon

What if prayer is not praying towards God but praying with God?
Graham Cooke

Communion is deeper than theology.
Samuel Chadwick

God welcomes our prayers. He is much more concerned about our hearts than our eloquence.
Billy Graham

The goal of prayer is the ear of God.
E.M. Bounds

We ought to act with God in the greatest simplicity, speak to Him frankly and plainly, and implore His assistance in our affairs.
Brother Lawrence

For the sun meets not the springing bud that stretches towards him with half that certainty as God, the source of all good, communicates Himself to the soul that longs to partake of Him.
William Law

I have learnt to love the darkness of sorrow; there you see the brightness of His face.
Madame Guyon

Prayer has features in common with all relationships that matter.
Phillip Yancey

It belongs to the very idea and nature of man to be in communion with God.
Unknown

Prayer is nothing more than turning our heart toward God and receiving in turn His love.
Madame Guyon

Speak as naturally and as easily as you would to a friend, since God is just that.
James Coburn

There can be no authentic relationship with God for people who prefer a mediator over and above personal encounters.
Bill Johnson

Discernment is merely God's conversation starter.
Shawn Bolz

The best way to get to know a new friend is to spend time with him, to talk with him. And the best way to get to know God better is to spend time with Him, to talk to Him. That is what prayer is — simply talking to God.
Stephen I. Spananoudis

I want constantly to be aware of Thy overshadowing Presence and to hear Thy speaking Voice.
A.W. Tozer

Prayer is not a thing you "say" but a conversation you have.
Jay Harris

Prayer is not artful monologue of voice uplifted from the son; it is love's tender dialogue between the soul and God.
John Richard Moreland

There are things that God only tells friends.
Bill Johnson

Prayer is spiritual communication between man and God, a two-way relationship in which man should not only talk to God but also listen to Him.
Billy Graham

Prayer connects us to God, fasting disconnects us from the world.
Stovall Weems

If you will go on the journey "with God" in understanding the prayer you are asking for, you will have much more intimacy than if He just gave you the answer.
Brian Clark

The unembarrassed interchange of love between God and redeemed men is the throbbing heart of the NT.
A.W. Tozer

Prayer is continuing a conversation that God has started through his Word and his grace, which eventually becomes a full encounter with him.
Tim Keller

I pray in astonished belief that God desires an ongoing relationship.
Phillip Yancey

I'd like to propose to you that revelation is not the product of laborious study, but it is the fruit of friendship with God.
Kris Vallotton

Prayer is not a discourse. It is a form of life, the life with God. That is why it is not confined to the moment of verbal statement.
Jacques Ellul

Prayer opens the channel between a soul and God; prayerlessness closes it.
Alan Redpath

Although we are to come before the Lord in an attitude of intimacy, there is still an element of separation.
R.C. Sproul

It's one thing to pray, but it's another thing to be heard.
John Bevere

Ask God to give you a greater hunger for Himself and a deeper desire for His fellowship. Then be honest about whatever is keeping you from prayer, and ask God to help you deal with it.
Billy Graham

Though in its beginnings prayer is so simple that the feeblest child can pray, yet it is at the same time highest and holiest work to which man can rise. It is fellowship with the unseen and most Holy One.
Unknown

Prayer is simply a two-way conversation between you and God.
Billy Graham

There is a great difference between praying to God about something and mentioning it to Him in passing.
John Blanchard

God wants us to pray, and He wants to hear our prayers - not because we are worthy, but because He is merciful.
Martin Luther

Let it be your business every day, in the secrecy of the inner chamber, to meet the holy God.
Andrew Murray

In prayer, do you converse with God or do you just leave Him a Voice Mail?
Jay Harris

Time with God leads us to make requests of Him.
Kevin Shorter

The first rule of right prayer is to have our heart and mind framed as becomes those who are entering into conversation with God.
John Calvin

Who will pray must know and understand that prayer is an earnest and familiar talking with God.
John Knox

The door of heaven is always open for the prayers of God's people.
Thomas Watson

Sometimes we need to say something to give God something to work with.
Steve Backlund

Entering God's Presence

God is always present but He is often not apparent.
Chuck Davis

The goal of prayer is to live all of my life and speak all of my words in the joyful awareness of the presence of God.
John Ortberg

God rescues and brings us into a 'spacious place' where we can stand 'surprised to be loved' (Ps 18:19 MSG).
Kathryn Scott

When I allow His presence to consume me, I surrender myself so completely to His will that my desires begin to line up with His.
Beni Johnson

When we pursue kingdom principles above His presence, we are looking for the kingdom without a king.
Bill Johnson

As you engage in steadfast prayer, you are building a habitation for God's will to be done completely in your life as a living temple of His Spirit.
Lance Wallnau

The goal of prayer is the ear of God, a goal that can only be reached by patient and continued and continuous waiting upon Him, pouring out our heart to Him and permitting Him to speak to us. Only by so doing can we expect to know Him, and as we come to know Him better we shall spend more time in His presence and find that presence a constant and ever-increasing delight.
E.M. Bounds

And surely it should be enough to restrain all 'lightness' and constrain an unceasing 'earnestness' did we apprehend the 'greatness of the Being' before whom we plead.
C.H. Spurgeon

True and absolute freedom is only found in the presence of God.
A.W. Tozer

Prayer revitalizes us with the atmosphere of God's presence.
Stephen Olford

Increased dependence on His presence can only result in His supernatural invasion into your circumstances.
Bill Johnson

How can we pray to Him without being with Him?
Brother Lawrence

There is a holy place where the divine presence becomes our shelter.
Francis Frangipane

His Presence is what you want, not results. Results happen in the Presence.
Allison Shorter

When we become what God meant us to be all along, we leave a wake of His presence behind us.
Allison Vesterfelt

Prayers of worshippers are powerful because they hang out in God's presence.
Kevin Shorter

What we need most is to be totally dependent on God showing up. We need His pure presence.
Heidi Baker

Worship is about encounter – coming into God's presence.
Jack Hayford

If we would just daily take the time to spend time in His presence, then He would so pour out His love on our hearts.
Trisha Cwir

Meet with the Lord personally and daily so that when you go into your day, it's with a sense of His presence.
James MacDonald

Lord, unless You break the glass and rescue my heart it will always be window shopping for your presence.
Kevin Adams

This is how the Master teaches us to pray: He brings us into the Father's living presence.
Andrew Murray

The ship of prayer may sail through all temptations, doubts and fears, straight up to the throne of God.
C.H. Spurgeon

So when we sing, 'Draw me nearer, nearer, blessed Lord,' we are not thinking of the nearness of place, but of the nearness of relationship. It is for increasing degrees of awareness that we pray, for a more perfect consciousness of the divine Presence. We need never shout across the spaces to an absent God. He is nearer than our own soul, closer than our most secret thoughts.
A.W. Tozer

It is not necessary to maintain a conversation when we are in the presence of God. We can come into His presence and rest our weary souls in quiet contemplation of Him. Our groanings, which cannot be uttered, rise to Him and tell Him better than words how dependent we are upon Him.
O. Hallesby

I want the presence of God Himself, or I don't want anything at all to do with religion... I want all that God has or I don't want any.
A.W. Tozer

Real prayer is simply being in the presence of God. When I am in trouble, and when I go to my friend, I don't want anything from him except himself. I just want to be with him for a time, to feel his comradeship, his concern, his caring round me and about me, and then to go out to a world warmer because I spent an hour with him. It must be that way with me and God. I must go to Him simply for Himself.
William Barclay

Ten minutes spent in the presence of Christ every day, aye, two minutes, will make the whole day different.
Henry Drummond

Prayer is nothing else than a sense of God's presence.
Brother Lawrence

We need to hear the 'sound from Heaven' that God is with us.
Jim Cymbala

Our spirit is strengthened in the presence of God.
Kevin Shorter

Christians pray as they feel; and in prayer they feel themselves in the presence of God, the Hearer of prayer, and the Searcher of hearts.
J.B. Johnson

Effective prayer is not getting what you ask, but entering into the throne room of God.
Kevin Shorter

As we see ourselves as God sees us, we are freed up from striving and we begin to simply enjoy His Presence.
Allison Shorter

All in God draws me; everything within and around drives me to the throne of grace.
Adolph Saphir

Prayer at its holiest moment is the entering into God [where] miracles seem tame... by comparison.
A.W. Tozer

Many of the greatest realities God has for us are gifts He has hidden in His heart. To obtain these blessings, God must be sought.
Francis Frangipane

Prayer is the very atmosphere of God's house.
Lance Wallnau

We can never expect to grow in the likeness of our Lord unless we follow His example and give more time to communion with the Father. A revival of real praying would produce a spiritual revolution.
E.M. Bounds

God doesn't send you anywhere that He doesn't want to go with you.
Kevin Shorter

If you are a God-seeker, you should expect to see the glory of God!
Francis Frangipane

If we would pray aright, the first thing we should do is to see to it that we really get an audience with God, that we really get into His very presence. Before a word of petition is offered, we should have the definite consciousness that we are talking to God, and should believe that He is listening and is going to grant the thing that we ask of Him.
R.A. Torrey

Once we draw near to God and prepared a place for Him, He comes. And when He comes, all things are now possible.
Kevin Shorter

I try to live in such a way that nothing gets bigger than my awareness of God's presence on my life.
Bill Johnson

Prayer is coming into perfect fellowship and oneness with God.
Oswald Chambers

The greatest privilege God gives to you is the freedom to approach Him at any time.
Wesley Duewel

The purpose of prayer is to reveal the presence of God equally present, all the time, in every condition.
Oswald Chambers

Always remember that even one brief encounter with His Presence can change destiny.
Tommy Tenney

We need only to realize that God is close to us and to turn to Him at every moment.
Brother Lawrence

Prayer is our way of entering into the happiness of God himself.
Tim Keller

You don't pray for the presence of God. You practice it. We are practicing the presence that we believe is present.
Graham Cooke

I don't get there by stress or striving; it is simply by surrendering to His presence.
Beni Johnson

Prayer opens heaven to us. Prayer brings us into the dimension of reality, as against the artificiality of the world outside.
Stephen Olford

Each day presents a new opportunity to experience God...this is a sacred expectation for us.
A.W. Tozer

As soon as you come in the presence of God, remain in respectful silence for a little while... Simply Enjoy God.
Madame Guyon

The closer the soul draws to God, the further she travels from her own wishes. In this way the influence on her life from her passions diminishes. The soul should have a pure and disinterested love, as it seeks nothing from God, but only to please him, and to do his will.
Madame Guyon

It is our privilege to bring the whole of our finite existence into the glory of His infinite presence.
R.C. Sproul

Prayer is the way we escape the gravitational pull of the flesh and enter God's orbit.
Mark Batterson

We must be focused and sitting in a place of peace, in heavenly places, and praying from a place of peace. Find God, and you find peace. Find peace, and you will find the answer.
Beni Johnson

Man was designed for the presence of God, not for His absence.
Francois du Toit

They must learn how to close their human eyes and how to open their spiritual eyes. Then they should concentrate on building up their inner spiritual being and, through their trust in their God who lives in them, come into the divine presence.
Madame Guyon

Shut the world out, withdraw from all worldly thoughts and occupations, and shut yourself in alone with God, to pray to Him in secret. Let this be your chief object in prayer, to realize the presence of your heavenly Father.
Andrew Murray

Open the window of prayer and invoke the presence of God in your world.
Max Lucado

God is near at hand when you do approach Him in prayer.
Octavius Winslow

Principles without Presence leads to Religion. Christian principles are to help us stay in God's presence to grow Relationship.
Kevin Shorter

Prayer is the window that God has placed in the walls of our world. Leave it shut and the world is a cold, dark house. But throw back the curtains and see His light. Open the window and hear His voice. Open the window of prayer and invoke the presence of God in your world.
Max Lucado

No prayer is complete without presence.
Mevlana Rumi

Men full of the Spirit can look right into heaven.
D.L. Moody

God is already present in my life and all around me; prayer offers the chance to attend and respond to that presence.
Phillip Yancey

An intimate encounter with Jesus is the most transforming experience of human existence.
John Eldredge

The purpose of God's wondrous stories is to draw you into the passionate pursuit of more of His presence.
Bill Johnson

To pray is to mount on eagle's wings above the clouds and get into the clear heaven where God dwells.
C.H. Spurgeon

It is so important that our kids not only hear about God but they should experience Him.
Kris Vallotton

There come times when I have nothing more to tell God. If I were to continue to pray in words, I would have to repeat what I have already said. At such times it is wonderful to say to God, "May I be in Thy presence, Lord? I have nothing more to say to Thee, but I do love to be in Thy presence."
O. Hallesby

The ideas we have of the divine being fall infinitely short of what he really is. A living faith in his presence is all we need.
Madame Guyon

Oh, to be known at the throne.
> Samuel Chadwick

God said He would never leave you nor forsake you. That means you have the presence of God whether you feel it or not!
> Graham Cooke

We experience the measure of presence we are willing to jealously guard.
> Bill Johnson

Prayer is actually a real encounter with the untamable God and Father of our Lord Jesus Christ, and therefore our experience of it should reflect the power, mystery, and even risk of entering into relationship with the Lord of the universe.
> Matt Woodley

[Intimacy with God] can be such union as make miracles seem tame and [answers] appear short of wonderful in contrast.
> A.W. Tozer

If you want the presence of God, you've got to learn to be present with God.
> Graham Cooke

I know when I am really in that place where I feel completely connected to God because I have an instant peace.
> Beni Johnson

Prophecy makes people feel what it might feel like in heaven, as if they have some of the hope that is in eternity now.
> Shawn Bolz

You need not cry very loud; he is nearer to us than we are aware of.
> Brother Lawrence

We are not at liberty in calling upon God to follow the suggestions of our own mind and will, but must seek God only in so far as He has invited us to approach Him.
> John Calvin

It's impossible to talk about God and Him not be present.
> Juan Carlos Montemayor Jr.

The Lord invites you into a relationship with Him that involves you loving yourself as much as He loves you.
> Graham Cooke

We should establish ourselves in a sense of God's presence by continually conversing with Him. It is a shameful thing to quit His conversation to think of trifles and fooleries.
> Brother Lawrence

The central significance of prayer is not in the things that happen as results, but in the deepening intimacy and unhurried communion with God at His central throne of control in order to discover a sense of God's need in order to call on God's help to meet that need.
> E.M. Bounds

Trying to be happy without a sense of God's presence is like trying to have a bright day without the sun.
A.W. Tozer

If fear comes, we must step back, take a breath of heaven, and find our peace and pray from there.
Beni Johnson

Communion with God that is what brings life more than anything.
Trisha Cwir

One of the sweetest lessons I ever learned about prayer is this: the prayer that gets to heaven is the prayer that starts in heaven. Our job is just to close the circuit.
Adrian Rogers

For what shall we do when we wake one day to find we have lost touch with our heart and with it the very refuge where God's presence resides?
John Eldredge

I believe that God's people have had it with cheap imitations...they long for the reality of God's presence.
A.W. Tozer

Prayer is practicing the presence of God, not mastering the mechanics of how to come to God.
Mark Water

We are not praying from a place of a slave, but we are seating in heavenly places. We already have the victory.
Matt Peterson

It's possible to go through life without touching Heaven as much as the Lord desires you to. Pay attention to the wonder of it all.
Graham Cooke

If the heart wanders or is distracted, bring it back to the point quite gently and replace it tenderly in its Master's presence. And even if you did nothing during the whole of your hour but bring your heart back and place it again in our Lord's presence, though it went away every time you brought it back, your hour will be very well employed.
St. Francis de Sales

We cannot merely pray down the presence of God, but we will attract Him by the quality of our relationships.
Graham Cooke

My destiny is to go to heaven, my responsibility is to bring heaven.
Bill Johnson

Connecting to what is going on in heaven fills the heart with what it is created to hold.
Mark Peterson

Fix Your Eyes on Him

We have to pray with our eyes on God, not on the difficulties.
Oswald Chambers

Prayer only works when the channels are open.
Woodrow Kroll

The presence of God is not a place to bypass your emotions — It's a place to process them.
Steven Furtick

To enter the gaze of the Holy is never to be the same.
Richard Foster

You can see God from anywhere if your mind is set to love and obey Him.
A.W. Tozer

We will always reflect the nature of the world we are most aware of.
Bill Johnson

We are called to be God's transmitters, to be completely separated from all thoughts which are contrary to His thinking, so that we may transmit His thoughts to others.
Hannah Hurnard

Prayer is the evidence that I am spiritually concentrated on God.
Oswald Chambers

Prayer gets us in on what God is doing.
Eugene Peterson

We must lock our mind into the words of prayer by force.
St. John of the Ladder

Every true prayer is a variation on the theme 'Thy will be done.'
John Stott

To pray is to expose the shores of the mind to the incoming tide of God.
Ralph Washington Sockman

Faith is not a once-done act, but a continuous gaze of the heart at the Triune God.
A.W. Tozer

We have to see what God is doing, not just what man is not doing or what the devil wants to do.
Shawn Bolz

The task is not to get God to do something I think needs done, but to become aware of what God is doing so that I can participate in it.
Eugene Peterson

When the eyes of the soul looking out meet the eyes of God looking in, heaven has begun right here on this earth.
A.W. Tozer

Something begins to inspire you when you see the world around you through God's heart for it.
Shawn Bolz

Be sure that your motive in praying is to glorify God.
Billy Graham

How can we be with Him without thinking of Him often?
Brother Lawrence

A concentrated mind and a sitting body make for better prayer than a kneeling body and a mind half asleep.
C.S. Lewis

As we pray and as our attention is turned toward God, we become more receptive to aligning our lives with His will.
Henry Blackaby

David gazed on God until he was enraptured and that rapture he could not always contain.
A.W. Tozer

Boldness, confidence, and faith will rise in your heart as you realize that God's supply is always greater than your need!
Andrew Wommack

If we only spent more of our time in looking at Him we should soon forget ourselves.
Martyn Lloyd-Jones

You may pray for an hour and still not pray. You may meet God for a moment and then be in touch with Him all day.
Fredrik Wisloff

It is not the body's posture, but the heart's attitude that counts when we pray.
Billy Graham

Only the prayer which comes from God can go to God.
C.H. Spurgeon

If we see what God sees, then we will pray with more hope and more accuracy than those that don't see it.
Matt Peterson

Since you can't imagine a place where He isn't, you might as well imagine Him with you.
Bill Johnson

Expectation sharpens our vision and focuses our attention towards God.
Allison Brown

Only divine praying can operate divine promises or carry out divine purposes.
E.M. Bounds

Reading seeks, meditation finds (meaning), prayer demands, contemplation tastes (God).
Beni Johnson

Constantly practice the habit of gazing inwardly upon God.
A.W. Tozer

True prayer is asking God what He wants.
William Barclay

Pastors must pay attention to God and then lead others to pay attention to God.
Eugene Peterson

The great thing in prayer is to feel that we are putting our supplications into the bosom of omnipotent love.
Andrew Murray

The purpose of prayer is emphatically not to bend God's will to ours, but rather to align our will to His.
John Stott

Faith looks not at what happens to him but at Him Whom he believes.
Watchman Nee

If God isn't answering your prayer right now, maybe you just need to modify it. Find out what God wants to do and ask Him to do it!
Graham Cooke

The most important aspect of Christianity is not the work we do, but the relationship we maintain and the surrounding influence and qualities produced by that relationship. That is all God asks us to give our attention to, and it is the one thing that is continually under attack.
Oswald Chambers

Often, we try to tell God what we want Him to do—but ask Him to help you guard against this, and to seek His will instead of your own. Pray and ask God to guide you.
Billy Graham

Our Lord prayed because He was concentrated on God; that is, He did not worship prayer.
Oswald Chambers

The reason many... close their eyes while praying is to shut out the affairs of the world so that their minds can be completely concentrated on God... it certainly lends itself to the attitude of prayer.
Billy Graham

To Know God

Our ordinary views of prayer are not found in the New Testament. We look upon prayer as a means for getting something for ourselves; the Bible idea of prayer is that we may get to know God Himself.
Oswald Chambers

If there is little energy for such prayer, and little consequent practice of it, this is a sure sign that as yet we scarcely know our God.
J.I. Packer

God is not only faithful to us but He will be faithful to them too.
Kris Vallotton

You will always "pray" if you always know that God is enjoying you!
Brian Clark

If God sees that my spiritual life will be furthered by giving the things for which I ask, then He will give them, but that is not the end of prayer. The end of prayer is that I come to know God Himself.
Oswald Chambers

Some people pray just to pray and some people pray to know God.
Andrew Murray

Acquaint thyself with God.
A.W. Tozer

The whole meaning of prayer is that we may know God.
Oswald Chambers

Prayer is not so much the listing of our requests but the breathing of our own deepest request, to be united with God as fully as possible.
Jeffrey Imbach

Every time I pray, I feel God so much closer.
Kevin Shorter

Our trust and faith in God grows in proportion to knowing His character, goodness and trustworthiness.
Steve Backlund

God's behavior towards me cannot be based upon my lifestyle. It has to be based on who He is.
Graham Cooke

If God doesn't want something for me, I shouldn't want it either. Spending time in meditative prayer, getting to know God, helps align my desires with God's.
Phillip Brooks

We can never know God as it is our privilege to know Him by brief repetitions that are requests for personal favors, and nothing more.
E.M. Bounds

When we properly position ourselves to receive God's love, then we can properly return His love back to Him.
Brian Clark

Once you get to know God, you never want to stop the conversation.
Graham Cooke

[God] wants to be known by his heart, personality, and Spirit.
Shawn Bolz

Men who know their God are before anything else men who pray.
J.I. Packer

Prayer also strengthens our bond to God. The more we think about him, talk to him, enter into his presence, the closer to him we will be.
Robert Harris

The more one knows God, the greater one desires to know Him.
Brother Lawrence

God alone is capable of making Himself known as He really is.
Brother Lawrence

The best prayer does not seek the God's gifts but the experience of His person.
Unknown

God wants us to understand His world and His Kingdom. He wants us to know all about Him and to know Him intimately. He wants to tell us His secrets and to share His heart with us.
Beni Johnson

Our understanding of God is the answer to prayer.
Oswald Chambers

Effective prayer is the fruit of a relationship with God, not a technique for acquiring blessings.
D.A. Carson

A comprehended God is no God.
John Chrysostom

Your relationship with [God] is the primary source and goal of revelation.
Shawn Bolz

We don't get to decide who God is.
Francis Chan

We are following a God who wants to be known and seems to wear His heart on His sleeve.
Kevin Shorter

We shall find every attribute of God Most High to be, as it were, a great battering-ram, with which we may open the gates of heaven.
C.H. Spurgeon

We pray not to inform God or instruct Him, but to become intimate with Him.
John Chrysastom

My prayer is Thy Will. Thou didst create it in me. It is Thine more than mine.
P.T. Forsyth

Your faith will only explore where you know God is good.
Bill Johnson

[Paul] does not see prayer as merely a way to get things from God but as a way to get more of God himself.
Tim Keller

Feeling His love for this world is a very intense feeling and will undo you every time.
Beni Johnson

3

THE ROLE OF THE FATHER

God Our Father

Prayer to God is like a child's conversation with his father. It is natural for a child to ask his father for the things he needs.
Billy Graham

An infinite God can give all of Himself to each of His children. He does not distribute Himself that each may have a part, but to each one He gives all of Himself as fully as if there were no others.
A.W. Tozer

When you beg God to do something that you already know is His will, then you don't know His nature.
Bill Johnson

God wants us... to talk to Him as to a friend or father - authentically, reverently, personally, earnestly.
Bill Hybels

Father God designed and intended our families to express the kind of relationship that God designed us to have with Him.
Danny Silk

If you understand that God is your Father, prayer makes a lot of sense and prayer becomes very easy.
Mark Driscoll

God's willingness to answer our prayers exceeds our willingness to give good and necessary things to our children, just as far as God's ability, goodness and perfection exceed our infirmities and evil.
E.M. Bounds

If a child approached his parents the way religion conditions us to approach God, they'd be accused of child abuse!
Andrew Wommack

The wonder is not that God hears prayer, but that He is our Father. The greater wonder includes the less.
Samuel Chadwick

No matter where we are, God is as close as a prayer. He is our support and our strength. He will help us make our way up again from whatever depths we have fallen.
Billy Graham

God wants to father all of us until we're dead sure of his approval, his guiding power and his promise of heaven.

Bill Hybels

Answered prayer is the interchange of love between the Father and His child.

Andrew Murray

The whole difficulty of embracing and seeing the miraculous has everything to do with our understanding of the Father.

Bill Johnson

The prayer of the poor in spirit can simply be a single word: Abba. Yet that word can signify dynamic interaction.

Brennan Manning

If Christ is dwelling in our hearts by faith: if the Holy Spirit is breathing into us our petitions, and we are praying in the Holy Ghost, ought we not to know that the Father hears us?

The Kneeling Christian

He who is born of God desires his Father's love while he is yet a child, and has no idea of waiting for it till he comes of age, and enters upon his estate.

C.H. Spurgeon

If God who sits in the heavens can laugh, His children on earth should be loyal enough to do exactly as their Father does.

C.T. Studd

When we connect with God, we make ourselves aware that He is right there all the time.

Beni Johnson

If you know your Father—how much he loves you and how gracious he has been to you—you're going to talk to him.

Mark Driscoll

Information doesn't matter; love does. Love covers even when we are wrong, because relationship bridges the gap that risks or immaturity create.

Shawn Bolz

All the storehouses of God are open to the voice of faith in prayer.

D.M. McIntyre

Everything we do for people is just to get them to experience the Father. Striving for a Christian only exists in the absence of realizing the Fathers love.

Bill Johnson

When we pray we must come with an expectation of God's love for us, else we will beg for His blessings.

Kevin Shorter

When the Father looks at you, He doesn't see anything wrong. He's not obsessed by sin; He's not like us. He is consumed by life!

Graham Cooke

Openness, honesty, and trust mark the communication of children with their father.

Richard Foster

We are called to discern the Father's heart, not just the black-and-white or the truth amongst lies.
Shawn Bolz

Success in prayer is not determined by length but recognition of your needs and His willingness to provide.
Kevin Shorter

God does not keep office hours.
A.W. Tozer

When I finally approach God, in fear and trembling, I find not a tyrant but a lover.
Phillip Yancey

The basis of prayer is sonship. Prayer is possible and reasonable because it is filial.
Samuel Chadwick

There is something about the Father that loves to give. When you are touched by the heart of the Father, you become a giver yourself.
Graham Cooke

As a loving father, He is ready to fully allow us to inherit blessings instead of reap more bad consequences for the mistakes in our lives.
Shawn Bolz

Prayer puts God's work in His hands-and keeps it there.
E.M. Bounds

To call God Father enhances everything you do in prayer. If you don't know that God is your Father, it flattens and reduces and thins out every prayer.
Tim Keller

When we receive His joy over us, our rejoicing increases.
Graham Cooke

Praise God He translates our earthly requests into something beyond our imagination!
Kevin Shorter

Go to your place of prayer not only to enjoy spiritual delights, but simply to please the Father.
Madame Guyon

Frustration comes in prayer when we confuse "Abba Father" for "Abracadabra".
Shawn Hayes

God's love is so incredible that it reaches us in our sinfulness and pulls us into His embrace. From there, we discover we are the Beloved.
Graham Cooke

Prayer crowns God with the honor and glory due to His name, and God crowns prayer with assurance and comfort. The most praying souls are the most assured souls.
Thomas Brooks

Sometimes we make things too complicated when we really need to remember that the kingdom belongs to children.
Heidi Baker

The best you can ask in prayer is eclipsed by God's desire to provide what's best for you?

Jay Harris

Don't let what you didn't get in your childhood keep you from what God provides for His children - a perfectly faithful Father.

Bill Johnson

Explanations don't bring comfort. The love and presence of God does.

Rick Warren

When in prayer you clasp your hands, God opens His.

John Blanchard

The more you love God, the more love you have received from Him (1 John 4:19).

Kevin Shorter

The most important purpose of prayer may be to let our true selves be loved by God.

Phillip Yancey

Our prayer simply aligns us with what is already God's great pleasure to give us.

Francis Frangipane

If God is For You...

- ..., His every approach to you is in love.
- ..., good things will come your way.
- ..., your future is bright.
- ..., you can expect His help as you live out your destiny.
- ..., He will always receive you.
- ..., who can discourage you?
- ..., He will become your focus and not what may hold you back.
- ..., bad things are never His will for you.
- ..., life is an exciting adventure.
- ..., addictions can be overcome.
- ..., you don't view yourself based on your sin.
- ..., He will hear your prayers.
- ..., you can expect things to get better.
- ..., He always wants to heal you.
- ..., doubt loses its grip on you.
- ..., you have no limitations.
- ..., delight yourself in Him.
- ..., joy is never-ending.
- ..., He will defend you.
- ..., He will redeem every bad thing that has happened to you.
- ..., you cannot out-dream God.
- ..., He is rooting for and enabling your success.
- ..., you always have hope.
- ..., stepping out in faith is natural.
- ..., He is not trying to make you feel bad for yourself.
- ..., He will give you the desires of your heart.

Kevin Shorter

One person walking with God is in the majority.
Graham Cooke

You may not know how God is going to come through but you hope because you know God's love for you.
Kevin Shorter

You are beautiful to God. Even in your weakness He loves you. So approach Him in confidence; don't hide from Him in shame.
IHOP

If you believe God loves you, has a plan for your life, and that His timing is always right, there is no need to envy anyone.
Joyce Meyer

If you know that God loves you, you should never question a directive from Him.
Henry Blackaby

Knowing that God is for us transforms any bad situation into hope.
Kevin Shorter

When we know God loves us even in our situation, fear releases its strangle hold over us.
Kevin Shorter

Since I know God loves me totally and wants what's best for me, I don't have to understand every move he makes in my life.
Rick Warren

You were handmade by someone who is crazy about you.
Lance Wallnau

Even in the lowest times, God never condemns. He doesn't want my disappointment in myself to keep me away.
Kelly O'Dell Stanley

You can have complete confidence with God because He is incredibly in love with you.
Kevin Shorter

Nothing can pluck you from God's hands - not even your wayward heart.
Kevin Shorter

If you don't have the strength to hold on to God, He has the strength to hold on to you.
Bryan Chapell

God's Desire in Prayer

We were made, not to hide from God, but to hide in God.
Leonard Sweet

When we know Him, we can be sure God hears our prayers. When troubles come may prayer be your automatic response.
Billy Graham

God's dream for us is that we would be immersed in the majesty of everything He feels for us.
Graham Cooke

The child asks of the Father whom he knows. Thus, the essence of Christian prayer is not general adoration, but definite, concrete petition. The right way to approach God is to stretch out our hands and ask of One who we know has the heart of a Father.
Dietrich Bonhoeffer

[God] wants to share with us every day and not just to fix something, but to walk with us.
Shawn Bolz

That is the ideal order of prayer: His glory before our wants.
Kent Hughes

We will always include God, but we will understand it is his joy to allow us to make powerful decisions.
Shawn Bolz

God has established a universal principle concerning His actions being dependent upon our prayers.
Morris Cerrulo

It might sound strange, but God wants to find me as much as, if not more than, I want to find God.
Henri Nouwen

God has not changed; and His ear is just as quick to hear the voice of real prayer, and His hand is just as long and strong to save; as it ever was.
R.A. Torrey

In prayer, even though He knows all the details, He wants to hear it from you.
Jay Harris

God formed us for His pleasure... He meant for us to see Him and live with Him and draw our life from His smile.
A.W. Tozer

I pray in trust that the act of prayer is God's designated way of closing the vast gulf between infinity and me.
Phillip Yancey

Trust is not a belief that God can bless or that He will bless, but that He does bless, here and now.
E.M. Bounds

In order to teach us the joy of utter dependence and trust, He waits for us to ask.
Hannah Hurnard

You are meant to live a life overwhelmed by the love of God.
Kevin Shorter

Paul was a man who knew he had weaknesses, but he used his weaknesses as a sign that he had to run to the Lord for strength. Religion, on the other hand, causes people to run away from God when they fail, due to guilt and shame. God, however, wants us to run to Him, so He can continue His work in our lives.
Don Nori, Sr.

God gives us promises that we may call upon His faithfulness to show how much He wants to give to us.
Kevin Shorter

If you believe prayer is how to make God do something, your prayer life rests on an extremely faulty foundation.
Andrew Wommack

There are two things we need to know, maybe above all else - our heart is good, and that our heart matters to God.
John Eldredge

We, one and all of us, have an instinct to pray; and this fact constitutes an invitation from God to pray.
Charles Sanders Peirce

Shame is the attempt of the strongman to prevent you accessing or enjoying what God has for you.
Alan Scott

Amazing, isn't it, that our prayers... can move the very heart of God who created the universe?
Joni Eareckson Tada

The nature of the divine goodness is not only to open to those who knock, but also to cause them to knock and ask.
Augustine

God's promises are to be our pleas in prayer.
Matthew Henry

Prayer shouldn't be a burden but a privilege—God wants our fellowship.
Billy Graham

We look for definite signs that we can't deny; God is looking for intimacy.
Kevin Shorter

Praying with an adversarial, demanding, self-righteous attitude toward the Lord is totally offensive to Him.
Andrew Wommack

He meant us to see Him and live with Him and draw our life from His smile.
A.W. Tozer

[God] speaks and gives us hints and understandings on potentially every subject.
Shawn Bolz

God delights in your holy boldness that will not take no for an answer. God counts it "great faith," and He then counts you His friend, for you understand His heart.
Wesley Duewel

Most of the Church is waiting for the next big command from God, but God is waiting for the dreams of His Church.
Bill Johnson

We pray when there's nothing else we can do, but God wants us to pray before we do anything at all.
Oswald Chambers

So much prayer is self-centered and can even be selfish - it's all about what we need for now with not forethought into our developing with God, His heart, and His love for us.
Shawn Bolz

The right way to pray is to stretch out our hands and ask of One who we know has the heart of a Father.
Dietrich Bonhoeffer

God answers prayers because He loves us. He desires us to pray out of love for Him.
Kevin Shorter

There isn't a single motivation, thought, act, or word that has slipped out of your being and escaped the full, undivided attention of God.
Bill Hybels

God always answers us in the deeps, never in the shallows of our soul.
Amy Carmichael

So we pray because we were made for prayer, and God draws us out by breathing Himself in.
P.T. Forsyth

God is more interested in your future and your relationships than you are.
Billy Graham

God is waiting to be put to the test by His people in prayer. He delights in being put to the test on His promises. It is His highest pleasure to answer prayer, to prove the reliability of His promises.
E.M. Bounds

The things God wants to share with you are not limited to things you could have figured out with more wisdom.
Kevin Shorter

I am deeply convince that the necessity of prayer, and to pray unceasingly, is not as much based on our desire for God as on God's desire for us. It is God's passionate pursuit of us that calls us to prayer.
Henri Nouwen

Prayer concerns God, whose purposes and plans are conditioned on prayer. His will and His glory are bound up in praying.
E.M. Bounds

God doesn't want to be unattainable; He wants intimacy.
Kevin Shorter

God wants to be loved for Himself, but that is only part. He also wants us to know that when we have Him we have everything.
A.W. Tozer

Believe it or not, the ultimate goal God has for us is not power but personal intimacy with Him.
Beth Moore

The call to prayer is a call to participate in the love that has forever burned in God's heart.
Mike Bickle

He wants you all to Himself to put His loving, divine arms around you.
Charles Stanley

It is always man's tendency to work, speak and run to earn God's approval. He wants is to sit and rest first to know His approval.
Kevin Shorter

Prayer is God's plan to supply man's great and continuous need with God's great and continuous abundance.
E.M. Bounds

God wants you to know that He has never not liked you.
Kevin Shorter

God doesn't want to be our habit, He wants to be our friend!
Kris Vallotton

God doesn't want to punish you.
Kevin Shorter

God is trying to call us back to that for which He created us, to worship Him and to enjoy Him forever.
A.W. Tozer

That which God abundantly makes the subject of His promises, God's people should abundantly make the subject of their prayers.
Jonathan Edwards

God wants you to pray so that He may confer His gifts on one who really desires them and will not regard them lightly.
Augustine

It is quite useless knocking at the door of heaven for earthly comfort; it's not the sort of comfort they supply there.
C.S. Lewis

God is looking for people to use, and if you can get usable, He will wear you out. The most dangerous prayer you can pray is this: 'Use me.'
Rick Warren

God is so good because He desires for us to experience His pleasures forever!
Brian Clark

Our prayers must be in accordance with the will of God for the simple reason that God knows better what is good for us than we know ourselves.
Billy Graham

God is looking for people who pursue Him with the same intensity that He pursues us.
Kevin Shorter

It takes no annointing to see what is wrong in people's lives.
Shawn Bolz

I don't have the right to tell God anything, but He gives me the privilege to ask in prayer. He is God and I am not.
Mel Blackaby

It is the revelation of the Father that gives confidence in prayer.
Andrew Murray

God doesn't want to be unattainable; He wants intimacy.
Kevin Shorter

If you want to experience all of God, you need to experience all of life because God uses everything in life to get you to experience more of Him.
Kevin Shorter

Prayer is the key to your relationship with God.
Jay Harris

God is looking for the open door to provide His solutions for our problems. We open that door through prayer.
Bill Johnson

Part of prayer is His desires becoming your dreams.
Vadim Mialik

In your times with God, you are the most important person to Him.
Kevin Shorter

When God intends great mercy for His people, the first thing He does is to set them a-praying.
Matthew Henry

Prayer is not wrestling with God's reluctance to bless us; it is laying hold on His willingness to do so.
John Blanchard

God thirsts to love and be loved by you - that is how precious you are to Him.
Mother Teresa

God's purposes move along the pathway made by prayer to their glorious designs.
E.M. Bounds

All that God is, and all that God has, is at the disposal of prayer.
R.A. Torrey

God is not solely looking for people to fill heaven. He is looking for more people to experience His abundant love.
Kevin Shorter

The Lord says, 'Without me, you cannot. But without you, I will not.'
Jack Hayford

God wants more than people gazing on Him at a distance and declaring how powerful and how great He is. He says to us, "Come closer!"
Mike Bickle

God wants to be loved. He wants to be a priority to someone.
John Eldredge

What God is Like

To pray rightly, you must make God your hope, stay, and all.
John Bunyan

One reason God can't reveal His glory to the church is because they cannot embrace how good He is.
Wendy Backlund

The glory of God is in His unending goodness. His goodness and His glory must fill the earth even as it fills Heaven.
Graham Cooke

Some people think God does not like to be troubled with our constant coming and asking. The only way to trouble God is not to come at all.
D.L. Moody

Our prayers aren't going anywhere if they don't start with a significant acknowledgement of who God is.
James MacDonald

I love Him because He first loved me, and He still does love me, and He will love me forever and ever.
Bill Bright

There are things that we may not like that God loves.
Kevin Shorter

Pray ye. Is an invitation to be accepted rather than a command to be obeyed.
The Kneeling Christian

Nothing is clearer than that prayer has its only worth and significance in the great fact that God hears and answers prayer.
E.M. Bounds

God is not mad at you. That's not what He does. He died so we can hang out with Him.
Trisha Cwir

When God's mercies are coming, their footfalls are our desires to pray.
C.H. Spurgeon

God is incapable of letting you down.
> *Jesse Skinner*

Do not be thinking of how little you have to bring God, but of how much He wants to give you.
> *Andrew Murray*

Revelation is given to us so we can carry a piece of God's heart from eternity into the world.
> *Shawn Bolz*

Spend your talents lavishly. It reflects the Father's heart who is generous.
> *Kevin Shorter*

We have hope and joy because we know the heart and character of the One in control of everything.
> *Kevin Shorter*

God answers our prayers not because we are good, but because He is good.
> *A.W. Tozer*

If we don't know our God and His ways, our prayer lives will be important and ineffective.
> *Kay Arthur*

Prayer delights God's ear; it melts His heart; and opens His hand. God cannot deny a praying soul.
> *Thomas Watson*

There is nothing in you that God doesn't love. Take risks to reveal more of yourself to others.
> *Kevin Shorter*

God tolerates even our stammering, and pardons our ignorance whenever something inadvertently escapes us - as, indeed, without this mercy there would be no freedom to pray.
> *John Calvin*

We don't need to twist God's heart to show Himself; it is His natural response to our offering ourselves to Him.
> *Kevin Shorter*

God resolutely ignores all of our negativity because He is seeing something that He is calling us up to.
> *Graham Cooke*

God loves and there is nothing we can do to cause His love to pull away from us.
> *Heidi Baker*

The only people who worry about stealing God's glory are those who don't know how glorious He is.
> *Wendy Backlund*

God's deep longing for more of our hearts is the same passion God wants us to have of Him.
> *Kevin Shorter*

God lives out Philippians 4:8 when He thinks about you. That's what you do when you are in love.
> *Kevin Shorter*

All that I know is that God is infinitely holy, righteous and happy; that all goodness is in Him.
> *Madame Guyon*

God loves you unconditionally, as you are and not as you should be, because nobody is as they should be.
Brennan Manning

God's cause is committed to men; God commits Himself to men. Praying men are the vice-regents of God; they do His work and carry out His plans.
E.M. Bounds

Getting your needs met is the baby end of life in the Spirit. We must learn to trust the Lord and be confident in His heart towards us.
Graham Cooke

God hears your prayers because He loves you.
Kevin Shorter

He is the Giver not only of the answer, but first of the prayer itself.
P.T. Forsyth

There is nothing God loves more than keeping promises, answering prayer, performing miracles, and fulfilling dreams.
Mark Batterson

True faith rests upon the character of God and asks no further proof than the moral perfections of the One who cannot lie.
A.W. Tozer

People who grow in the prophetic the quickest are the people who are already naturally encouraging everyone around them.
Shawn Bolz

Nothing can separate you from God's love and His grace is always available for you to access.
Kevin Shorter

God never stops loving me, so I will never stop loving Him.
Kevin Shorter

God has everything ready and planned in order to meet all our needs before ever we realise what they are.
Hannah Hurnard

God put Himself in a box so that the Israelites could dwell with Him.
Trisha Cwir

If we want to know what God is like let us spend more time in prayer.
Stephen Olford

We cannot expect too little from man, nor too much from God.
Matthew Henry

God never motivates us by withholding His love from us.
Kevin Shorter

God is always relentless. He is relentless against the enemy. He is relentless towards his people in terms of his kindness and goodness.
Graham Cooke

Freedom is a top priority in Heaven, because it makes relationship possible.
Danny Silk

God did not promise to answer our prayers once we became robots. He actually makes Himself vulnerable to the desires of His people. This is easier to understand in friendship over servanthood.
Bill Johnson

The air which our body requires envelops us on every hand. The air which our souls need also envelops all of us at all times and on all sides. God is round about us in Christ on every hand, with his many sided and all-sufficient grace. All we need to do is to open our hearts.
O. Hallesby

There is no pit so deep that the love of God is not deeper still.
Corrie ten Boom

God is too good to be unkind and He is too wise to be mistaken.
C.H. Spurgeon

We are not punished because of our sin. We are punished by our sin! That is why God hates sin.
Kris Vallotton

The love of God encompasses everything within itself and everything that is rooted in love stems from God.
Madame Guyon

The value God places on a willing heart is so high that He willingly made Himself vulnerable to rejection by it.
Kevin Adams

Is it not the very unchangeableness of God which is our greatest encouragement to pray?
A.W. Pink

You don't have to convince God to bless you. You have to convince yourself to receive it.
Steve Backlund

We please God most, not by frantically trying to make ourselves good, but by throwing ourselves into His arms.
A.W. Tozer

If we could see how much the Lord loves us—and truly feel it— none of us would be the same again.
R.T. Kendall

You can always get God's attention. Can He get yours?
Kevin Shorter

We don't want to bother [God] with requests for small things that would be nice to have but aren't necessary... God cares about all aspects of our lives. God is so big, and is very capable of blessing you with the thing your heart desires.
Heidi Baker

When we have substandard view of God, we actually detract from His glory.
Graham Cooke

God is good all the time. Prayer makes you more alert to those times.
Kevin Shorter

If it matters to you, it matters to him.
Bill Johnson

Joy is the experience of knowing that you are unconditionally loved.
Henri Nouwen

God's love is never-ending. How much of it do you want? Just enough or overwhelming?
Kevin Shorter

Being with God is the only way to know Him.
Brian Clark

His nature is such that our often coming does not tire him. The whole burden of the whole life of every man may be rolled on to God and not weary him, though it has wearied man.
Henry Ward Beecher

If God answers prayer it's because God is good. From His goodness, His lovingkindness, His good-natured benevolence, God does it! That's the source of everything.
A.W. Tozer

We do not pray to inform God. Neither do we pray to persuade Him, for His love needs neither to be induced nor coaxed.
Samuel Chadwick

God Himself is the power that makes prayer work.
Billy Graham

Prayer opens the heart of God, and is a means by which the empty soul is filled.
John Bunyon

God puts His ear so closely down to your lips that He can hear your faintest whisper.
Thomas De Witt Talmage

We cannot have a expression of love for God that is greater than any He has for us.
Kevin Shorter

God is not a destination; He is the abundant life.
Kevin Shorter

God warms His hands at man's heart when he prays.
John Masefield

It is impossible to over-exaggerate the goodness of God.
Sean Feucht

God is still on His throne, we're still His footstool, and there's only a knee's distance between!
Jim Elliot

Prayer is no more inconsistent with the unchangeable purposes of God, than the use of any other means; for God in forming his purposes had respect to all appropriate means of producing the intended ends, and among these prayer has an important place.
Archibald Alexander

When God can trust you with His heart, He can then trust you with His power.
Kevin Shorter

You are incapable of letting God down. He always thinks highly of you.
Kevin Shorter

If the Gospel is about anything, it is about a God who meets us where we are, and not where we ought to be.
Robert Capon

God is our fortress and our hiding place. To step back into His kindness has been my salvation in countless circumstances!
Graham Cooke

God is greater than His promises, and often gives more than either we desire or deserve — but He does not always do so.
The Kneeling Christian

And if there is one terrible disease in the Church of Christ, it is that we do not see God as great as He is. We're too familiar with God.
A.W. Tozer

Our prayer is to be a reflex action to God's prior initiative upon the heart.
Richard Foster

We must be changed by the heart of God before we can become representative of it.
Graham Cooke

God is not like the "friend" who must be badgered (Luke 11:5-8).
Andrew Wommack

May you be aware of the love of God in everything that happens today.
Kevin Shorter

God allows in His wisdom what He could easily prevent by His power.
Graham Cooke

God can never be expected to undertake a cause which is unworthy of defence.
John Calvin

In seeking blessings from God we own that He is the Author and Fountain of every good and perfect gift.
A.W. Pink

The only power that God will yield to is that of prayer.
Leonard Ravenhill

4

THE ROLE OF THE SON

Jesus' Role in Prayer

A glad Jesus messes up many people's theology.
Steve Backlund

We must bear in mind that mere resolutions to take more time for prayer and to conquer reluctance to pray will not prove lastingly effective unless there is a whole hearted and absolute surrender to the Lord Jesus Christ.
The Kneeling Christian

Jesus wills of His own accord to come into us and, in His own power, to deal with our needs. It is not necessary for us to constrain Him by our prayers to take an interest in us.
O. Hallesby

To pray is nothing more involved than to open the door, giving Jesus access to our needs and permitting Him to exercise His own power in dealing with them.
O. Hallesby

Prayer as it comes from the saint is weak and languid; but when the arrow of a saint's prayer is put into the bow of Christ's intercession it pierces the throne of grace.
Thomas Watson

God's hearing of our prayers doth not depend upon sanctification, but upon Christ's intercession; not upon what we are in ourselves, but what' we are in the Lord Jesus; both our persons and our prayers are acceptable in the beloved [Eph 1.6]."
Thomas Brooks

Remember, Jesus endured the cross for the joy set before Him. Always look past the obedience to the joy.
Judy Franklin

Our prayers are heard, not because we are in earnest, not because we suffer, but because Jesus suffered.
Oswald Chambers

The results of prayer are, therefore, not dependent upon the powers of the one who prays.
O. Hallesby

Never will man pray as he ought unless the Master will guide both his mouth and his heart.
John Calvin

You may never know that JESUS is all you need, until JESUS is all you have.
Corrie ten Boom

In the Kingdom, peace is the presence of a Person.
Bill Johnson

The name of Jesus, the power of his blood, and the prayer of faith have never lost their power over the centuries.
Jim Cymbala

And many shall think they are praying to the Father in my name, whilst deceiving themselves.
The Kneeling Christian

Prayer is the one prime, eternal condition by which the Father is pledged to put the Son in possession of the world. Christ prays through His people. Had there been Importunate, universal, and continuous prayer by God's people, long ere this the earth had been possessed for Christ.
E.M. Bounds

Avail yourself of the greatest privilege this side of heaven. Jesus Christ died to make this communion and communication with the Father possible.
Billy Graham

Prayer in Jesus' name puts the crowning crown on God, because it glorifies Him through the Son and it pledges the Son to give to men 'whatsoever and anything' they shall ask.
E.M. Bounds

f Jesus Christ be God and died for me, then no sacrifice can be too great for me to make for Him.
C.T. Studd

[Jesus] prayed briefly when He was in a crowd; He prayed a little longer when He was with His disciples; and He prayed all night when He was alone. Today, many in the ministry tend to reverse that process.
Billy Graham

Prayer means that I come in contact with an almighty Christ, and almighty results happen along the lines He laid down.
Oswald Chambers

Jesus life isn't our standard; He wants it to be our baseline.
Kevin Shorter

We are the hope of the nations, because we have been sent by Jesus.
Kevin Shorter

We have no right to come before God at all, apart from the finished work of Christ.
R.C. Sproul

In Jesus we see that God would rather be killed than kill.
Phil Drysdale

Jesus is the promised abundant life.
Kevin Shorter

Sitting at the feet of Jesus will lead you to wash the feet of others.
Kevin Shorter

Prayer for Jesus Christ, formed the brackets in which He accomplished His earthly work. It fortified Him with wisdom and power before action occurred, and it renewed, refreshed, and revived Him when His human strength was exhausted. On the front end, He prayed for fruit, in the middle, He bore fruit. Afterwards, He thanked God for fruit.

Dan Hayes

Truth is whatever Jesus declares true.

Kevin Shorter

The Lord Jesus makes intercession for us (Hebrews 7:25), and God cannot say Him Nay.

The Kneeling Christian

Jesus Christ teaches the importance of prayer by His urgency to His disciples to pray.

E.M. Bounds

Jesus died on the cross that we may be free to live.

Kevin Shorter

Prayer is the open admission that without Christ we can do nothing.

John Piper

Jesus didn't come to remove the evil and put in the good; He came to remove the evil so that the good could fully shine (Isaiah 60:1).

Kevin Shorter

The man who, despite the teaching of Scripture, tries to pray without a Savior, insults the deity.

C.H. Spurgeon

It has well been said that Christ's life in heaven is His prayer for us. It is what He is that determines what He does.

Warren Wiersbe

Above all the grace and the gifts that Christ gives to his beloved is that of overcoming self.

Francis of Assisi

The cross doesn't excuse sin so that I can carry on as before. It pays in full so that I can be set completely free.

Kathryn Scott

Religious people pray things like "God, kill me," not realizing [Jesus came to die that we didn't have to].

Kris Vallotton

The Emmanuel who came to earth 2,000 years ago still wants to be the God with us today. Pursue Him and He will draw near to you.

Kevin Shorter

We offer our prayers in weakness but they ascend in power because of the blood of Jesus.

Mike Bickle

Know this fundamental truth as you begin [praying]. When Jesus prays for God's Kingdom to come, remember that He said, 'the kingdom of God is within you.

Madame Guyon

Nothing means so much to our daily prayer life as to pray in the name of Jesus. If we fail to do this, our prayer life will either die from discouragement and despair or become simply a duty which we feel we must perform.

O. Hallesby

When we pray in Jesus' name, we also speak with His voice to the Father.

Bryan Chapell

It is inconsistent to have Jesus pay a price for healing and for us to believe it is not God's intention to heal.

Bill Johnson

Jesus came that we may have life abundantly. Prayer is communicating with Him. Therefore prayer should be the most life-giving, exciting thing we can do.

Kevin Shorter

You were saved when you believed in Jesus, but you got transformed when you realized He believed in you.

Kris Vallotton

Prayer as it comes from the saint, is weak and languid; but when the arrow of a saint's prayer is put into the bow of Christ's intercession it pierces the throne of grace.

Thomas Watson

Jesus loves you and is for you. What are you afraid of?

Kevin Shorter

God proved his love on the cross. When Christ hung, and bled, and died it was God saying to the world — I love you.

Billy Graham

Notice carefully every word here. It is not our prayer which draws Jesus into our hearts. Nor is it our prayer which moves Jesus to come in to us. All He needs is access. He enters in of His own accord, because He desires to come in. To pray is nothing more involved than to let Jesus into our needs, and permitting Him to exercise His own power in dealing with them. And that requires no strength. It is only a question of our wills. Will we give Jesus access to our needs?

O. Hallesby

Jesus is praying for us exactly what we'd pray for ourselves, if we knew what He knows.

Scotty Smith

Jesus has no teaching on unanswered prayer because He has no experience with it.

Bill Johnson

Let's don't waste our lives living beneath the life Jesus died to give us.

Kevin Shorter

Your knowledge of Christ, your relationship, and your union with Him through prayer is the source (the foundation) of your strength.

Morris Cerrulo

God put you in a place where He would always accept you and approve. He put you in the safest place ever. He put you in to Jesus!
Graham Cooke

Our prayers don't have to be perfect to accomplish God's purposes. They are effective because of the blood of Jesus not eloquent speech.
IHOP

God does not empower you to become like Jesus. He dwells within you to become like Jesus.
Graham Cooke

Prayer is the risen Jesus coming in with His resurrection power, given free reign in our lives, and then using His authority to enter any situation and change things.
O. Hallesby

What sin has ruined, Christ is going to redeem.
Graham Cooke

Our prayers are always a result of Jesus' knocking at our heart's doors.
O. Hallesby

He wants us to be more childlike, more humble, more grateful in prayer, to remember we all belong to the mystical body of Christ, which is praying always.
Mother Teresa

In my name (John 14:13,14; 15:16; 16: 23, 24, 26). Evidently something very important is here implied. It is more than a condition — it is also a promise, an encouragement, for our Lord's biddings are always His enablings.
The Kneeling Christian

There's no place for judgment in our hearts. Our words should heal and release people because it is for freedom that Christ has set us free!
Graham Cooke

Calling yourself a sinner, a worm, nobody special is not being humble; it's an insult to Jesus.
Kevin Shorter

If we really loved each other with the kind of love Jesus loved with, we wouldn't be able to fit everyone in the church.
Joyce Meyer

If [Jesus] felt that He had to pray, how much more do we need to pray!
Billy Graham

Anything you think you know about God, that you can't find in the person of Jesus, you have reason to question.
Bill Johnson

Jesus Christ carries on intercession for us in heaven; the Holy Ghost carries on intercession in us on earth; and we the saints have to carry on intercession for all men.
Oswald Chambers

God was the painter, you are the painting, and Jesus was the model.
Kris Vallotton

[Jesus] didn't treat [people] as He hoped they would one day be; He treated them as if they were already restored.
Shawn Bolz

On the ground of our own goodness we cannot expect to have our prayers answered. But Jesus is worthy, and for His sake we may have our prayers answered.
George Müller

If His presence changes things, shouldn't ours?
Bethany Forman

Live life to the full. Anything less is an insult to Christ's suffering.
Kevin Shorter

Christ did not just make our joy possible, he died to become the supreme object of our joy (2 Cor 4:4-6).
John Piper

When He puts the resurrected Christ in you, He immediately expects you to conquer something.
Bill Johnson

The wonderful revelation the Son came to make of His Father as our Father too.
Andrew Murray

Christians are to pray for the manifestation of the reign of Christ and the emergence of His kingdom.
R.C. Sproul

Our souls can only be renewed when we are passive towards the Spirit who alone can renew us. For who can restore the image of God within us in its original form, except for Jesus Christ himself who is the essential image of his Father?
Madame Guyon

Praying in Jesus' name is not merely the postscript to a good prayer; it is the prelude to God's providing the best of all things for his loved ones.
Bryan Chapell

If I could hear Christ praying for me in the next room, I would not fear a million enemies. Yet distance makes no difference. He is praying for me.
Robert Murray M'Cheyne

To pray is to let Jesus come into our hearts. It is not our prayer which moves the Lord Jesus. It is Jesus who moves us to pray.
O. Hallesby

God has placed this light in our hearts to display the face of Christ. To seek His face, we need to dive into our hearts and find Christ there.
Kevin Shorter

What comes with Jesus' completeness on the cross is that we can now fight from victory not for victory.
Beni Johnson

Jesus Christ has promised to be our ever-present Teacher and Guide. His voice is not hard to hear. His direction is not hard to understand.
Richard Foster

Thou are not a spectator God. Your wounded feet are still walking the trails of earth, then we shall not give way to hopelessness.
Catherine Marshall

No one will love you better than Jesus - not your friends, fears, addictions, self, etc.
Kevin Shorter

Jesus is moved to happiness every time He sees that you appreciate what He has done for you. Grip His pierced hand and say to Him, "I thank Thee, Saviour, because Thou has died for me." Thank Him likewise for all the other blessings He has showered upon you from day to day. It brings joy to Jesus.
O. Hallesby

The greatest book in the world is Jesus Christ himself. He will teach you everything that can be readily understood by the inner self.
Madame Guyon

[Jesus] had only three years of public ministry, but He was never too hurried to spend hours in prayer. No day began or closed in which He was not in communion with His Father.
Billy Graham

Jesus took what I deserved so I could get what He deserved.
Bill Johnson

Next time you wonder if God hears you when you pray, remember you are in Christ.
Bill Johnson

Jesus demonstrated the importance of prayer by His own example. His whole ministry was saturated with prayer.
Billy Graham

If we imitate Jesus, people will see Him when they look at us.
Heidi Baker

The weight of our own cross can only be carried under the gravity of grace – His sacrifice makes all others weightless.
Kevin Adams

In prayer, because of our sonship, provided by the redeeming work of Jesus, we can rightfully address God as "Father"!
Jay Harris

Fix Your Eyes On Jesus

See the incense of the Lord's intercession and your prayer will rise up with and in His prayer.
Adolph Saphir

How the outlook changes when Jesus comes!
Smith Wigglesworth

Most of our prayers become pleas for God to act because we are more focused on what we want Him to do than we are of Him.
Kevin Shorter

Worry sees the problem, but it doesn't see God.
Joyce Meyer

A lifestyle of prayer is simply an addiction to a desire to be with Jesus!
Brian Clark

Our rest lies in looking to the Lord, not to ourselves.
Watchman Nee

Whatever we focus on, we give power to. Take your eyes off the negative and you will disempower it.
Graham Cooke

Focus on how much God loves you - your love for Him will grow from that.
Kevin Adams

Nothing can separate you from the love of Christ, so don't let it get far from your mind.
Kevin Shorter

We need to keep our eyes on Jesus when we're praying.
Kelly O'Dell Stanley

The revelation of our spiritual standing is what we ask in prayer; sometimes what we ask is an insult to God; we ask with our eyes on the possibilities or on ourselves, not on Jesus Christ.
Oswald Chambers

God will answer all our questions in one way and one way only. Namely, by showing us more of his Son.
Watchman Nee

Wherever faith has eyes to see, there is a smiling presence of the Son of God.
A.W. Tozer

Prayer is vital for the fight to be more like Jesus.
John Piper

Brilliant prayer is about having a fantastic perspective.
Graham Cooke

All of the focus of God is on something that is good. Why? Because God is good.
Graham Cooke

Prayer is not a convenient device for imposing our will upon God, or bending His will to ours, but the prescribed way of subordinating our will to His.
John Stott

How do you seek God when He's always with you? You learn to look for Him in every situation and become committed to that insight.
Graham Cooke

Focusing on Christ in the midst of seemingly-hopeless circumstances allows us to rise above them.
Bob Hartley

To the Son of God prayer was more important than the assembling of great throngs... He often withdrew into the wilderness and prayed [Luke 5:15-16].
Billy Graham

Pray for and work for fullness of life above every thing; full red blood in the body; full honesty and truth in the mind; and the fullness of a grateful love for the Saviour in your heart.
Phillip Brooks

To pray in the name of Christ is to pray as one who is at one with Christ, whose minid is the mind of Christ, whose desires are the desires of Christ, and whose purpose is one with that of Christ.
Samuel Chadwick

The more you keep your eyes on Jesus, the more His hope directs your life.
Jud Wilhite

The real purpose of prophecy is to tie you to your eternal calling to be in Jesus.
Shawn Bolz

Of all the things Christ wants for us, loving Him and focusing our attention on Him are the most important.
Charles Stanley

The things you let your mind dwell on are the things you train your heart to want.
Kevin Shorter

5

THE ROLE OF THE HOLY SPIRIT

What the Holy Spirit Does

The goal of the prophetic is to see people the way God always longed for them to be seen and, from that revelation, to treat them out of His culture of love so that they will want to be the version of themselves we see.
Shawn Bolz

The biggest thing God ever did for me was to teach me to pray in the Spirit.
Samuel Chadwick

The Spirit does not lead you to pray for useless goals.
Wesley Duewel

Jesus chose not to remain on Earth in human form so that the Spirit of Christ could draw near to you.
John Bevere

The Holy Spirit as the Spirit of Life ends our deadness in prayer.
Leonard Ravenhill

"Lord, make me sensitive" is a prayer that should always be on our hearts.
Dennis J De Haan

All true prayer is exercised in the sphere of the Holy Spirit, motivated and empowered by Him.
Jay Mack

All prayer comes from the Spirit— be it disciplined prayer or spontaneous prayer.
R.T. Kendall

Prayer lays hold of God's plan and becomes the link between His will and its accomplishment on earth. Amazing things happen, and we are given the privilege of being the channels of the Holy Spirit's prayer.
Elisabeth Elliot

If the Spirit prays in us, shall we not share His groanings in prayer?
The Kneeling Christian

The indwelling Spirit shall teach him what is of God and what is not. This is why sometimes we can conjure up no logical reason for opposing a certain teaching, yet in the very depth of our being arises a resistance.
Watchman Nee

Joy is the environment of Heaven, and nobody embodies that joy more than the Holy Spirit.
Graham Cooke

God wants His people to be ablaze with Holy Ghost activity.
Smith Wigglesworth

It is in the atmosphere of prayer that the Holy Spirit nurtures and develops our faith or redirects our wills.
Unknown

The Holy Spirit longs to talk to you and is talking to you more than you know.
Allison Shorter

To have Christ the Son, and the Spirit of the Son, dwelling within us and revealing the Father makes us true, spiritual worshippers.
Andrew Murray

But it is the Holy Spirit of God Who is prayer's great Helper.
The Kneeling Christian

The Holy Spirit compensates for our sensory limits by enabling us to conceive of things we cannot perceive with our five senses.
Mark Batterson

Prayer brings the spirit, the life, the power.
David Stoner

Why do you think Jesus gave us a Comforter? He knew His ways would make us uncomfortable first.
Bill Johnson

I believe that God hears your prayers because there is a secret work of the Spirit going on within you teaching you to pray.
C.H. Spurgeon

The primary purpose of the Spirit's words is to reveal the love of our Father and our relationship with him.
Shawn Bolz

True prayer is God the Holy Spirit talking to God the Father in the name of God the Son, and the believer's heart is the prayer-room.
Samuel M. Zemer

The same Spirit of faith which teaches a man to cry earnestly, teaches him to wait patiently.
John Mason

The same power that stopped the sun and raised Christ from the grave lives in every believer.
Steven Furtick

Our praying, however, needs to be pressed and pursued with an energy that never tires, a persistency which will not be denied, and a courage which never fails.
E.M. Bounds

Our assignment has never been about what we can do for God, but what can God do through us!
Bill Johnson

The Spirit, when He prays through us, or helps us to meet the mighty oughtness of right praying, trims our praying down to the will of God.
R.A. Torrey

The true spirit of prayer is no other than God's own Spirit dwelling in the hearts of the saints. And as this spirit comes from God, so doth it naturally tend to God in holy breathings and pantings. It naturally leads to God, to converse with him by prayer.
Jonathan Edwards

The Holy Spirit's voice is calm, peaceful, authoritative, and harmonizes with the Truth.
Rachel DiPaolo

The Holy Spirit turns prayer from activity into energy.
John Blanchard

There is no such thing as another Pentecost. The Holy Spirit comes to stay.
Reinhard Bonnke

Our prayers must spring from the indigenous soil of our own personal confrontation with the Spirit of God in our lives.
Malcolm Boyd

In our prayer God returns from His projection in Nature to speak with Himself. When we speak to God it is really the God who lives in us speaking through us to Himself. His Spirit returns to Him who gave it; and returns not void, but bearing our souls with Him.
P.T. Forsyth

The gifts of the Spirit are the love language of God.
Kris Vallotton

The Holy Spirit as the Spirit of Power helpeth our infirmity in prayer.
Leonard Ravenhill

The Spirit not only conforms our prayers to God's purposes but in doing so confirms how precious we are to God.
Bryan Chapell

Our minds can be kept free of anxiety as we dump the load of our cares on the Lord in prayer.
Charles Swindoll

The Holy Spirit as the Spirit of Fire delivers us from coldness in prayer.
Leonard Ravenhill

The Holy Spirit as the Spirit of Might comes to our aid in our weakness as we pray.
Leonard Ravenhill

God gave us the Comforter because His plan was to call us places where we would have to deal with things that were uncomfortable to us.
Kevin Shorter

One way the Holy Spirit comforts us is by giving us hope through our prayers.
Kevin Shorter

Nothing is more calculated to begat a spirit of prayer than to unite in social prayer with one who has the Spirit Himself.
Wesley Duewel

The Bible knows nothing about air in a jar, only wind in motion. It knows nothing about the Holy Spirit except in action, in manifestation.
Reinhard Bonnke

Grace is the empowering presence of God that enables you to become what He sees when He looks at you.
Graham Cooke

The Spirit imparts a sense of sonship and acceptance that creates freedom and confidence in the presence of God.
Unknown

The Holy Spirit often uses promptings to draw us to the important task of praying. We need to learn how to identify these signals so that we will be alerted: It's time to pray. The life situations... that call us to prayer include those times when we're anxious, joyful, tempted, concerned, or angry.
Jim Nicodem

When the Spirit is absent, our excuses always seem right, but in the presence of the Spirit our excuses fade away.
R.T. Kendall

It must be because I live too little in the Spirit that my prayer is to little in the Spirit.
Andrew Murray

The spirit of prayer is the fruit and token of the Spirit of adoption.
John Newton

Prayer is an art which only the Spirit can teach us. He is the giver of all prayer.
C.H. Spurgeon

All difficulties are to teach us about our relationship with the Holy Spirit as our comforter.
Graham Cooke

Our self-oblation stands on His; and the spirit of prayer flows from the gift of the Holy Ghost, the great Intercessor.
P.T. Forsyth

That "the Spirit Himself intercedes" indicates that it is actually God pleading, praying, and mourning through us.
Billy Graham

The Spirit of God, when he is poured out as a spirit of prayer in the most glorious measures, does not contradict the rules of a natural and reasonable method, although His methods may have infinite variety in them.
Isaac Watts

If the spirit of prayer departs, it is a sure indication of a backslidden heart, for while the first love of a Christian continues he is sure to be drawn by the Holy Spirit to wrestle much in prayer.
Charles Finney

True prayer rises in the spirit of the Christian from the Spirit who indwells us.
J. Oswald Sanders

His Holy Spirit puts fresh ideas into the minds of praying people.
The Kneeling Christian

You have a glorious helper — the Holy Ghost — and by his power you may accomplish miracles of holiness.
C.H. Spurgeon

Prayer has mighty power to move mountains because the Holy Spirit is ready both to encourage our praying and to remove the mountains hindering us. Prayer has the power to change mountains into highways.
Wesley Duewel

When a man has found the Lord, he no longer has to use words when he is praying, for the Spirit Himself will intercede for him with groans that cannot be uttered.
John Climacus

Groanings which cannot be uttered are often prayers which cannot be refused.
C.H. Spurgeon

God can pick sense out of a confused prayer.
Richard Sibbes

If the spiritual life be healthy, under the full power of the Holy Spirit, praying without ceasing will be natural.
Andrew Murray

Participating with the Holy Spirit

There's a huge difference between a good idea and a God-inspired idea.
Craig Groeschel

We cannot expect divine revelation to be what we imagine; if it was, there would be no need of divine revelation at all.
Reinhard Bonnke

You cannot live the life God planned for you without prayer because the things He has planned require His involvement which is found in prayer.
Kevin Shorter

I am always an amazing counselor and speaker when God shows up!
Shawn Bolz

We want our spirit as strong as it can be because it is the part of us that is always desiring agreement with the things of God.
> *Kevin Shorter*

To pray rightly is a rare gift.
> *John Calvin*

Is his Holy Spirit promised to teach pray; and shall a Christian be careless or unwilling to receive such divine teaching?
> *Isaac Watts*

Virtues are formed by prayer. Prayer draws into the soul the Holy Spirit, and raises man to Heaven.
> *St. Ephraem*

We know not the matter of the things for which we should pray, neither the object to whom we pray, nor the medium by or through whom we pray; none of these things know we, but by the help and assistance of the Spirit.
> *John Bunyan*

Fasting reduces the power of self so that the Holy Spirit can do a more intense work within us.
> *Bill Bright*

We have the Holy Spirit to help us pray. God never intended for us to pray on our own.
> *Kevin Shorter*

We want to be so humble that we are irresistible to the Holy Spirit.
> *Heidi Baker*

All who desire to pray may pray without difficulty as they are strengthened by those universal graces and gifts of the Holy Spirit which all men and women possess.
> *Madame Guyon*

The starting place is ask. And then in doing that, to draw on the energy and power of the Holy Spirit to do that asking because we need help to go beyond anything we can pray on our own.
> *Jack Hayford*

We miss a lot of mighty things God wants to do in us and through us because we think we can't.
> *Ron Hutchcraft*

When Jesus prayed, heaven opened, and the Holy Spirit descended upon Him.
> *Henry Blackaby*

Jesus spoke of rivers of living water which would flood out from our innermost being. So don't pray to be filled. Pray for overflowing!
> *Graham Cooke*

If the spirit does not move me, I move the Spirit.
> *Smith Wigglesworth*

If I wanted to dance with the Holy Spirit, I needed to know how He was dancing and fall into step with Him. Otherwise I would be doing my own thing, in my own strength, and without the grace that comes from following His lead.
> *Judy Franklin*

The Church is not looking for better methods; God is looking for better men. The Holy Ghost does not flow through methods, but through men. He does not come on machinery, but on men. He does not anoint plans, but men... Men of prayer.
E.M. Bounds

A man of prevailing prayer must be filled with the Spirit of God.
The Kneeling Christian

The measure of God's giving the Spirit is our asking.
Andrew Murray

When we let the Holy Spirit help us in prayer, sometimes with the understanding, sometimes praying in the Spirit, that then, the Bible says, all things will work together for good.
Jack Hayford

We know not what we should pray for as we ought, and if prayer waits for understanding it will never begin.
Samuel Chadwick

When you don't know what to say or how to pray, the Spirit of Christ living in you does.
John Bevere

You can have the correct theology of the Holy Spirit, but not be filled with the Holy Spirit.
Jim Cymbala

The Holy Spirit comes in answer to believing prayer.
Andrew Murray

When the Spirit is absent, we will find excuses not to pray.
R.T. Kendall

What the Church needs today is not more or better machinery, not new organizations or more and novel methods, but men whom the Holy Ghost can use—men of prayer, men mighty in prayer. The Holy Ghost does not flow through methods, but through men. He does not come on machinery, but on men. He does not anoint plans, but men —men of prayer.
E.M. Bounds

The oil of the Holy Spirit will never cease to flow so long as there are empty vessels to receive it.
The Kneeling Christian

If you want to increase in the life of God, then you must settle it in your heart that you will not at any time resist the Holy Spirit. The Holy Ghost and fire - the fire burning up everything that would impoverish and destroy you.
Smith Wigglesworth

He that lives without prayer or prays without life, has not the Spirit of God.
John Mason

It is when we have failed and know not what prayers to offer or in what way, that the Holy Spirit is promised as our Helper.
The Kneeling Christian

It is when we pray, that the Holy Spirit takes of the things of Christ and reveals them unto us (John 16:15).
The Kneeling Christian

As we pray, we will also learn that 'less' is often 'more' as the Lord guides our steps.
Jim Cymbala

God bestows His Holy Spirit in His fullness only on men of prayer.
The Kneeling Christian

We need to ask questions to know God's secrets.
Shawn Bolz

As we choose to love, we become more attractive to the Holy Spirit and more of Him will come upon you.
Kevin Shorter

Many prayers are thought to be God's will that are only selfish desires. May we be more sensitive to the Spirit.
Kevin Shorter

Jesus taught his disciples that the highest exercise of prayer was in obtaining God's divinest bestowment, the gift of the Holy Spirit.
William Patton

God is inside you, so He lives in your heart. He speaks in your spirit and then what's in your spirit rises up into your conscious mind and you get to hear it and feel it and then it's a simple thing to open your mouth and say it.
Graham Cooke

Prayer brings increased fullness and power of the Holy Spirit.
Kent Hughes

If we rely on the Holy Spirit, we shall find that our prayers become more and more inarticulate; and when they are inarticulate, reverence grows deeper and deeper.
Oswald Chambers

Prayers prayed in the Spirit never die until they accomplish God's intended purpose.
Wesley Duewel

To effect such a radical change in our lifestyles as will make more time for prayer will call for strength of purpose and a deep dependence on the Holy Spirit.
J. Oswald Sanders

If you don't feel like praying, ask the Holy Spirit how He would like to pray and follow the lead!
Graham Cooke

How true it is that without the guidance of the Holy Spirit intellect not only is undependable but also extremely dangerous, because it often confuses the issue of right and wrong.
Watchman Nee

When we learn to pray in the Holy Ghost, we find there are some things for which we cannot pray, there is a sense of restraint. Never push and say, I know it is God's will and I am going to stick to it. Beware, remember what is recorded of the children of Israel: He gave them their request; but sent leanness into their soul.
Oswald Chambers

If we were more disposed today to mind the voice of conscience, we would not be as defeated as we are.
Watchman Nee

Your understanding of the Holy Spirit will mature as your devote yourself to time in His presence.
John Bevere

Understanding the language of the Spirit is essential to your connection with God.
Allison Shorter

Only in the power of the Holy Spirit can we possibly live up to God's expectations.
A.W. Tozer

A spiritual Christian must experimentally know the Holy Spirit in his spirit.
Watchman Nee

If we follow his impulse, the Holy Spirit will always lead us to pray.
R.T. Kendall

If you do not sense the Holy Spirit's power in your life, you may not be spending adequate time in prayer.
Henry Blackaby

If you develop sensitivity to the Holy Spirit, you won't need guilt as a motivation; love will be your motivation.
Graham Cooke

One way to re-collect the mind easily in the time of prayer and preserve it more in tranquility, is not to let it wander too far at other times.
Brother Lawrence

He has mastered but little of prayer who knows little of the Spirit-groaning which cannot be uttered.
Payne

Prayer for the in-dwelling of the Spirit, with all the fullness of his sanctifying grace, ought then to be the most natural and continual of the petitions of the Christian.
William Patton

Since the days of Pentecost, has the whole church ever put aside every other work and waited upon Him for ten days, that the Spirit's power might be manifested? We give too much attention to method and machinery and resources, and too little to the source of power.
Hudson Taylor

Keep our hearts open to the inflowing Spirit and we will not become exhausted by the outflow.
A.W. Tozer

Interaction with the Holy Spirit enables you to operate on a level far above your own abilities.
John Bevere

Any structure we create is designed to host the presence of the Holy Spirit. We celebrate the wine not the wine skin.
Bill Johnson

God is not just an audience for our prayers but a partner in our prayers.
Rob Jacobs

Some people like to read their Bibles in the Hebrew; some like to read it in the Greek; I like to ready it in the Holy Spirit.
Smith Wigglesworth

Pray a little each day in a childlike way for the Spirit of prayer. If you feel that you know, as yet, very little concerning the deep things of prayer and what prayer really is, then pray for the Spirit of prayer. There is nothing He would rather do than unveil to you the grace of prayer.
O. Hallesby

By neglecting fasting and prayer you are blocking a dynamic means by which the Holy Spirit brings change.
Bill Bright

We are never really men of prayer in the best sense, until we are filled with the Holy Ghost.
Samuel Chadwick

The Father has ordained that His ideas must be spoken, and when they are spoken, the Spirit releases power.
IHOP

The Holy Spirit is imprisoned in the bodies of unbelieving believers.
Bill Johnson

It's much more fun to pray with God than merely to pray to Him.
Bill Johnson

His power + your effort = supernatural synergy.
Mark Batterson

6

OUR RESPONSIBILITY IN PRAYER

The Role of Holiness

No man's prayer is acceptable with God whose life is not well pleasing before God.
Alexander Whyte

Prayer quiets our flesh and builds up our inner person.
John Bevere

Prayer will promote our personal holiness as nothing else, except the study of the Word of God.
R.A. Torrey

Of course our prayers are limited by our sin. If you want powerful prayers, get the sin out of your life.
John Eldredge

Holiness is not to love Jesus and do whatever you want. Holiness is to love God and do what He wants.
C. Peter Wagner

Believing prayer from a wholly-cleansed heart never fails.
The Kneeling Christian

Prayer will make a man cease from sin, or sin will entice a man to cease from prayer.
John Bunyon

May our prayers today, and every day, be from our hearts and with the focus of our whole being.
Billy Graham

Spend your time in nothing which you know must be repented of; in nothing on which you might not pray for the blessing of God; in nothing which you could not review with a quiet conscience on your dying bed; in nothing which you might not safely and properly be found doing if death should surprise you in the act.
Richard Baxter

Overindulgence in pleasure always affects the prayer life.
Henrietta Mears

Unless we are living the Victorious Life we cannot truly pray in the name of Christ, and our prayer-life must of necessity be feeble, fitful and oft-times unfruitful.
The Kneeling Christian

We put it as our most sober judgment that the great need of the Church in this and all ages is men of such commanding faith, of such unsullied holiness, of such marked spiritual vigor and consuming zeal, that their prayers, faith, lives, and ministry will be of such a radical and aggressive form as to work spiritual revolutions which will form eras in individual and Church life.
E.M. Bounds

Our praying, to be strong, must be buttressed by holy living. The life of faith perfects the prayer of faith.
E.M. Bounds

We need to be firm and stable in our connection with God and other people so we can pray into things without our own problems getting in the way.
Allison Shorter

Holy living is essential preparation for prayer.
E.M. Bounds

He only can truly pray who is all aglow for holiness, for God, and for heaven.
E.M. Bounds

God uses prayer to educate His people and to produce holiness of character in them.
Harold Lindsell

Unless the heart is right the prayer must be wrong.
The Kneeling Christian

Fasting is abstaining from anything that hinders prayer.
Andrew Bonar

We actually give a constant 'no' to the world every time we take time to what the world would call nothing.
Trisha Cwir

Every man is as holy as he really wants to be.
A.W. Tozer

Prayer - secret, fervent, believing prayer - lies at the root of all personal godliness.
William Carey

Spend one hour each day in adoration of your Lord, and never do anything you know is wrong. Follow this and you'll be fine.
Mother Teresa

Prayer is an ordinance of God, that must continue with a soul so long as it is on this side glory.
John Bunyan

Holiness is not you ceasing to sin, but firmly holding to what Jesus gave you.
Kevin Shorter

It is only when whatsoever we do is done in His name that He will do whatsoever we ask in His name.
The Kneeling Christian

What prayer most often changes is the wickedness and the hardness of our own hearts.
R.C. Sproul

When I don't get an answer [to prayer], I first look at my life. I look at my relationship with my wife. I check my motives.
Francis Chan

Every time I pray, I pray my best.
Smith Wigglesworth

The first step toward God is a step away from the lies of the world.
Eugene Peterson

Self turns what would otherwise be a pure and powerful prayer into a weak and ineffective one.
A.W. Tozer

He [Jesus] has a right to interrupt your life. He is Lord. When you accepted Him as Lord, you gave Him the right to help Himself to your life anytime He wants.
Henry Blackaby

Unless we are willing to pay the price, and sacrifice time and attention and what appears legitimate or necessary duties, for the sake of the heavenly gifts we need not look for a large experience of the power of the heavenly world in our work.
Andrew Murray

The conditions of praying are the conditions of righteousness, holiness, and salvation.
E.M. Bounds

Sincerity is the prime requisite in every approach to the God who... hates all hypocrisy, falsehood, and deceit.
Geoffrey B. Wilson

If we do not love one another, we certainly shall not have much power with God in prayer.
D.L. Moody

I can offer no worship wholly pleasing to God if I know that I am harboring elements in my life that are displeasing to Him.
A.W. Tozer

Because sin has been dealt with, we need to manage our freedom responsibly.
Danny Silk

The farther you go with God the less you can take with you.
Bill Johnson

Prayer is the guide to perfection, and prayer delivers us from every vice, and gives us every virtue; for the one way to become perfect is to walk in the presence of God.
Madame Guyon

He who prays as he ought, will endeavor to live as he prays.
John Owen

To begin our prayer with a petition for the hallowing of God's name and to have no real and prime place for holiness in our life or faith is not sincere.
P.T. Forsyth

Prayer is the touchstone of true godliness.
The Kneeling Christian

One sin allowed in the life wrecks at once our usefulness and our joy, and robs prayer of its power.
The Kneeling Christian

Prayer and a holy life are one. They mutually act and react. Neither can survive alone. The absence of the one is the absence of the other.
E.M. Bounds

A life growing in its purity and devotion will be a more prayerful life.
E.M. Bounds

If you're tolerating sin in your life, my friend, don't waste your breath praying unless it's a prayer of confession.
Bill Hybels

If you have integrity down and priorities central, then you are ready for a spirit of wisdom and revelation to give you glimpses into the greater things.
Bill Johnson

The first and last stages of holy living are crowned with praying.
E.M. Bounds

8 obstacles to prayer: No plan, no praise, no pattern, no purity, no peace, no passion, no persistence, no partner.
Jim Nicodem

The prayer preceding all prayers is "May it be the real I who speaks."
C.S. Lewis

Prayer as a relationship is probably your best indicator about the health of your love relationship with God. If your prayer life has been slack, your love relationship has grown cold.
John Piper

We must lay before Him what is in us, not what ought to be in us.
C.S. Lewis

The efficacy of prayer depends on uprightness of life and motive, wholehearted and sustained earnestness in the person praying, and how far it conforms to God's revealed purposes and ways.
J.I. Packer

Our Savior's call to prayer is simply a clarion call to holiness. Be ye holy! for without holiness no man can see God, and prayer cannot be efficacious.
The Kneeling Christian

Prayer is a serious thing. We may be taken at our words.
D.L. Moody

The thing about prayer that reaches God's ear is that it comes from a sincere heart that wants to walk in the light and is looking to God in faith.
Jim Cymbala

Cease to pray and thou will begin to sin.
William Gurnall

It is hard to hold God accountable to His promises if we value ours too little.
Kevin Shorter

Before prayer changes others, it first changes us.
Billy Graham

Our true character comes out in the way we pray.
Oswald Chambers

The goal of Revelation is so simple: see what God sees, hear what God hears, and speak what God speaks so we can all love the way God loves.
Shawn Bolz

The prayer of a person living right with God is something powerful to be reckoned with.
Eugene Peterson

All hindrance to prayer arises from ignorance of the teaching of God's Holy Word on the life of holiness He has planned for all His children or from an unwillingness to consecrate ourselves fully to Him.
The Kneeling Christian

Holiness is as indispensable for a spiritual warrior as is eyesight for a military fighter pilot.
C. Peter Wagner

Pride infects all our prayers, no matter how well worded they may be.
E.M. Bounds

God will never tell us to do something that gratifies the flesh.
Charles Stanley

I pray on the principle that wine knocks the cork out of a bottle. There is an inward fermentation, and there must be a vent.
Henry Ward Beecher

God only requires of his adult children, that their hearts be truly purified, and that they offer him continually the wishes and vows that naturally spring from perfect love. For these desires, being the genuine fruits of love, are the most perfect prayers that can spring from it.
John Wesley

He must set his heart to conquer by prayer, and that will mean that he must first conquer his own flesh, for it is the flesh that hinders prayer always.
A.W. Tozer

Perfectionism is fathered by fear. But excellence is fathered by His excellency.
Kris Vallotton

The desert call is to swap the saying of prayers for the being of our prayers.
Jane Williams

God will hear His people at the beginning of their prayers if the condition of their heart is ready for it.
C.H. Spurgeon

A consecrated life is both a prayer life and a thanksgiving life.
E.M. Bounds

Sin quenches prayer, affliction quickens it.
John Mason

Purity is vital to faith.
Smith Wigglesworth

Our lives must be as holy as our prayers.
Andrew Murray

The stream of praying cannot rise higher than the fountain of living.
E.M. Bounds

Prayer at its best is the expression of the total life, for all things else being equal, our prayers are only as powerful as our lives.
A.W. Tozer

How great is the position of the man who is born of God, born of purity, born of life, born of power!
Smith Wigglesworth

Is the prayer of my lips really the prayer of my life?
Andrew Murray

God does not discipline us to subdue us, but to condition us for a life of usefulness and blessedness.
Billy Graham

Is there any proof that a man is a man of God like the fact that he is a man of prayer? Of Elijah it is said that he 'prayed in his prayer' (James 5: 17).
Samuel Chadwick

The Role of Belief

Joy and hope are always attached to a belief system.
Wendy Backlund

The question is not 'Lord, tell me what to do.' The question is 'Lord, tell me what to believe.'
Steve Backlund

The reason why we obtain no more in prayer is because we expect no more. God usually answers us according to our own hearts.
Richard Alleine

A person who wholly follows the Lord is one who believes that the promises of God are trustworthy, that He is with His people, and that they are well able to overcome.
Watchman Nee

Your prayers are only limited by your belief of God - even then He may surprise you.
Kevin Shorter

If the truth sets us free, it is a lie that holds us in bondage.
Lance Wallnau

Your prayer life demonstrates what you really believe about God.
Darrin Patrick

Unbelief is perhaps the most widespread sin tolerated by Christians today.
Francis Frangipane

It is a totally wrong and fatal idea for one who would really pray to think of God as reluctant or unwilling to bless.
Albert D. Belden

We have permission to be hopeless about anything God is hopeless about.
Wendy Backlund

There is one door that can always stand in our way and keep us from receiving our miracle. It is the door of unbelief.
Daniel Kolenda

Believe that when you come into the presence of God you can have all you came for. You can take it away, and you can use it, for all the power of God is at your disposal in response to your faith.
Smith Wigglesworth

Fear of God failing us leads us to "cover for God." This means we ask, expect, and are satisfied with less.
Francis Chan

I believe that is scarcely a failure [in sin] that cannot be traced finally to imperfect ignoble thoughts about God.
A.W. Tozer

Our beliefs are the doors that keep shutting the passage to the realities that God has promised.
Kevin Shorter

What do I need to believe to have hope in this situation?
Wendy Backlund

The truths that I know best I have learned on my knees. I never know a thing well, till it is burned into my heart by prayer.
John Bunyon

We won't contend for anything we don't believe is ours to own.
Wendy Backlund

It is as natural and reasonable for a dependent creature to apply to its Creator for what it needs, as for a child thus to solicit the aid of a parent who is believed to have the disposition and ability to bestow what it needs.
Archibald Alexander

Blessed are those who believe when there is no evidence of an answer to prayer.
David Wilkerson

What we believe is more important than what we do.
Steve Backlund

We spend way too much time trying to change our emotions instead of trying to change the beliefs behind the emotions.
Wendy Backlund

Wisdom is believing that God hears you when you pray.
Mario Murillo

We must trust Him by not being worried, anxious or fearful. When we speak out our trust, our spirit pushes away the negative.
Graham Cooke

Our interpretations of our experiences in life result in our beliefs.
Kevin Shorter

It is no sin to doubt some things, but it may be fatal to believe everything.
A.W. Tozer

As believers, you don't need to pray for a new heart, you need to pray for a new head.
Andrew Wommack

Beware in your prayers, above everything else, of limiting God, not only by unbelief, but by fancying that you know what He can do. Expect unexpected things 'above all that we ask or think.
Andrew Murray

Your past isn't your problem. Your current beliefs are.
Steve Backlund

The way you think either expresses or undermines faith.
Bill Johnson

Trust perfected is prayer perfected. Trust looks to receive the thing asked for and gets it.
E.M. Bounds

It is really important for us to travel with God in joy, in laughter and in delight because He is faithful, powerful, and intentional!
Graham Cooke

God's past faithfulness is your present promise of His continual loving care.
Leah Dipascal

One can believe intellectually in the efficacy of prayer and never do any praying.
Catherine Marshall

The Kingdom of God is not advanced by good conduct. It's moved forward by good beliefs.
Steve Backlund

Apart from believing a lie, a Christian would not sin.
Bill Johnson

I want to help you decide that, by the power of God, you will not be ordinary.
Smith Wigglesworth

Hope believes explicitly in the nature of God. It is a solid defense that opens us up to all that God has purposed.
Graham Cooke

Your wildest imagination is nowhere near God's dream for you.
Graham Cooke

Believing lies empowers a disempowered devil.
Steve Backlund

The one thing most of us need to live in the destiny God has given us is to believe in ourselves the way God does.
Kevin Shorter

The degree with which we don't know our own heart is the degree that we will be hindered in knowing God's.
Kevin Shorter

We must never have a thought about God that does not magnify His love.
Graham Cooke

Christianity wants us to think less of ourselves else we get prideful, yet God always says we are better than we could even imagine.
Kevin Shorter

Beloved, it is not our long prayers but our believing God that gets the answer.
John G. Lake

If you don't know who you are, you are not going to pray what you should.
Kevin Shorter

If you believe that God will take care of all your needs, then why do you worry?
Wendy Backlund

Christians: Doesn't matter where you've been, God already sees you as you will be eternally: a saint with Christ.
Mark Driscoll

Never lose consciousness of the God that invades the impossible.
Bill Johnson

Words create worlds when they are an internal reality within yourself.
Kris Vallotton

There is nothing more important than what you think about God.
Graham Cooke

Wrong core beliefs hinder confidence in the power of our prayers.
Steve Backlund

Prayer frees us from anxiety because it teaches us to trust. And the result is peace.
Richard Foster

Before God can deliver us we must undeceive ourselves.
Augustine

Faith means believing that being in it with God is better than being anywhere else without Him.
Kelly O'Dell Stanley

A lot of prayer is actually an expression of unbelief.
Bill Johnson

You can't believe a lie when you are speaking the truth.
Steve Backlund

A lot of what we call our personality is really just bad beliefs.
Steve Backlund

Any revelation that does not bring us into greater encounter only trains us to be more religious.
Bill Johnson

The more we don't believe in the greatness God put in us we are sabotaging God's plan of redemption for your area of influence.
Kevin Shorter

Frustration is a sign of hopelessness.
Wendy Backlund

It is impossible to renew your mind and not be transformed.
Wendy Backlund

If we believe all circumstances are good, we will subconsciously think prayer is pointless.
Steve Backlund

Laughter is a powerful weapon to break off the absurdity of what we believe.
Steve Backlund

Fear often looks like wisdom to those in unbelief.
Bill Johnson

What comes into our minds when we think about God is the most important thing about us.
A.W. Tozer

Our hope levels are indicators of whether we are believing truth or lies.
Steve Backlund

Experience will catch up to beliefs; the gap time is called faith.
Steve Backlund

Don't pray out of need, but out of identity and inheritance. You'll get a much bigger response.
Graham Cooke

Fear of who you may become will keep you from who God made you to be.
Kevin Shorter

My heart can go where my head can't fit.
Bill Johnson

The essence of idolatry is the entertainment of thoughts about God that are unworthy of Him.
A.W. Tozer

Asking things of God shows a dependence on Him, a belief that He will come through for us, and a confidence that He is more than able.
Kevin Shorter

Before a word of petition is offered, we should have the definite and vivid consciousness that we are talking to God and should believe that He is listening to our petition and is going to grant the thing that we ask of Him. We should look to the Holy Spirit to really lead us into the presence of God and should not be hasty in words until He has actually brought us there.
R.A. Torrey

Make your thoughts and conversations consistent with your prayers.
Bill Johnson

The question is not what should I do. The question is what should I believe. Because if I believe the right things then I will do the right things.
Wendy Backlund

You are who Jesus says you are. You do what you think you are. Do they line up?
Kevin Shorter

What you pray, reflects what you believe about God.
Craig Groeschel

Even in "prayer," your words produce either death or life. Praying God's solution from the Word releases life, but praying negatively and focusing on your problems only energizes and strengthens them—whether you realize it or not!
Andrew Wommack

The problem with most Christians is that we trust more in the blackness of our hearts than the goodness of God's heart for us.
Kevin Shorter

If you have a distorted image of God, you will have a distorted image of yourself. That's why we must focus on being Christlike.
Graham Cooke

What they heard was dependent upon whom they believed Jesus to be.
Judy Franklin

Truth that doesn't set you free is not truth.
Graham Cooke

What we believe after we pray is just as important as what we believe when we pray.
Steve Backlund

If we pray little, it is probably because we do not really believe that prayer accomplishes much at all.
Wayne Grudem

We can't consistently do what we don't believe we are.
Steve Backlund

Unbelief is safe, because it takes no risk and almost always gets what it expects.
Bill Johnson

God's voice brings change in us as it transforms our mind.
Kevin Shorter

If I truly believe nothing is impossible, then I have a lifestyle where I will take risks.
Bill Johnson

Misinterpretations of life and wrong beliefs about ourselves, God, and others create fear that keep us from living from our hearts.
Kevin Shorter

We need to believe God for great things. God is just waiting for us to believe Him for even greater dreams.
Bill Bright

God's sovereignty does not negate our responsibility to pray, but rather makes it possible to pray with confidence.
Jerry Bridges

For this reason the gravest question before the Church is always God Himself, and the most portentous fact about any man is not what he at a given time may say or do, but what he is in his deep heart conceives God to be like.
A.W. Tozer

Never be afraid to trust an unknown future to a known God.
Corrie ten Boom

No one can believe how powerful prayer is and what it can effect, except those who have learned it by experience.
Martin Luther

No matter what I preach or what we claim to believe in our heads, the future will depend upon our times of prayer.
Jim Cymbala

Renewing our mind means we must learn the Holy Spirit's pleasure and enthusiasm in canceling out our old belief about ourselves.
Graham Cooke

Any burden too small to be turned into a prayer is too small to be made into a burden.
Corrie ten Boom

Fear is a powerful demotivator. It reveals what we really believe.
Kevin Shorter

The reason people don't go to God is they don't believe He is for them.
Kevin Shorter

A "prayer warrior" is a person who is convinced that God is omnipotent—that God has the power to do anything, to change anyone and to intervene in any circumstance. A person who truly believes this refuses to doubt God.
Bill Hybels

Any area that doesn't have an expectation of good is under the influence of a lie.
Bill Johnson

You will know you believe something if your emotions line up with it even in the face of opposition.
Wendy Backlund

The Role of Faith

Your fear is the greatest limitation to experiencing the abundant life God has promised you.
Kevin Shorter

Don't ask someone who has a history of being negative for advice about your step of faith that doesn't make sense.
E.M. Bounds

Is it a sign of unbelief to repeat our prayer? That is a mistake. It is little use praying in the first place without faith.
Reinhard Bonnke

Faith is always praying... Prayer is always believing.
Shirley Dobson

The soul seeks God by faith, not by the reasonings of the mind and labored efforts, but by the drawings of love; to which inclinations God responds, and instructs the soul, which co-operates actively. God then puts the soul in a passive state where He accomplishes all, causing great progress, first by way of enjoyment, then by privation, and finally by pure love.
Madame Guyon

Provision is a consequence to a promise believed.
Graham Cooke

Faith in the nature of God is what keeps you moving even when situations are against you because you KNOW that God is faithful.
Graham Cooke

Real faith not only does something for us, but it also does something to us.
A.W. Tozer

Worry is not believing God will get it right, and bitterness is believing God got it wrong.
Tim Keller

Too much faith hasn't been a problem. Our problem has been believing too little.
Francis Frangipane

Faith honors God by counting Him righteous and accepts His testimony against the very evidence of its own senses.
A.W. Tozer

When trust is perfect and there is no doubt, prayer is simply the outstretched hand ready to receive. Trust perfected is prayer perfected.
E.M. Bounds

Faith is the pathway through which we access the supernatural ways of God.
Kevin Shorter

Faith is generated in the atmosphere of experiencing truth.
Bill Johnson

Unless there is an expectancy, faith is not fully in exercise.
A.W. Pink

The nature of faith is you believe something before you see it.
Steve Backlund

Fear is faith in the power of the enemy!
Wendy Backlund

The prayer that is faithless is fruitless.
Thomas Watson

It matters little what form of prayer we adopt or how many words we use. What matters is the faith which lays hold on God, knowing that He knows our needs before we even ask Him. That is what gives Christian prayer its boundless confidence and its joyous certainty.
Dietrich Bonhoeffer

Faith is deliberate confidence in the character of God whose ways you may not understand at the time.
Oswald Chambers

It is good to have the laugh of faith. When doubt whines and cries, faith laughs.
C.T. Studd

When we have a problem, we can worry about it, or we can choose to trust God.
Joyce Meyer

The problem isn't God's willingness or ability to give, but rather our ability to believe and receive.
Andrew Wommack

The door is closed to prayer unless it is opened with the key of trust.
John Calvin

Worry is imagining your future as if God doesn't show up.
Wendy Backlund

Everyone experiences what seem to be unanswered prayers. But in God's economy, no one's faith is ever wasted.
Steven Furtick

To pray rightly is a rare gift. Doubtful prayer is no prayer at all. Prayer is the chief exercise of faith.
John Calvin

It is one thing to have faith that God can do something, it is quite another to believe that we can do the same thing in His name.
Steve Backlund

Here is the definition for the fear of God: to care more about what God thinks than anyone else.
Kevin Shorter

Faith is not presumption but assumption. You rightly assume that God will never let you down—and thus "enter into rest."
Reinhard Bonnke

Faith is the vital principle of prayer.
Reinhard Bonnke

Joy makes way for hope, which leads to faith that creates the atmosphere for God's miraculous answers.
Kevin Shorter

Pray, hope, and don't worry. Worry is useless. God is merciful and will hear your prayer.
Padre Pio

The life of faith is grabbing hold of God's promises and living as if they are true.
Kevin Shorter

Pray according to faith, not circumstances.
Woodrow Kroll

When we pray from a place of peace and not fear, we will see fruit.
Beni Johnson

We will never overcome this world if we are living in fear of it.
Kevin Shorter

Imagination is the place to develop faith because faith isn't blind, it's visionary.
Kris Vallotton

As we battle spiritual forces, it is important to distinguish between the burden of the Lord and the weight of unbelief.
Wendy Backlund

When you do business with people you need money. When you do business with God you need faith.

Faith is the currency of the Kingdom of God.
Reinhard Bonnke

If you want to pray in faith, you have to get rid of your fear.
Wendy Backlund

As you let your mind focus on God's goodness, your faith will rise up.
Kevin Shorter

Can you imagine a life with no fear? What if faith, not fear, was your default reaction to threats?
Max Lucado

The promises are the ground of faith, and faith, when strengthened, will make thee fervent, and such fervency ever speeds and returns with victory out of the field of prayer.
William Gurnall

Faith in a prayer-hearing God will make a prayer-loving Christian.
Andrew Murray

Do we have to see it to believe it? Yes. Faith needs to see it in our hearts.
Kevin Shorter

Faith moves Heaven, so that Heaven will move earth.
Bill Johnson

You have to live by faith. You have to believe that God is there when everything says that He is not.
Graham Cooke

God's promises are the cork to keep faith from sinking in prayer.
Thomas Watson

The stretching of our faith prepares us to receive the promise.
Kevin Shorter

Audacious faith is the raw material that authentic Christianity is made of. It's the stuff that triggers ordinarily level-headed people like you and me to start living with unusual boldness.
Steven Furtick

There are two main principles I've picked up over the years as they pertain to cultivating the type of faith that moves mountains. The first is this: Faith comes by looking at God, not at the mountain. The second is this: God gives us faith as we walk by his side.
Bill Hybels

It is not the length, but heartfelt faith that makes your prayer a quality effective prayer.
Andrew Wommack

Natural ability and educational advantages do not figure as factors in this matter of prayer; but a capacity for faith, the power of a thorough consecration, the ability of self-littleness, an absolute losing of one's self in God's glory and an ever present and insatiable yearning and seeking after all the fullness of God.
E.M. Bounds

Faith feeds from the invisible world towards our visible one.
Bill Johnson

Hope gives room for faith and faith prepares a place for God to move.
Kevin Shorter

Visualizing a victory or working up a "feeling" of faith is a pathetic human attempt to get something to happen. Real faith lays hold of the Faith-giver (Eph. 2:8), who holds all power for every need, and trusts Him to answer our prayer as He promised He would do.
Jack Hayford

If you can't see it, you won't have the faith to pray for it.
Kevin Shorter

A dump truck of desire will not move God but a pinch faith will.
Kevin Adams

Great faith is the full trust in the love and goodness of God for you.
Kevin Shorter

Praying men must be strong in hope, and faith, and prayer.
E.M. Bounds

We are good at praying but not good at receiving. We are to receive it all by faith.
Wendy Backlund

Prayer and faith enable us to take possession of those promises and appropriate them in our lives.
Morris Cerrulo

Having faith often means doing what others see as crazy. Something is wrong when our lives make sense to unbelievers.
> *Francis Chan*

Great faith is the product of great fights.
> *Smith Wigglesworth*

Do you know what prayer is? It is not begging God for this and that. The first thing we have to do is to get you beggars to quit begging until a little faith moves in your souls.
> *John G. Lake*

To the man of faith, there is not a thing that is not opportunity.
> *Smith Wigglesworth*

Prayer is asking for rain; faith is carrying the umbrella.
> *John Mason*

When faith sets prayer on work, prayer sets God on work.
> *Thomas Watson*

Without faith your prayer can actually be sin.
> *Daniel Kolenda*

Faith sees the invisible, believes the unbelievable, and receives the impossible.
> *Corrie ten Boom*

Abiding faith attracts the promises of God.
> *Bill Johnson*

Bold faith stands on the shoulders of quiet trust.
> *Bill Johnson*

Neither the length nor eloquence of your prayers causes God to answer. God responds to faith.
> *Rick Warren*

Just like you don't pull the trigger on a gun unless it's aimed and loaded, neither should you pray your prayer unless you know you're in faith!
> *Andrew Wommack*

I have learned that faith means trusting in advance what will only make sense in reverse.
> *Phillip Yancey*

Faith generally means openly taking some sort of risk and of being willing to look a fool before others.
> *Hannah Hurnard*

Prayer is faith in action.
> *Reinhard Bonnke*

Doubtful prayer is no prayer at all.
> *John Calvin*

It is only when Christ's words abide in us that our prayers will be answered. Then we can ask what we will and it shall be done, because we shall will only what He wills.
> *John Stott*

I am not here to entertain you, but to get you to the place where you can laugh at the impossible.
> *Smith Wigglesworth*

When you magnify the promises instead of the problems, that's your faith being released.
Joel Osteen

Unbelief creates a vacuum in your life that the enemy is more than willing to fill.
Graham Cooke

[The prayer of faith] is a prayer willing to believe and prevail for God's answer in a situation that is utterly impossible. Regardless of the difficulty of the situation, you require no external confirmation but believe God in spite of appearance. Your eyes are on God, not on the situation.
Wesley Duewel

Only God can move mountains, but faith and prayer can move God.
E.M. Bounds

The reason you are hopeless about yourself is because your faith is in YOU.
Steve Backlund

When entering the prayer chamber, we must come filled with faith and armed with courage.
A.W. Tozer

Just as our faith strengthens our prayer life, so do our prayers deepen our faith. Let us pray often, starting today, for a deeper, more powerful faith.
Shirley Dobson

The breath of prayer comes from the life of faith.
John Mason

Without faith, God's grace is wasted, and without grace, faith is powerless.
Andrew Wommack

Faith is at the root of all true worship, and without faith it is impossible to please God.
A.W. Tozer

Joy is an act of faith in God's goodness, and it creates a landing platform for the arrival of God's answers and provisions.
Kevin Shorter

True prayer is the voice of faith!
Morris Cerrulo

The reason so many struggle with faith is that they lack hope. If you have no hope, faith has nothing to give substance to.
John Bevere

If we don't know the extent of God's love for us, we will not be fully convinced of His love for other people.
Kevin Shorter

Faith thrives in an atmosphere of prayer.
E.M. Bounds

Faith is like radar that sees through the fog ....the reality of things at a distance that the human eye cannot see.
Corrie ten Boom

Faith is visionary not blind. You have seen it in the unseen realm.
Wendy Backlund

Faith is the offspring of grace.
Bill Johnson

The life of faith is only comfortable because of the One you have faith in. He makes faith the only comfortable place.
Kevin Shorter

Faith is not the absence of doubt, it's the means to overcome it.
Steven Furtick

Prayer is not telling God what to do; it's standing in faith for the things God has promised while circumstances tell us He has forgotten all about us.
Kevin Shorter

Unbelief is easier than faith because it only demands denial.
Graham Cooke

Prayer assumes the sovereignty of God. If God is not sovereign, we have no assurance that He is able to answer our prayers. Our prayers would become nothing more than wishes. But while God's sovereignty, along with His wisdom and love, is the foundation of our trust in Him, prayer is the expression of that trust.
Jerry Bridges

Trust always operates in the present tense. Hope looks toward the future. Trust looks to the present. Hope expects. Trust possesses.
E.M. Bounds

Faith never knows where it is being led, but it loves and knows the One who is leading.
Oswald Chambers

Many a person is praying for rain with his tub the wrong side up.
Sam Jones

Any faith that must be supported by the evidence of the senses is not real faith.
A.W. Tozer

Faith is believing that He sees and believing that He rewards.
Misty Edwards

Praying in faith is a God ordained way to receive His blessing in both our internal lives and our external circumstances.
Mike Bickle

Either worrying drives out prayer, or prayer drives out worrying.
D.A. Carson

Worry is so deadly because it saps the strength from your faith.
Kevin Shorter

Prayer goes by faith into the great orchard of God's exceeding great and precious promises, and with hand and heart picks the ripest and richest fruit.
E.M. Bounds

Our prayers reveal our faith (or lack of) in God's power over our world.
Kevin Shorter

Fear looks; faith jumps. Faith never fails to obtain its object.
Smith Wigglesworth

God does not require you to have great faith. You simply are to have faith in a great God.
Bill Bright

Faith doesn't deny a problems existence. It denies it a place of influence.
Bill Johnson

Faith is the fountain of prayer, and prayer should be nothing else but faith exercised.
Thomas Manton

Faith is a gift of God. Without it there would be no life. And our work, to be fruitful, and to be all for God, and to be beautiful, has to be built on faith — faith in Christ, who has said, I was hungry, I was naked, I was sick, and I was homeless, and you ministered to me. On these words of His, our work is based.
Mother Teresa

The man who prays without faith has a radical defect in his character.
Thomas Manton

Faith removes the mountains which unbelief creates.
Reinhard Bonnke

Prayer is more than a wish turned heavenward... It is the voice of faith directed Godward.
Billy Graham

Faith isn't just what you believe, it's what you expect.
Joaquin Evans

Prayer is the chief exercise of faith.
John Calvin

Faith never denies reality but leaves room for God to grant a new reality.
Jim Cymbala

Praying without faith is like shooting without a bullet; it makes a noise but does no execution.
Francis Burkitt

The truth is that faith and worry cannot inhabit the same space at the same time. One of them has to go, and we get to choose.
Graham Cooke

Trust receives what prayer acquires. So, what prayer needs, at all times, is abiding and abundant trust.
E.M. Bounds

If we don't get what we believed in faith, hope keeps us safe by believing something better is coming.
Wendy Backlund

The reason that our prayers are not answered is that we are not stupid enough to believe what Jesus says.
Oswald Chambers

Fear actually creates static in the spirit realm that prevents us from hearing God's voice clearly.
Wendy Backlund

Faith is not the absence of doubt; it is the presence of belief.
Bill Johnson

There are no depths from which the prayer of faith cannot reach heaven.
John Blanchard

Those who do not believe do not pray. This is a good functional definition of faith. Faith prays, unbelief does not.
John A. Hardon

God has never been nervous about his ability to live up to our faith in him.
Steven Furtick

Faith is taking hold of what is unseen and making it visible.
Kevin Shorter

If faith fails, prayer perishes.
Augustine

It's very important to pray out of a place of peace.
Beni Johnson

You can laugh in the face of hardships because they are really just opportunities for God to show His faithfulness to you.
Kevin Shorter

Hope is where you hear God and obey whether it is understood.
Bob Hartley

Praying without faith is like trying to cut with a blunt knife - much labor expended to little purpose.
James Fraser

I believe that prayer mixed with faith is the answer to everything.
David Wilkerson

Jesus put some disciples outside the room when he needed to raise the dead. In a crisis you need to detach from those with doubt.
Lance Wallnau

Hindrances to following God: the things I love, the things I fear and the things I doubt.
Kris Vallotton

Faith provides eyes to the heart. Faith sees.
Bill Johnson

Hope is the joyful anticipation of good.
Bill Johnson

Prayer is the supreme activity of all that is noblest in our personality, and the essential nature of prayer is faith.
Oswald Chambers

That prayer brings glory to God is further seen from the fact that prayer calls faith into exercise, and nothing from us is so honoring and pleasing to Him as the confidence of our hearts.
A.W. Pink

A declaration is a faith statement about what's true whether it is in our experience or not.
Steve Backlund

When we choose faith that God is going to show up over what looks impossible, God is greatly pleased.
Kevin Shorter

Our faith may be resting on a wrong basis: faith in faith or faith in prayer rather than faith in God.
Ivan French

Keep on praying for faith, it is through prayer that you develop all your wonderful qualities of soul.
Myrtle Fillmore

Praying with faith and expectancy will always attract the presence and power of God just as the absence of these key elements will repel the presence and power of God.
Daniel Kolenda

Prayer is the very natural breath of faith.
William Gurnall

The real reason my prayers were weak was that my faith was weak.
Bill Hybels

Our faith can only go as far as our awareness of God's goodness.
Bill Johnson

Faith is the power line, but prayer switches it on.
Reinhard Bonnke

Our intimacy and relationship with Him will have a direct correlation to our level of faith; not because it "earns" us more authority, but because it gives something for our faith to stand on.
Wendy Backlund

Faith is a leap into the light, not a step into the darkness.
Reinhard Bonnke

The Role of Listening

We need to find God, and He cannot be found in noise and restlessness. God is the friend of silence. See how nature—trees, flowers, grass—grows in silence; see the stars, the moon and the sun, how they move in silence... We need silence to be able to touch souls.
Mother Teresa

The goal of reading the Word is to listen for the voice of the God who speaks.
Eugene Peterson

The wise man comes to God without saying a word and stands in awe of Him.
Francis Chan

Nothing deafens a hearing heart more quickly than unwillingness to keep open to further light.
Hannah Hurnard

Prophecy bridges the gap from [God's] heart to ours and helps us go from small-mindedness to a big picture.
Shawn Bolz

Samuel prayed "Speak Lord, I'm listening!" Too often we pray "Listen Lord, I'm speaking!" Prayer is LISTENING too.
Rick Warren

We are trying not so much to make God listen to us as to make ourselves listen to Him; we are trying not to persuade God to do what we want, but to find out what He wants us to do.
William Barclay

Hearing God doesn't have to be mystical. I like to think of the supernatural things of God as being a natural part of our lives. That would make us naturally supernatural!
Doug Addison

With an anxious heart we make petition but only with a rested heart can we truly learn to listen.
Kevin Adams

The great principle of the hearing heart is that we become as little children, utterly dependent and always ready to obey.
Hannah Hurnard

How great is it that God wants to speak to us. Our greatest limitation is not believing that He will.
Kevin Shorter

If God isn't saying anything, go back over what He has said.
Graham Cooke

The way to hear God's voice is by talking to Him and then sitting and listening.
Justin Rizzo

If you do all the talking when you pray, how will you ever hear God's answers?
A.W. Tozer

There is no one way or method for hearing God. He is mutlifaceted, and when we try to put Him in a box, we will miss the unlimited power and creativity available to us.
Doug Addison

God speaks in the silence of the heart. Listening is the beginning of prayer.
Mother Teresa

The world's screaming at us that we are worthless and we have believed it. God is whispering it is not true.

Kevin Shorter

God is always preparing and positioning us for divine appointments. And prayer is the way we discern our next move.

Mark Batterson

Nothing holds greater power to transform your inner life than that moment when God's voice touches your heart with revelation of who He is.

IHOP

Prayer is putting oneself under God's influence.

Harry Emerson Fosdick

The facts are that God is not silent, has never been silent. Its the nature of God to speak.

A.W. Tozer

Hearing God's voice should be as natural to a believer as taking a breath.

Kevin Shorter

It so often happens that in prayer we are really saying, 'Thy will be changed,' when we ought to be saying, 'Thy will be done.' The first object of prayer is not so much to speak to God as to listen to Him.

William Barclay

To pray is to listen to the One who calls you "my beloved daughter," "my beloved son," my beloved child."

Henri Nouwen

The sheep hear His voice, but the sons do what they see Him doing!

Brian Clark

We can miss God's still, gentle voice if we do not slow down enough to listen.

Doug Addison

Get into the habit of saying, "Speak, Lord," and life will become a romance.

Oswald Chambers

Prayer at its highest is a two-way conversation and for me the most important part is listening to God's replies.

Frank Laubach

Many times He doesn't talk to me because He can't wait to see what I'll choose.

Shawn Bolz

Every person should have a hunger to hear the voice of God.

Bill Johnson

For everything you discern, there is a deeper, more original thought about it in God's heart.

Shawn Bolz

Sometimes we can fill our time with activities that appear worthwhile but actually hinder us from spending time hearing God.

Doug Addison

Yieldedness is vital in listening to what He has to say.
Charles Stanley

How can God speak to us if we don't take time to listen? Quietness is essential to listening. If we are too busy to listen, we won't hear. It takes time and quietness to prepare to listen to God (Psalm 62:5).
Charles Stanley

Everything you see, even if you feel like you are only imagining it, has significance. That is why it is important for you to know that you can go back to a scene during prayer, revisit it, and ask God to show you more about what you are seeing.
Judy Franklin

God wants to speak to you about your life and help bring context to what He's doing in you.
Shawn Bolz

A season of silence is the best preparation for speech with God.
Samuel Chadwick

Life doesn't come from revelation; it comes from the encounter brought about by the revelation.
Bill Johnson

Every work undertaken in obedienced to a divine command, whether the work be that form of conflict with the powers of darkness that we call prayer, or whether it be the action that follows, leads sooner or later to a new demand on personal devotion to our Lord Jesus Christ.
Amy Carmichael

A hearing heart and a listening ear produce a fruitful life. It's just that simple. Have you heard Him lately?
Dutch Sheets

Did Jesus say "I only do what the Scriptures tell me to do?" NO. He said: "I only do what the Father tells me to do, what I see Him do!"
Kris Vallotton

Prayer - if it be a monologue, you be the one listening.
Jay Harris

If you aren't willing to listen to everything [Holy Spirit] has to say, you won't hear anything He has to say.
Mark Batterson

Jesus is not idle, nor has he developed laryngitis.
Richard Foster

Most people don't want to get in touch with God, because they're convinced He is just going to talk badly to them.
Graham Cooke

[Jesus and the apostles] obviously believed that they knew the will of God was before they prayed the prayer of faith.
Richard Foster

The man who has gotten God's word in the prayer closet neither seeks nor expects encouragement from men for the delivery of that word. The Spirit himself bears witness of the approval.
Leonard Ravenhill

Prayer is speaking to God—but sometimes He uses our times of prayerful silence to speak to us in return.
Billy Graham

Every time God speaks to you, it is to put a smile on your face.
Graham Cooke

Listen to your heart; the eyes will deceive.
Bill Bright & Ted Dekker

While we are waiting for Him to speak to our mind, He is waiting for an opportunity to speak to our heart.
Wendy Backlund

The main thing that God asks for is our attention.
Jim Cymbala

[Meditation is] the detachment from the confusion all around us in order to have a richer attachment to God.
Richard Foster

[In our fast-paced life] we have no time for contemplation. We have no time to answer God when He calls.
A.W. Tozer

Every believer has the ability to receive inspiration from God because we are His sheep and we know His voice.
Allison Shorter

When you have a heart for God, you have access to the secrets of God.
Bill Johnson

We can have no deep, ongoing fellowship with God unless we obey Him - totally.
Bill Hybels

There are so many voices and opinions speaking into our lives every day. We have to fight to keep God's voice as the loudest and clearest.
Justin Rizzo

God doesn't speak to your head. Why would He speak to the hardest part of you?
Graham Cooke

If you want to hear the voice of God, listen to your wife.
John Wimber

Let us give God the chance of putting His mind into us, and we shall never doubt the power of prayer again.
The Kneeling Christian

An unschooled man who knows how to meditate upon the Lord has learned far more than the man with the highest education who does not know how to meditate.
Charles Stanley

God never ceases to speak to us, but the noise of the world without and the tumult of our passions within bewilder us and prevent us from listening to Him.
François Fénelon

God always talks to your heart first not your head. You asked Him into your heart; not your head.
Graham Cooke

The voice of the Lord is like a whisper at times. That's why being still is important to prophecy. In the peace of God, revelation flows.
Graham Cooke

In prayer, more is accomplished by listening than by talking.
Jane Frances de Chantal

God's voice is still and quiet and easily buried under an avalanche of clamour.
Charles Stanley

God sometimes seems to speak to us most intimately when He catches us, as it were, off our guard.
C.S. Lewis

You need to rejoice. Don't put pressure on yourself to hear. The pressure is on God to speak, not on you to hear. If you rejoice, you will hear!
Graham Cooke

You belong to God. This makes you fully capable of hearing His voice.
John Bevere

Prayer is humbling work. It abases intellect and pride, crucifies vainglory and signs our spiritual bankruptcy, and all these are hard for flesh and blood to bear.
E.M. Bounds

You have to believe what you hear in your spirit even when you see just the opposite. This is what faith is all about.
Joel Osteen

We must forget ourselves and all self-interest, and listen, and be attentive to God.
Madame Guyon

Those who love most, see most.
Hannah Hurnard

A joyful heart finds it easy to trust and to hear the voice of God.
Graham Cooke

Our prayer life will become restful when it really dawns upon us that we have done all we are supposed to do when we have spoken to Him about it. From the moment we have left it with Him, it is His responsibility.
O. Hallesby

Through practice and knowing what to look for, we can become confident in our ability to hear His voice.
Wendy Backlund

Expect our children to hear from God. Ask them what Jesus would say if He walked into the room. Teach them to think how God thinks.

Kris Vallotton

If God said it, I believe it, and that jolly well settles it! That has to be enough. It's always going to be enough.

Graham Cooke

We remove the fear of making a mistake [in hearing God] by making our God bigger than any mistake we can make.

Wendy Backlund

Hearing from God isn't supposed to be a hard subject.

Shawn Bolz

I believe we try to make hearing God so difficult that we create an environment where we can no longer hear Him.

Kevin Shorter

If your life is rushing in many directions at once, you are incapable of the kind of deep, unhurried prayer that is vital to the Christian walk.

Bill Hybels

God can't help but speak His mysteries and inner thoughts, downloading them to those He loves.

Shawn Bolz

God aims to exalt Himself by working for those who wait for Him. Prayer is the essential activity of waiting for God.

John Piper

The real "work" of prayer is to become silent and listen to the voice that says good things about me.

Henri Nouwen

If Jesus Christ is bringing you into the understanding that prayer is for the glorifying of His Father, He will give you the first sign of His intimacy-silence.

Oswald Chambers

When the voice of God speaks to you, it comes with courage.

Banning Liebscher

I love how hearing from God gives you opportunities you never would have had without his voice.

Shawn Bolz

Men would pray better if they lived better. They would get more from God if they lived more obedient and well-pleasing to God.

E.M. Bounds

When you are in the dark, listen, and God will give you a very precious message.

Oswald Chambers

To people in the fast lane, determined to make it on their own, prayer is an embarrassing interruption.

Bill Hybels

We are on the whole disposed to emphasize activity in prayer too much.

                                    O. Hallesby

Talk in prayer is essential but it is also partial. Silence is essential.

                         Eugene Peterson

What God is saying is always the right answer – much more efficient to develop our listening skills than our intelligence.

                                Kevin Adams

God always speaks to your potential, not your actual.

                              Graham Cooke

The call of God is not just for a select few but for everyone. Whether I hear God's call or not depends on the condition of my ears, and exactly what I hear depends upon my spiritual attitude.

                         Oswald Chambers

Never assume what God may do. Assumption kills relationship; it breaks connection and leads to rules.

                              Kevin Shorter

The Quaker habit of prayer was sitting in complete silence in His presence, lifting our hearts to Him and asking Him to cleanse our thoughts and show us if there was anything to confess or put right before we began to pray together. Then we began to pray together, simply and informally, as though we were holding conversation with the Lord.

                         Hannah Hurnard

God's voice speaking tenderly to our hearts today is the same voice that powerfully called creation into being.

                                A.W. Tozer

If you really listen you will discover that God has much to say to you.

                                  Jay Harris

Since God knows our future, our personalities, and our capacity to listen, He isn't every going to say more to us than we can deal with at the moment.

                            Charles Stanley

The essence of meditation is a period of time set aside to contemplate the Lord, listen to Him, and allow Him to permeate our spirits.

                            Charles Stanley

The value of consistent prayer is not that He will hear us, but that we will hear Him.

                            William McGill

Prayer is speaking to God, but sometimes He uses our times of prayerful silence to speak to us in return.

                              Billy Graham

No matter what we pray for, whether it be temporal or spiritual things, little things or great things, gifts for ourselves or others, our prayers should resolve themselves into a quiet waiting for the Lord in order to hear what it is the Spirit desires to have us pray for at that particular time.
O. Hallesby

Prayer is the very way God Himself has chosen for us to express our conscious need of Him and our humble dependence on Him.
John Stott

A hearing heart depends upon an utter willingness to obey.
Hannah Hurnard

You have no right to believe anything about yourself that God did not say about you.
Kevin Shorter

Why would God speak to your old man when the new man is so much more compelling to Him?
Graham Cooke

The Lord has taught us that nobody can know God unless God teaches him.
Irenaeus

What hinders me from hearing is that I am taken up with other things. It is not that I will not hear God, but I am not devoted in the right place. I am devoted to things, to service, to convictions, and God may say what He likes but I do not hear Him.
Oswald Chambers

If God is speaking to your heart, don't let your mind get in the way of what God wants you to do.
Mark Batterson

One of the most important features of being a minister unto the Lord is to have a heart for the voice of God.
Bill Johnson

Too often our problem is that we listen to the news rather than sitting and listening to the voice of God in our own circumstances!
Graham Cooke

When people hear the thoughts and emotions of God toward them, they believe in his love for them.
Shawn Bolz

God delights in showing us exciting new alternatives for the future.
Richard Foster

Our challenge with faith is not an inability to hear God's voice, it's our willingness to listen to other voices.
Bill Johnson

Before we can pray, "Thy Kingdom come," we must be willing to pray, "My kingdom go."
Alan Redpath

The more we give the Holy Spirit's presence a place of honor in our lives, the more sensitive we become to His voice.
Daniel Kolenda

Fall on your knees and grow there. There is no burden of the spirit but is lighter by kneeling under it. Prayer means not always talking to Him, but waiting before Him till the dust settles and the stream runs clear.
F.B. Meyer

We put ourselves down trying to make God look better. But that's not what God does. He's trying to tell us how great we are.
Kevin Shorter

God wants us to hear His voice more than we want to hear it, so He is persistent!
James Goll

Strict adherence to your plans will cause you to miss God's unconventional ways.
Kevin Shorter

Some people want God to speak to them about everything because they have no identity.
Shawn Bolz

Caring for your heart is also how you protect your relationship with God... The heart is where we commune with him. It is where we hear his voice.
John Eldredge

Often people who are naturally gifted with a lot of common sense and organising ability find it very difficult to believe that any guidance can be right which looks foolish or contrary to common sense, and are never willing to accept such guidance. In that case it is difficult for them to develop the hearing heart, and they go through life largely dependent on their judgement.
Hannah Hurnard

The true waiting for the Lord, and going forth to meet the Bridegroom, is hidden from outward observation.
Adolph Saphir

If you have trouble hearing God speak, you are in trouble at the very heart of your Christian experience.
Henry Blackaby

Hearing from God does not come through effort; it comes through surrender.
Bill Johnson

Listening to God's voice is the secret of the assurance that He will listen to mine.
Andrew Murray

Unconsciously, we limit God from speaking to us because we are straining to hear words.
Wendy Backlund

Rejecting God's voice is rejecting His face as it rejects the opportunity for an authentic relationship with Him.
Bill Johnson

Sometimes loving God with all your heart simply means listening to your heart instead of your head.
Mark Batterson

Most Christians do believe that God still speaks to people today, just not necessarily to them. If we change our focus and accept that God loves us and longs to speak to us, there is a good chance we will begin to hear God in ways we never thought possible.
Doug Addison

The process of learning to distinguish between the voice of our spirit and the voice of our mind is a journey of trial and error.
Wendy Backlund

Why is it that when we talk to God, it's called 'prayer,' but when God speaks to us, it's called schizophrenia?
Henry Blackaby

People could be built far greater in the Lord and be more wonderfully established if they would move out sometimes and think over the graces of the Lord.
Smith Wigglesworth

God is not forcing you to listen to Him; that is what the enemy does. God is waiting for His people to ask.
Matt Peterson

Real prayer is always an answer to God's revelation.
Tim Keller

The lover of silence draws close to God. He talks to Him in secret and God enlightens him.
John Climacus

I am convinced that God is trying to speak to us all, but we have just not been trained to listen.
Doug Addison

God longs to talk to His children and show us secrets of the Kingdom.
Allison Shorter

Until you hear the voice of God, you won't be able to sing His song.
Mark Batterson

Prayer is a discipline, preceded by the foundation of listening.
Graham Cooke

But we first need to behold God. In waiting, we look at Him and not the problem or request. We abide in Him; then in turn He abides in us. That's when the fresh wind of God can blow on us.
Beni Johnson

Prayer is the most tangible expression of trust in God.
Jerry Bridges

Attuning ourselves to divine breathings is spiritual work, but without it our prayer is vain repetition.
Richard Foster

The trouble with nearly everybody who prays is that he says 'Amen' and runs away before God has a chance to reply. Listening to God is far more important than giving Him our ideas.
Frank Laubach

We should not open our mouths too hastily upon approaching God. On the contrary, we first must ask God to show us what and how to pray before we make our request known to Him. Have we not consumed a great deal of time in the past asking for what we wanted? Why not now ask for what God wants?
Watchman Nee

Since God is creative, don't limit Him to one way of communicating with you.
Allison Shorter

Often times God wants us to sit before Him in quietness. He doesn't want us to do all the talking. As Isaiah 30:15 says In quiet and confidence will be your strength.
Charles Stanley

Prayer is God's answer to our poverty, not a power we exercise to obtain an answer.
Oswald Chambers

The soul needs its silent spaces. It is in them we learn to pray.
Samuel Chadwick

The same voice that spoke order into chaos at the dawn of creation is still doing it. He can speak order into the chaos of your life.
Mark Batterson

You should easily be able to connect in an exciting and real way to his voice!
Shawn Bolz

Where does the sound of God's voice begin? Perhaps in the place where common sense ends.
Kevin Adams

Prayer is alien to our proud human nature.
Bill Hybels

God is often silent. This silence doesn't mean disapproval; in fact, when God is quiet it is generally an indication that He is happy with us. He doesn't need to constantly reassure His mature sons and daughters when they are doing well; He just lets us be until we look like we're heading off track.
Graham Cooke

I do not think that prayer is ever evasion, that prayer saves us from having to face things that we do not want to face and that are going to hurt if we face them. Jesus in Gethsemane discovered that there was no evasion of the cross.
William Barclay

When we have no personal discipline of rest, we are seriously behind in terms of our development. Rest allows us to see into the spirit.
Graham Cooke

Prayer is also when God speaks to us through dreams and desires and promptings and impressions and ideas.
Mark Batterson

Prayer is putting oneself in the hands of God, and listening to His voice in the depth of our hearts.
Mother Teresa

If God speaks when you are striving with effort, He would only reaffirm flesh and carnality and not the genuineness of who you are in Christ.
Bill Johnson

All the teaching in the world will not overcome the huge deficit created in the new believer that can't hear the voice of God for themselves.
Kevin Shorter

The purpose of us hearing God is to know Him better and help others do the same.
Doug Addison

HURRY destroys prayer. INNER CALM opens my INTER-COM to God. "Be still..." Ps 46:10
Rick Warren

Have you ever said, "Well, all we can do now is pray"? When we come to the end of ourselves, we come to the beginning of God.
Billy Graham

Why is it so important that you are with God and God alone on the mountain top? It's important because it's the place in which you can listen to the voice of the One who calls you the beloved. To pray is to listen to the One who calls you my beloved daughter, my beloved son, my beloved child. To pray is to let that voice speak to the center of your being, to your guts, and let that voice resound in your whole being.
Henri Nouwen

You will find it hard to hear from God until you let go your rights and your agenda.
John Eldredge

When God speaks, all of the sudden He brings you into the present with Him of what He originally designed you to be.
Shawn Bolz

God is speaking to you daily and longs for you to pay attention to the small nudges He is already giving you.
Doug Addison

Some people's theology would be radically changed if they just listened to what God was saying about them.
Kevin Shorter

We need to fully believe that God can compensate for our apparent spiritual deafness.
Wendy Backlund

To have God speak to the heart is a majestic experience, an experience that people may miss if they monopolize the conversation and never pause to hear God's responses.
Charles Stanley

If you spend anytime in prayer listening to the words God speaks to you, you will know He thinks very highly of you.
Kevin Shorter

It was obvious He used one's own mental faculties to receive the thoughts He wanted to give, and it was therefore natural to suppose that He would use the sort of vocabulary I had acquired in which to clothe those thoughts.
Hannah Hurnard

A voice of fear, guilt or condemnation isn't God's voice to a believer.
Rachel DiPaolo

Prayer is never the first word; it is always the second word. God has the first word.
Eugene Peterson

Listening to the Lord is the first thing, second thing, and the third thing necessary for successful intercession.
Richard Foster

The pulpit of this day is weak in praying. The pride of learning is against the dependent humility of prayer. Prayer is with the pulpit too often only official—a performance for the routine of service. Prayer is not to the modern pulpit the mighty force it was in Paul's life or Paul's ministry. Every preacher who does not make prayer a mighty factor in his own life and ministry is weak as a factor in God's work and is powerless to project God's cause in this world.
E.M. Bounds

If you would have God hear you when you pray, you must hear Him when He speaks.
Thomas Brooks

God does not stand afar off as I struggle to speak. He cares enough to listen with more than casual attention. He translates my scrubby words and hears what is truly inside. He hears my sighs and uncertain gropings as fine prose.
Timothy Jones

Sometimes believers mistake the enemy's voice for their own, and are surprised to find that God's voice can also be confused with their own.
Wendy Backlund

If men and women are not willing to assume a listening attitude, there will be no meeting with God in living, personal experience.
A.W. Tozer

The root cause of ineffective prayer is some form of disobedience.
Charles Swindoll

Jesus was never motivated to use revelation to shame anyone.
Shawn Bolz

This filter in our minds telling us what God may do will hinder God's leading in our lives.
Kevin Shorter

When I am praying the most eloquently, I am getting the least accomplished in my prayer life. But when I stop getting eloquent and give God less theology and shut up and just gaze upward and wait for God to speak to my heart He speaks with such power that I have to grab a pencil and a notebook and take notes on what God is saying to my heart.
A.W. Tozer

God's acquaintance is not made hurriedly.
E.M. Bounds

[Prophecy] empowers people to fully say yes to God and to take on His nature so they can be amazing now, not just in eternity.
Shawn Bolz

The Role of Obedience

The spirit of prayer should rule our spirits and our conduct.
E.M. Bounds

We waste most of our time trying to get God to do something He has already done—or praying for God to do something He told us to do.
Jacquelyn K. Heasley

It is good for us to keep some account of our prayers, that we may not unsay them in our practice.
Matthew Henry

I used to ask God to help me. Then I asked if I might help Him. I ended up by asking Him to do His work through me.
Hudson Taylor

I feel that very frequently prayer is made a refuge to dodge the action of faith.
John G. Lake

In matters of faith... remember that the parachute doesn't open until you jump!
Kevin Adams

The deeper the experience of the free grace of God, the more generous we must become.
Tim Keller

Discipline is only important if I have a relationship God not so I can have one.
Kris Vallotton

Obedience out of love is joy.
Heidi Baker

Obedience out of fear is for slaves; obedience out of love is for heirs and friends.
Kevin Shorter

Let a man set his heart ONLY on doing the will of God and he is instantly free.
A.W. Tozer

God is less interested in compliance and more interested in love.
Danny Silk

Holy joy will be oil to the wheels of our obedience.
Matthew Henry

Faith is the willingness to look foolish.
Mark Batterson

God usually doesn't reveal the second step until we take the first step.
Mark Batterson

You stop hearing God's voice through disobeying what you have already heard.
Kevin Shorter

It is truer to say that we live the Christian life in order to pray than that we pray in order to live the Christian life.
P.T. Forsyth

The will of God will never take us where the grace of God cannot sustain us.
Billy Graham

Never use prayer as an excuse to procrastinate doing what you already know is the right thing to do.
Rick Warren

Too many have accepted "doing things" as more important than prayer. They only pray when there is nothing urgent to do.
Kevin Shorter

To be absorbed in God's will and to be earnest about doing His will, is a symptom of a believer who prays effectively.
Shirley Dobson

It is easy to follow God when we don't understand if its toward something we want. Would we still follow if we think we won't like the outcome? (Abraham & Isaac)
Kevin Shorter

So many Christians are immobilized in their lives because they are afraid to get too far in front of God.
Kevin Shorter

Christian meditation, very simply, is the ability to hear God's voice and obey his word.
Richard Foster

We cannot talk to God strongly when we have not lived for God strongly. The closet cannot be made holy to God when the life has not been holy to God.
E.M. Bounds

And the real adventure was not taking the land God had given them, but finding out how God wanted them to take the land.
Kevin Shorter

God is not mocked. He does not answer prayers if He has already given us the answer and we are not willing to use it.
William MacDonald

God gives revelation to those He knows will do whatever He says.
Bill Johnson

It is possible that we can get so busy doing work 'for' the Lord that we have no time FOR the Lord.
A.W. Tozer

The overflow of our love for God is obedience. The overflow of God's love for us is revelation.
Kevin Shorter

An idol is anything you have to check with before you say yes to God.
Kris Vallotton

God is waiting on people who will pray and dream big prayers, and work hard to see them come to pass.
Mark Batterson

Waiting in prayer is a disciplined refusal to act before God acts.
Eugene Peterson

What use is it going to one prayer meeting after another to pray for power if you never do anything that needs power, or your prayers are steeped in disobedience and unbelief? Faith does not come by logic. Remember the feeding of the 5,000? Miracles flow only through hands that distribute bread. Faith and obedience is the vehicle, which carries believers – even timid ones – into the miracle zone.
Reinhard Bonnke

Prayer is the supreme way to be workers together with God.
Wesley Duewel

Prayer strikes the winning blow; service is simply picking up the pieces.
S.D. Gordon

Our response to things is almost always more important than the thing that is happening.
Steve Backlund

Sometimes we lack the victory because His way doesn't make sense to us so we don't follow His plan.
Bill Johnson

Small things, done in great love, bring joy and peace.
Mother Teresa

All that a Christian does, even in eating and sleeping, is prayer, when it is done in simplicity, according to the order of God, without either adding to or diminishing from it by His choice.
John Wesley

If prayer leads us into a deeper unity with the compassionate Christ, it will always give rise to concrete acts of service.
Henri Nouwen

It may not seem obvious at first glance, but the way we make decisions in life tells a lot about the kind of faith we have in Jesus Christ.
Jim Cymbala

Prayer will become effective when we stop using it as a substitute for obedience.
A.W. Tozer

Instead of praying and waiting, why don't we pray and engage?
Steve Thompson

Our choices should reflect our hopes not our fears!
Antje Jordan

The pathway of greatness with God is journeyed by a continual process of saying yes to Him.
Kevin Shorter

Those eternally seeking the will of God are overrun by those who DO the will of God.
Reinhard Bonnke

Prayer is never an acceptable substitute for obedience. The sovereign Lord accepts no offering from His creatures that is not accompanied by obedience. To pray for revival while ignoring or actually flouting the plain precept laid down in the Scriptures is to waste a lot of words and get nothing for our trouble.
A.W. Tozer

Obedience is the master key to effectual prayer.
Billy Graham

To truly walk with God, we must be willing to leave the known and follow Him in unknown places.
Rick Joyner

Faith is stepping out in obedience with the outcome not guaranteed.
Kevin Shorter

It is through relationships with others that we see how well our relationship with God has taken root in our lives.
Kevin Shorter

The most eloquent prayer is the prayer through hands that heal and bless.
Billy Graham

See that you do not use the trick of prayer to cover up what you know you ought to do.
Oswald Chambers

Service as a substitute for worship is idolatry.
Richard Foster

The more willing we are to courageously trust God with our life, the more willing He is to trust us with His plan.
Kevin Adams

Sometimes, God is more interested in what He is doing in us than what He is doing through us.
Kris Vallotton

To pray is to change. Prayer is the central avenue God uses to transform us. If we are unwilling to change, we will abandon prayer as a noticeable characteristic of our lives.
Richard Foster

If we become more consumed with our task than we are with our love for God, our lives will eventually become brittle and desolate.
Francis Frangipane

The most eloquent prayer is often prayed through hands that heal and bless.
Billy Graham

When God speaks, oftentimes His voice will call for an act of courage on our part.
Charles Stanley

We are as strictly obliged to adhere to God by action in the time of action, as by prayer in its season.
Brother Lawrence

We all copy/mimic the God we really believe in through how we treat people.
Dr. Darrell Johnson

Prayer prompts and nurtures obedience, putting the heart into the proper "frame of mind" to desire obedience.
R.C. Sproul

I have seen many men work without praying, though I have never seen any good come out of it; but I have never seen a man pray without working.
Hudson Taylor

The difficulty is not in knowing His will but doing it.
Reinhard Bonnke

The work we do is nothing more than a means of transforming our love for Christ into something concrete.
Mother Teresa

Wherever faith has accepted the Father's love, obedience accepts the Father's will.
Andrew Murray

Boldness in prayer is the result of faithfulness in life and service.
Warren Wiersbe

Faith offends the stationary.
Bill Johnson

Straight praying is never born of crooked conduct.
E.M. Bounds

His voice leads us not into timid discipleship but into bold witness.
Charles Stanley

He isn't going to show you everything at once, but as you go.
Graham Cooke

A life taught in the Scriptures, and tuned in to God in prayer, produces an outflowing of grace and power.
Billy Graham

He who prays as he ought will endeavour to live as he prays.
John Owen

It is not my ability, but my response to God's ability, that counts.
Corrie ten Boom

Believing prayer will lead to wholehearted action.
Hudson Taylor

In prayer, God loves to hear "Yes, Lord!"
Jay Harris

When facing God, results are not important. Faithfulness is what is important.
Mother Teresa

Praying which does not result in pure conduct is a delusion. We have missed the whole office and virtue of praying if it does not rectify conduct. It is in the very nature of things that we must quit praying, or quit bad conduct.
E.M. Bounds

Praying that does not result in right thinking and right living is a farce. We have missed the whole office of prayer if it fails to purge our character and correct conduct. We have failed entirely to understand the virtue of prayer, if it does not bring about the revolutionizing of life. In the very nature of tings, we must either quit praying or quit our bad conduct.
E.M. Bounds

Obedience is measured by our response to God's voice.
Bill Johnson

We must alter our lives in order to alter our hearts, for it is impossible to live one way and pray another.
William Law

It is not what a man does that determines whether his work is sacred or secular, it is why he does it. The motive is everything.
A.W. Tozer

We cannot expect to live defectively and pray effectively.
John Blanchard

Prayer without action grows into powerless pietism, and action without prayer degenerates into questionable manipulation.
Henri Nouwen

Obedience leads us to the heart of God and even to knowing our own hearts.
Kevin Shorter

Praying for God to work is fine, but praying for Him to do what we should be doing is pointless.
Reinhard Bonnke

A person who does not pray cannot follow God (see John 10:4).
Kevin Shorter

We can do more than pray after we have prayed, but we cannot do more than pray before we have prayed.
John Bunyan

Whenever God shows you the outcome, you know it is about the process. The outcome is guaranteed; the process is the pleasure we find in getting there.
Graham Cooke

But the misfortune is that people wish to direct God instead of resigning themselves to be directed by Him.
Madame Guyon

Faith is the capacity to step out without caution. Faith is not risk, it is an assurance built on hope.
Graham Cooke

If I've learned anything about prayer, it's that desperation drives discipline.
Bill Hybels

When you ask God to do something impossible, He usually instructs you to do something uncomfortable.
Steven Furtick

Sometimes we have to pray for the answer, but sometimes we have to pray to be the answer.
Bill Johnson

The Role of Thanksgiving

God has two dwellings; one in heaven, and the other in a meek and thankful heart.
Izaak Walton

Thanksgiving is not casual; it's intentional. So let's thank the Lord for who He is, His goodness, His kindness. He's brilliant!
Graham Cooke

Praise and thanksgiving not only open the gates of heaven for me to approach God, but also prepare a way for God to bless me.
The Kneeling Christian

Thanking God after he answers a prayer is gratitude. Thanking him in advance is faith.
Rick Warren

Perhaps it takes a purer faith to praise God for unrealized blessings than for those we once enjoyed or those we enjoy now.
A.W. Tozer

Even if circumstances have not changed, thankfulness will alter our perspective from doubt to faith.
Steve Backlund

We must open ourselves up to who God is for us. The most consistent way to do that is by rejoicing, giving thanks and joyful prayer.
Graham Cooke

Most of us get started with great works for the Lord out of deep and sincere gratitude. However thanksgiving will not keep us in the race for the long haul. At some point love must be the driving force in our lives.
Kevin Shorter

The thankful heart sees the best part of every situation. It sees problems and weaknesses as opportunities, struggles as refining tools, and sinners as saints in progress.
Francis Frangipane

Give thanks for all things being confident that He who began a good work in you will bring it to completion.
Kevin Shorter

Prayer is an act of worship, not just an expression of our wants and needs. There should be reverence in our hearts as we pray to God.
Warren Wiersbe

We have short memories in magnifying God's grace. Every blessing that God confers upon us perishes through our carelessness, if we are not prompt and active in giving thanks.
John Calvin

Rejoicing gives us the opportunity to hear God. When we enter His presence with thanksgiving, we open more of ourselves to His voice.
Graham Cooke

Oh, what a cause of thankfulness it is that we have a gracious God to go to on all occasions... Oh, what an unspeakable privilege is prayer!
Lady Maxwell

Amazement and rapture should be our reaction to the God revealed as Love.
Brennan Manning

Thanksgiving in all things opens us up to God's redemption.
Kevin Shorter

Joy is who God is; rejoicing is our response to who God is!
Graham Cooke

My earnest wish is to paint in true colors the goodness of God to me, and the depth of my own ingratitude.
Madame Guyon

Rejoicing and giving thanks from the heart will always overpower anything negative.
Graham Cooke

A sensible thanksgiving for mercies received is a mighty prayer in the Spirit of God. It prevails with Him unspeakably.
John Bunyan

Praise lies upon a higher plain than thanksgiving. When I give thanks, my thoughts still circle around myself to some extent. But in praise my soul ascends to self-forgetting adoration, seeing and praising only the majesty and power of God, His grace and redemption.
O. Hallesby

Thanksgiving creates the context to keep your prayers on focus.
Bill Johnson

Abundant gratefulness is a sign of a flourishing soul.
Steve Backlund

Wherever there is true prayer, there thanksgiving and gratitude stand hard by ready to respond to the answer when it comes.
E.M. Bounds

Thankfulness hones the precision in our prayer life because it keeps it about Him.
Bill Johnson

Keep praying, but be thankful that God's answers are wiser than your prayers!
William Culbertson

Giving thanks is the oil that prepares you for and keeps you in the fullness of the Spirit.
Kevin Shorter

We ought to be as earnest and frequent in our prayers of thanksgiving when the cupboard is full as we would be in our prayers of supplication if the cupboards were bare.
Jerry Bridges

The greater our gratitude the more we will experience of God.
Kevin Shorter

In all your prayers forget not to thank the Lord for his mercies.
John Bunyon

Instead of focusing on your unworthiness, thank Him for His goodness.
Andrew Wommack

By thanking God in the midst of circumstances that seem awful, we are showing faith in God's goodness.
Kevin Shorter

The Bible tells us that whenever we come before God, whatever our purpose or prayer request, we are always to come with a thankful heart.
David Jeremiah

A thankful person isn't without trouble. They just stay in wonder at the provision around them rather than complain about what is lacking.
Matt Peterson

1 Thessalonians 5 puts prayer in the middle of a thanksgiving sandwich.
Graham Cooke

A mature Christian moves in thanksgiving and praise even before the answer comes.
Graham Cooke

Thanksgiving was never meant to be shut up in a single day.
Robert Caspar Lintner

A single grateful thought toward heaven is the most complete prayer.
Gotthold Lessing

If we are to have our prayers answered, we must give God the glory.
Billy Graham

Prayers of gratitude remind us of just how much we receive at his hands.
Robert Harris

Gratitude leads you to His presence.
Lance Wallnau

Sometimes I go to God and say, God, if Thou dost never answer another prayer while I live on this earth, I will still worship Thee as long as I live and in the ages to come for what Thou hast done already. God's already put me so far in debt that if I were to live one million millenniums I couldn't pay Him for what He's done for me.
A.W. Tozer

If the only prayer you said in your whole life was, "thank you," that would suffice.
Meister Eckhart

The Role of Worship

Praise gives proper perspective for prayer. You may at times lack words for prayer but you never lack words for praise.
Gabriel Allred

A little lifting of the heart suffices; a little remembrance of God, one act of inward worship are prayers which, however short, are nevertheless acceptable to God.
Brother Lawrence

They came to the temple to worship, pray and give offering. Not to hear preaching. Church isn't a place to receive, but to give.
Graham Cooke

The Father seeks worshippers: our worship satisfies His loving heart and is a joy to Him.
Andrew Murray

Ascribe to the Lord the glory due to his name; worship the Lord in the splendor of his holiness (Psalm 29:2). This is the key verse to the book of Psalms. The door into the temple of praise and prayer is open. Go in with the psalmist to rest and pray. It is a real privilege to go apart during the rush of earthly things… The Psalms are for the closet of prayer.
Henrietta Mears

Don't let the "how to's" of worship distract you from the "who to."
Bill Johnson

The supreme thing is worship. The attitude of worship is the attitude of a subject bent before the King…the fundamental thought is that of prostration, of bowing down.
Campbell Morgan

Worship involves an opening of ourselves to the adventurous life of the Spirit.
Richard Foster

In worship, God imparts himself to us.
C.S. Lewis

Prayer can no more be divorced from worship than life can be divorced from breathing.
R.T. Kendall

Intertwined with our petitions should be praise and marveling that we are able to approach God, and be welcomed in Christ.
Tim Keller

The glue that holds confidence and endurance together is praise.
Graham Cooke

I did not see that it is the process of being worshipped that God communicates His presence to men.
C.S. Lewis

The prayers of the great saints, the prayer warriors of church history, are marked by their fervent adoration of God.
R.C. Sproul

Can you worship a God who isn't obligated to explain His actions to you?
Francis Chan

We are tempted to treat God as an asset, and to exploit him. But true prayer, thinking most of the Giver, quells the egoism and dissolves it in praise.
P.T. Forsyth

Without worship, we go about miserable.
A.W. Tozer

Yes, I pray that my pain might be removed, that it might cease; but more so, I pray for the strength to bear it, the grace to benefit from it, and the devotion to offer it up to God as a sacrifice of praise.
Joni Eareckson Tada

Prayer is listening as well as speaking, receiving as well as asking; and its deepest mood is friendship held in reverence. So the daily prayer should end as it begins - in adoration.
George Buttrick

My prayer life consists of generous stretches of praise and adoration. My main purpose is fellowship with Him.
Tim Keller

Prayer without worship lacks confidence.
Kevin Shorter

God gives promises so that we will pray the promise back to Him and wait and worship until He fulfills that which He has said.
Jim Cymbala

Worship is the highest and noblest activity of which man, by the grace of God, is capable.
John Stott

If God was small enough for us to understand, He wouldn't be big enough for us to worship.
Unknown

If we long to go where God is going and do what God is doing, we will move into deeper, more authentic worship.
Richard Foster

Learn to worship God as the God who does wonders, who wishes to prove in you that He can do something supernatural and divine.
Andrew Murray

The Christian man at prayer is the secretary of Creation's praise.
P.T. Forsyth

Christians are made to glorify God. We are never in our element until we are praising Him.
C.H. Spurgeon

Isn't it a comfort to worship a God we cannot exaggerate?
Francis Chan

Although God certainly knows all our needs, praying for them changes our attitude from complaint to praise and enables us to participate in God's personal plan for our lives.
Ray Stedman

Worship also means to express in some appropriate manner what you feel. And what will be expressed? A humbling but delightful sense of admiring awe and astonished wonder. It is delightful to worship God, but it is also a humbling thing.
A.W. Tozer

Worshipping God is the great essential of fitness. If you have not been worshipping... when you get to work you will not only be useless yourself, but a tremendous hindrance to those who are associated with you.
Oswald Chambers

Yes, worship of the loving God is man's whole reason for existence.
A.W. Tozer

There is more healing joy in five minutes of true worship than in five nights of revelry.
A.W. Tozer

Worship means to feel in the heart. A person that merely goes through the form and does not feel anything is not worshipping.
A.W. Tozer

Don't let what's wrong with you keep you from worshiping what's right with God.
Mark Batterson

Praising God is one of the highest and purest acts of religion. In prayer we act like men; in praise we act like angels.
Thomas Watson

In worship we don't escape the real world, we introduce the real world.
Alan Scott

In almost everything that touches our everyday life on earth, God is pleased when we're pleased. He wills that we be as free as birds to soar and sing our maker's praise without anxiety.
A.W. Tozer

Worship lifts us out of our fear and renews our faith in God and His goodness towards us.
Kevin Shorter

Rejoicing is a way of praising God until the heart is sweetened and rested, releasing its grip on anything else it thinks it needs.
Tim Keller

Worship is the act of the abandoned heart adoring its God.
John Eldredge

We are presumptuous not when we marvel at His grace, but when we reject it.
Max Lucado

The most powerful prayers are always filled with worship, knowing that He is "enthroned on the praises of His people" (Ps. 22:3).
Adrian Rogers

Mixing worship into intercession helps the intercessor keep perspective of how much greater God is than the problem.
Paul Rapley

To omit adoration is to cut the heart out of prayer.
R.C. Sproul

We cannot worship God any way we wish; our worship must always conform to God's pleasure.
A.W. Tozer

If you stand, worship, and love God in the midst of lack and difficulty, you will never lose.
Heidi Baker

Prayer and praise are the oars by which a man may row his boat into the deep waters of the knowledge of Christ.
C.H. Spurgeon

The more you praise, the more vigor you will have for prayer; and the more you pray, the more matter you will have for praise.
J.I. Packer

Praise reminds you of all that God is able to do and of great things He has already done.
Wesley Duewel

Each time you intercede, be quiet first and worship God in His glory. Think of what He can do, of how He delights to hear Christ, of your place in Christ, and expect great things.
Andrew Murray

In true worship the Father must be first, must be all.
Andrew Murray

Real prayer is preceded and followed by a celebration of who God is for us.
Graham Cooke

Worship clears the airwaves so we can hear again.
Brian Johnson

We must resist wandering thoughts in prayer. Raising our hands reminds us that we need to raise up our minds to God, setting aside all irrelevant thoughts.
John Calvin

Worship is pure or base as the worshiper entertains high or low thoughts of God.
A.W. Tozer

To gather with God's people in united adoration of the Father is as necessary to the Christian life as prayer.
Martin Luther

Worship and intercession must go together, the one is impossible without the other. Intercession means that we rouse ourselves up to get the mind of Christ about the one for whom we pray.
Oswald Chambers

Worship changes the worshiper into the image of the One worshiped.
Jack Hayford

Worship, in a very real sense of the word, opens a doorway to the power of His presence, confounding dark powers and overthrowing sin's destructive operations.
Jack Hayford

Worship is a way of gladly reflecting back to God the radiance of His worth.
John Piper

Worship is the human response to the divine initiative.
Richard Foster

Why did Christ come? In order that He might make worshippers out of rebels.
A.W. Tozer

When I cannot pray, I always sing.
Martin Luther

When we praise God for the negative, we release His power into the situation.
Ney Bailey

To worship God in truth is to recognize Him for being who He is, and to recognize ourselves for what we are.
Brother Lawrence

Worship begins in holy expectancy, it ends in holy obedience.
Richard Foster

We always become like the one we worship.
Bill Johnson

Prayer and praise are to the Christian as the two wings are to the bird. Don't expect the bird to fly if one wing is broken. Even so the Christian needs both prayer and praise.
J. Wesley Adcock

We should dedicate ourselves to becoming in this life the most perfect worshippers of God we can possibly be, as we hope to be through all eternity.
Brother Lawrence

God does not ask much of you : a little remembrance from time to time, a little adoration.
Brother Lawrence

The Role of Forgiveness

One thing we can't do in prayer is have a spirit of anger or resentment or unforgiveness toward another person because the whole philosophy of prayer, the whole approach to the throne of grace, is that I'm only there, sinful as I am, I'm only there and can pray in Jesus' name because God has been so merciful to me and to you.
Jim Cymbala

Forgiveness is the key which unlocks the door of resentment and the handcuffs of bitterness.
Corrie ten Boom

How many times will God pick you up when you fall? Every time!
Kevin Shorter

Every kind of prayer, not intercessory prayer only, which is the highest kind of prayer, but all prayer, from the lowest kind to the highest, is impossible in a life of known and allowed sin.
Alexander Whyte

If we rationalize our problems when He points them out, we will spend less and less time meditating because we won't want to face God in that area of our lives.
Charles Stanley

Our prayers are the shadows of mercy.
C.H. Spurgeon

For a good confession three things are necessary: an examination of conscience, sorrow, and a determination to avoid sin.
St. Alphonsus Liguori

The closer we are to God, the more the slightest sin will cause us deep sorrow.
R.C. Sproul

Have we not more often been brought to tears of repentance by undeserved kindness than by severe rebuke?
John Piper

Forgiveness is not trust. Forgiveness takes a moment, but trust is built over time.
Mark Driscoll

When God promises us that He will forgive us, we insult His integrity when we refuse to accept it.
R.C. Sproul

Leaving our sins hidden in darkness exposes lies we believe about God's forgiveness.
Kevin Shorter

Repentance removes old sins and wrong attitudes, and it opens the way for the Holy Spirit to restore our spiritual health.
Shirley Dobson

You know forgiveness is starting to settle in when you begin wanting good things for those who have hurt you the most.
Allison Vesterfelt

The unbeliever rationalizes his sinfulness, but the Christian is sensitive to his unworthiness. Confession takes up a significant portion of his prayer time.
R.C. Sproul

You may have every right to not to forgive, but nothing will hinder you from experiencing the fullness of God more.
Kevin Shorter

The Christian life is not a constant high. I have my moments of deep discouragement. I have to go to God in prayer with tears in my eyes, and say, 'O God, forgive me,' or 'Help me.'
Billy Graham

Isaiah found out his deficiencies in God's presence. But after one touch he was ready to be sent out.

Kris Vallotton

Forgiveness breaks the chains of bitterness and the shackles of selfishness.

Corrie ten Boom

In continuing the practice of conversing with God throughout each day, and quickly seeking His forgiveness when I fell or strayed, His presence has become as easy and natural to me now as it once was difficult to attain.

Brother Lawrence

Children's failure doesn't move the parent because they are so convince the child can do what the parent can do. (God feels the same about His child.)

Wendy Backlund

To forgive is to set a prisoner free. That prisoner is you.

Corrie ten Boom

As we release forgiveness on others, we open ourselves up to more of the love of God.

Kevin Shorter

Prayer is an offering up of our desires unto God for things agreeable to His will, in the name of Christ, with confession of our sins and thankful acknowledgment of His mercies.

The Kneeling Christian

Most Christians repent enough to get forgiven, but not enough to see the Kingdom.

Bill Johnson

Years of repentance are necessary in order to blot out a sin in the eyes of men, but one tear of repentance suffices with God.

French Proverb

Every temptation is an invitation to depend on Christ.

Craig Groeschel

The one thing above all others that bolts and bars the way into the presence chamber's of prayer is unwillingness to forgive from the heart.

Samuel Chadwick

If Joseph hadn't forgiven his brothers, he would have killed the line that Jesus came from. That's the power of forgiveness.

Kevin Shorter

As we pour out our bitterness, God pours in his peace.

F.B. Meyer

God delights in our temptations and yet hates them. He delights in them when they drive us to prayer; He hates them when they drive us to despair.

Martin Luther

To forgive ourselves after God has forgiven us is a duty as well as a privilege.

R.C. Sproul

God is always going to focus on your new nature because He killed your old one.
Graham Cooke

Sin saddens God's heart not angers Him; He loves us so much He wants us to experience all of the joy in His heart for us.
Kevin Shorter

Let no sense of your unworthiness prevent your taking hold of the boundless and all-sufficient grace of God.
Unknown

I forgave you, even if they didn't. You are forgiven and you should act like it.
Judy Franklin

When grace moves in... guilt moves out.
Max Lucado

Let no one pray for a mighty baptism of power who is not prepared for deep heart searchings and confession of sin.
Evan Roberts

Admit sin, and you banish prayer. But, on the other hand, entertain, and encourage, and practice prayer, and sin will sooner or later flee before it.
Alexander Whyte

Confession begins in sorrow, but it ends in joy.
Richard Foster

Shame of sin can only be healed once it is exposed and met with loving acceptance.
Kevin Shorter

The best prayer I ever prayed had enough sin to damn the whole world.
John Bunyan

We do not have to make God willing to forgive. In fact, it is God who is working to make us willing to seek his forgiveness.
Richard Foster

It is so much easier to repent when you don't feel that God is mad at you.
Judy Franklin

I can't repeat this point enough, because it is where so many people struggle: if you are praying with unrepented sin in your life, you are wasting your breath! Your prayers are getting no higher than the ceiling lights.
Adrian Rogers

God doesn't want to talk to you about sin. He wants to talk about the righteousness you lack in that area.
Graham Cooke

A Heart for God

If the target of our prayers is not for the glory of God, then the answers may turn us away from our Father.
Kevin Shorter

[God] speaks through parables, so that we have to seek his heart to know his mind.
Shawn Bolz

Don't let anything you do for God or think about Him become greater than your love for Him and those He loves.
Kevin Shorter

The best prayers often have more groans than words.
John Bunyan

When you're in love with God, you're not afraid to yield your life to Him.
Heidi Baker

As you pursue the heart of God, you will gain His heart for you, your friends, and the world.
Kevin Shorter

This is what prayer is all about: not what I can get from God, but to have my heart so radically changed by Him that I come to want only what God wants for me.
Richard Burr

The more we have of God's glory, the less shall we seek His gifts.
The Kneeling Christian

The more we live as citizens of Heaven, the more Heaven's activities infect our lifestyles!
Bill Johnson

Prayer does not consist in the elegance of the phrase, but in the strength of the affection.
John Mason

When we in prayer seek only the glorification of the name of God, then we are in complete harmony with the Spirit of prayer. Then our hearts are at rest both while we pray and after we have prayed. Then we can wait for the Lord.
O. Hallesby

Devotion to prayer and intimacy with God is the only setting in which we can completely step into the fullness of God's purposes.
Bill Johnson

All fruitfulness flows from intimacy.
Heidi Baker

God looks not at the pomp of words and variety of expression, but at the sincerity and devotion of the heart. The key opens the door, not because it is gilt but because it fits the lock.
Billy Graham

Questions asked in trust lead to revelation; questions asked in distrust lead to separation.
Bill Johnson

The impulse to pursue God originates with God.
A.W. Tozer

Intimate lovers of God are full of power and passion.
Heidi Baker

There is no joy in the soul that has forgotten what God prizes.
Oswald Chambers

Prayer from the heart is not interrupted by the thoughts from a person's mind. Indeed nothing can interrupt this prayer except for ungodly inclinations.
Madame Guyon

A prayerful heart and an obedient heart will learn, very slowly and not without sorrow, to stake everything on God Himself.
Elisabeth Elliot

Prayer continues in the desire of the heart, though the understanding be employed on outward things.
John Wesley

Besides the potent magnetism of the centre itself, there is, in every creature, a corresponding tendency to reunion with its own particular centre, and this is vigorous and active in proportion to the spirituality and perfection of the subject.
Madame Guyon

Our only business is to love and delight ourselves in God.
Brother Lawrence

Real prayer comes not from gritting our teeth but from falling in love.
Richard Foster

The most excellent method of going to God is that of doing our common business without any view of pleasing people but purely for the love of God.
Brother Lawrence

Drawing nigh to God is the most concentrated energy of the soul.
D.A. Carson

We don't need to be afraid of the reproach of God, provided we are sincerely seeking His will in a given situation.
R.C. Sproul

Let us think often that our only business in this life is to please God.
Brother Lawrence

We exalt God because it gives God room to exalt us.
Kevin Shorter

The outworking of that impulse [to pursue God] is our following hard after Him.
A.W. Tozer

Royalty is my identity. Servanthood is my assignment. Intimacy with God is my life source.
Bill Johnson

If I had it to do over again, I'd spend more time in meditation and prayer and telling the Lord how much I love him and adore him and looking forward to the time we are going to spend together for eternity.
> Billy Graham

The prayer life does not consist of perpetual repetition of petitions. The prayer life consists of life that is always upward and onward and Godward.
> George Campbell Morgan

The strength in prayer is not that you complain or bellyache about a problem; it's that you joined your heart to His to see His kingdom come and His purposes work out on the earth.
> Bill Johnson

It is not the mouth that is the main thing to be looked at in prayer, but whether the heart is so full of affection and earnestness in prayer with God, that it is impossible to express their sense and desire; for then a man desires indeed, when his desires are so strong, many, and mighty, that all the words, tears, and groans that can come from the heart, cannot utter them.
> John Bunyan

Love opens the eyes of our understanding and enables us to see more of the truth than can those blinded by self-love.
> Hannah Hurnard

Prayer thrives in the atmosphere of true devotion.
> E.M. Bounds

What would happen if we sought God's face as earnestly as we seek pleasure?
> A.W. Tozer

The wisest thing you'll ever do in this life is to draw close to God and to seek Him with all your heart.
> Bob Sorge

Amazing things happen when we are more aware of the glory of God than we are of any other thing.
> Joel Hill

Prayer is first and foremost an act of love. ...[It] is born of a desire to be with Jesus.
> Brennan Manning

In prayer it is better to have a heart without words than words without a heart.
> John Bunyon

The most dangerous trap is just living and forgetting that God exists.
> A.W. Tozer

We can never fully love that which we fear.
> Kevin Shorter

The amount of time we spend with Jesus-meditating on His Word and His majesty, seeking His face-establishes our fruitfulness in the kingdom.
> Charles Stanley

We are called to an everlasting preoccupation with God.
A.W. Tozer

Christians who want a productive prayer life must keep a pure heart.
Charles Swindoll

If we are to pray aright, perhaps it is quite necessary that we pray contrary to our own heart.
Dietrich Bonhoeffer

Those who want to be close to God on earth will be the closest to God in heaven.
Kevin Shorter

If we pray only because we want answers, we will become irritated and angry with God.
Oswald Chambers

Importunate praying is the earnest inward movement of the heart toward God.
E.M. Bounds

Prayer is the application of the heart to God, and the internal exercise of love... To attract and draw the soul into the rest of love, and not into the many ways of the self.
Madame Guyon

An attitude of reverence toward God is vital to the effectiveness of our prayers.
R.C. Sproul

Do your utmost to guard your heart, for out of it comes life.
Walter Hilton

Prayerlessness proves that the person has very little love for God.
Wesley Duewel

We become practical atheists when we start to believe that we must please people more than we should please God.
Craig Groeschel

Don't go out and share Jesus unless you are in love with Him. When you are in love with Jesus, then all you do will radiate Him.
Heidi Baker

I henceforth take Jesus Christ to be mine. I promise to receive Him as a husband to me. And I give myself to Him, unworthy though I am, to be His spouse. I ask of Him, in this marriage of spirit with spirit, that I may be of the same mind with Him--meek, pure, nothing in myself, and united in God's will. And pledged as I am to be His, I accept, as a part of my marriage portion, the temptations and sorrows, the crosses and the contempt, which fell to Him.
Madame Guyon

We hope in God because He is worthy of our hope, our trust and our love.
Bob Hartley

Whether we think of, or speak to, God, whether we act or suffer for him, all is prayer, when we have no other object than his love, and the desire of pleasing him.
John Wesley

In order to know God, we must often think of Him; and when we come to love Him, we shall then also think of Him often, for our heart will be with our treasure.
Brother Lawrence

The primary requirement [for the Disciples of faith] is a longing after God.
Richard Foster

Our love for God is tested by whether we seek Him or His gifts.
Ralph Sockman

Lord, thou madest us for thyself, and we can find no rest till we find rest in thee.
Augustine

Let your religion be less of a theory and more of a love affair.
G.K. Chesterton

We should not pray for God to be on our side, but pray that we may be on God's side.
Billy Graham

The effective prayer of faith comes from a life given up to the will and the love of God.
Andrew Murray

When we accept His passion for us we can love Him with all our heart!
Graham Cooke

The grace to let go and let God be God flows from trust in His boundless love.
Brennan Manning

God loves it when we pray the things that are on His heart more than our own.
Daniel Kolenda

Through prayer I become one in love with Christ.
Mother Teresa

Spending time in meditative prayer, getting to know God, helps align my desires with God's.
Phillip Yancey

People seek methods of learning to know God. Is it not much shorter and more direct to simply do everything for the love of Him? There is no finesse about it. One only has to do it generously and simply.
Brother Lawrence

Be wholehearted in your love of God and your capacity to see Him will grow accordingly.
Graham Cooke

You cannot be a continually prophetic voice if you are in conflict with the world that God loves.
Shawn Bolz

Prayerlessness means unavailability to God.
Wesley Duewel

Every time you pray, if your prayer is sincere, there will be new feeling and new meaning in it which will give you fresh courage, and you will understand that prayer is an education.
Fyodor Dostoyevsky

In prayer, we begin to think God's thoughts after him: to desire the things he desires, to love the things he loves, to will the things he wills.
Richard Foster

In each prayer to the Father I must be able to say that I know of no one whom I do not heartily love.
Andrew Murray

Prayerlessness reveals a heart that doesn't enjoy being with God.
Paul Miller

God does not contradict Himself. It is true that he who seeks God, yet is unwilling to forsake his sins, will not find Him. But he who seeks God and forsakes sin will certainly find Him.
Madame Guyon

Prayer is a gift to Christians that enhances our intimacy with God.
Kevin Shorter

Prayer in the Spirit is prayer whose supreme object is the glory of God; only in a secondary sense does it seek a blessing for self or for others.
J. Oswald Sanders

We are made for intimacy with God, not just knowledge about him.
John Eldredge

If we would have God in the closet, God must have us out of the closet. There is no way of praying to God, but by living to God.
E.M. Bounds

Are we willing to trade our divided pursuits: livelihood, personal identity, & happy marriage for a wholehearted pursuit of God instead?
Kevin Adams

The chief purpose of prayer is that God may be glorified in the answer.
R.A. Torrey

Christians may speak of God's love, but they prefer to distance themself from Him experientially out of fear.
Kevin Shorter

Pray that you do not lose your first love.
Kevin Shorter

The prayer of the saints is never self-important, but always God-important.
Oswald Chambers

The heart attitude behind prayer interests God much more than the actual words you say.
Andrew Wommack

You must keep all earthly treasures out of your heart, and let Christ be your treasure, and let him have your heart.
C.H. Spurgeon

Everything God does makes us want to fall in love with Him all over again.
Graham Cooke

To have found God and still pursue Him is the soul's paradox of love.
A.W. Tozer

To the soul that is athirst for God, nothing can be more delightful.
A.W. Tozer

True prayer is the trading of the heart with God.
C.H. Spurgeon

The Role of Perseverance

It is atheism to pray and not wait on hope.
Richard Sibbes

It is not lost time to wait upon God!
Hudson Taylor

One of the greatest strains in life is the strain of waiting for God.
Oswald Chambers

Because we know God can answer, we never quit. We keep praying even when everything seems black.
Elmer Towns

No matter how dark and hopeless a situation might seem, never stop praying.
Billy Graham

Importunate perseverance is a prerequisite to success in prayer, because it has an intimate connection with the preparation of a right spiritual condition in us.
William Patton

The ministry of prayer, if it be anything worthy of the name, is a ministry of ardor, a ministry of unwearied and intense longing after God and after his holiness.
E.M. Bounds

The purpose of God is not to answer our prayers, but by our prayers we come to discern the mind of God.
Oswald Chambers

Prayer and perseverance are necessary in our daily conflicts. The best remedy to the weariness is diligence in prayer.
John Calvin

A delayed answer to your prayer DOESNT mean God is unconcerned but rather He has a larger purpose for his timing. Trust him!
Rick Warren

You shall find this to be God's usual course: not to give His children the taste of His delights till they begin to sweat in seeking after them.
Richard Baxter

Sometimes the power of prayer is the power to carry on. It doesn't always change your circumstances, but it gives you the strength to walk through them.
Mark Batterson

We press our pleas because we must have them, or die.
E.M. Bounds

The meaning of prayer is that we get hold of God, not of the answer.
Oswald Chambers

The only way you can fail is if you stop praying.
Mark Batterson

The great point is never to give up until the answer comes. I have been praying for sixty-three years and eight months for one man's conversion. He is not converted yet, but he will be! How can it be otherwise?
George Müller

Persistence purifies our prayers. If I'm not willing to pray for something more than once, it's a whim, not a real desire.
Rick Warren

Prevailing prayer makes men invincible.
Samuel Chadwick

Persistence in prayer doesn't change God. It shapes us for the answer.
Bill Johnson

It is not enough for the believer to begin to pray, nor to pray correctly; nor is it enough to continue for a time to pray. We must patiently, believingly continue in prayer until we obtain an answer.
George Müller

Hurry is the death of prayer.
Samuel Chadwick

Waiting for an answer to prayer is often part of the answer.
John Blanchard

Waiting is a sustained effort to stay focused on God through prayer and belief.
Max Lucado

The faith that relentlessly asks God, also pleases God.
Francis Frangipane

Prayer is me looking at God and God looking at me.
St. John Vianney

Sometimes when we do not receive comfort in our prayers, when we are broken and cast down, that is when we are really wrestling and prevailing in prayer.
C.H. Spurgeon

Continuing in prayer is not for persuading God but for changing us and changing our spiritual environment.
Bill Johnson

Sometimes He delays so that greater glory may be brought to Himself.
The Kneeling Christian

No principle is more definitely enforced by Christ than that prevailing prayer must have in it the quality which waits and perseveres, the courage that never surrenders, the patience which never grows tired, the resolution that never wavers.
E.M. Bounds

Don't quit. For if you do, you may miss the answer to your prayers. God's solution is a prayer away!
Max Lucado

It is not enough to begin to pray, nor to pray aright; nor is it enough to continue for a time to pray; but we must patiently, believingly, continue in prayer until we obtain an answer.
George Müller

Jesus taught that perseverance is the essential element in prayer.
E.M. Bounds

I think Christians fail so often to get answers to their prayers because they do not wait long enough on God. They just drop down and say a few words, and then jump up and forget it and expect God to answer them. Such praying always reminds me of the small boy ringing his neighbor's door-bell, and then running away as fast as he can go.
E.M. Bounds

Prayer unaccompanied by perseverance leads to no result.
John Calvin

Persistence in prayer is not an attempt to change God's mind but to get ourselves to the place where He can trust us with the answer.
Warren Wiersbe

If we prevail in prayer, God will do only what he can do.
Jim Cymbala

True prayer will achieve just as much as it costs us.
Samuel Zwemer

We must persevere in prayer that He may not permit our hearts to faint.
John Calvin

Prayer is the acid test of the inner man's strength. A strong spirit is capable of praying much and praying with all perseverance until the answer comes. A weak one grows weary and fainthearted in the maintenance of praying.
Watchman Nee

We don't want to wait for God to resolve matters in His good time because His idea of 'good time' is seldom in sync with ours.
Oswald Chambers

Pursuing prayer is prayer on a mission. It is diligent, fervent, constant, persevering, determined, and convinced.
David Bryant

Prevailing prayer is prayer that not only takes the initiative but continues on the offensive for God until spiritual victory is won.
Wesley Duewel

Prevailing prayer is when intellect, emotion, and will unite to take hold of God.
Unknown

It is hard to wait and press and pray, and hear no voice, but stay till God answers.
E.M. Bounds

Sometimes through persistence in prayer, we find out we need to change how we are praying.
Bill Johnson

Delays are as much a part of God plan as answered prayers. God wants you to trust Him.
Rick Warren

The reason so many people do not pray is because of its cost. The cost is not so much in the sweat of agonizing supplication as in the daily fidelity to the life of prayer.
Samuel Chadwick

And truly, my own experience tells me, that there is nothing that prevails more with God than persistence.
John Bunyon

Patience in prayer is nothing but faith spun out.
Thomas Watson

Instead of yielding to fatalism, hear the call: 'Keep praying, even when tough stuff happens,' and do this by invading the difficult with thanksgiving, because the truth larger than the problem is that God's power can transform any mess when He is invited into it.
Jack Hayford

Sometimes God takes years in answering one prayer.
R.T. Kendall

Sometimes the Lord wants us to keep on asking so that we could get closer to the real prayer He most wants to answer.
Graham Cooke

It is always too soon to quit praying, even when praying is the last thing we seem able to do.
Harold Lindsell

When you go to private prayer your first thought must be: The Father is in secret, the Father waits me there.
Andrew Murray

It is true that Bible prayers in word and print are short, but the praying men of the Bible were with God through many a sweet and holy wrestling hour. They won by few words but long waiting.
E.M. Bounds

Whole days and weeks have I spent prostrate on the ground in silent or vocal prayer.
George Whitefield

But to the man who withdraws himself from all that is of the world and man, and prepares to wait upon God alone, the Father will reveal Himself.
Andrew Murray

Don't be afraid to wait with faith and patience, and not feel pressured to have an immediate answer from God.

Joyce Meyer

The short prevailing prayer cannot be prayed by one who has not prevailed in a mightier struggle of long continuance.

E.M. Bounds

A lack of endurance is one of the greatest causes of defeat, especially in prayer.

Dutch Sheets

Perseverance is an essential element in successful praying, as in every other realm of conflict.

E.M. Bounds

The Role of Passion

If you would move me with your preaching, or with your praying, or with your singing, first be moved yourself.

Alexander Whyte

There is only one requirement that you must follow at all times [in prayer]. This simple requirement is you must learn to pray from your heart and not your head.

Madame Guyon

Prayer is an exercise of passion, not of indifference.

R.C. Sproul

Prayer creates a vehicle that moves our heart, mind, soul and spirit into alignment with God's heart.

Jurgen Matthesius

When I live out of discipline, I'm admired; when I live out of passion, I'm contagious.

Bill Johnson

We are not called to be passive. We are called to passionately pursue God.

Kevin Shorter

When thou prayest, rather let thy heart be without words, than thy words without a heart.

John Bunyon

There is neither encouragement nor room in Bible religion for feeble desires, listless efforts, lazy attitudes; all must be strenuous, urgent, ardent. Flamed desires, impassioned, unwearied insistence delight heaven. God would have His children incorrigibly in earnest and persistently bold in their efforts. Heaven is too busy to listen to half-hearted prayers or to respond to pop-calls. Our whole being must be in our praying.
E.M. Bounds

Mediocrity is always invisible until passion shows up and exposes it.
Graham Cooke

It is necessary to iterate and reiterate that prayer, as a mere habit, as a performance gone through by routine or in a professional way, is a dead and rotten thing.
E.M. Bounds

Fire always falls on sacrifice. Are you willing to become that living sacrifice for His fire to rest upon?
Bill Johnson

Cold prayers always freeze before they reach heaven.
Thomas Brooks

If you stay humble and stay hungry, there is nothing God cannot do in you and through you.
Mark Batterson

Desire tends to open the eyes as well as the heart.
Bill Bright & Ted Dekker

Persevere in prayer. Persevere, even when your efforts seem barren. Prayer is always fruitful.
St. Josemaría Escrivá

Most of what you need will come to you; most of what you want you'll have to go get.
Bill Johnson

You cannot see the kingdom of God unless you first want to.
Bill Bright & Ted Dekker

Incense can neither smell nor ascend without fire; no more does prayer unless it arises from spiritual warmth and fervency.
Acker

Whatever a man wants badly and persistently enough will determine the man's character.
A.W. Tozer

There is a mighty lot of difference between saying prayers and praying.
John G. Lake

Yank some of the groans out of your prayers, and shove in some shouts.
Billy Sunday

In a similar way when our emotions are set on fire, if we try to stir them up even more, we extinguish the flame, and the soul is deprived of its nourishment. We should, therefore, in stillness and quiet, with respect, confidence, and love, swallow the blessed food that we have tasted.

Madame Guyon

Those prayers God likes best which come seething hot from the heart.

Thomas Watson

Our prayers are weak because they are not impassioned by an unfailing and resistless will.

E.M. Bounds

It is only when the whole heart is gripped with the passion of prayer that the life-giving fire descends, for none but the earnest man gets access to the ear of God.

E.M. Bounds

Follow your own way of speaking to our Lord sincerely, lovingly, confidently, and simply, as your heart dictates.

Jane Frances de Chantal

Prayer must be aflame. Its ardor must consume. Prayer without fervor is as a sun without light or heat, or as a flower without beauty or fragrance. A soul devoted to God is a fervent soul, and prayer is the creature of that flame. He only can truly pray who is all aglow for holiness, for God, and for heaven.

E.M. Bounds

In souls filled with love, the desire to please God is continual prayer.

John Wesley

Shall I come into your presence, O my God, and mock You with cold-hearted words?

C.H. Spurgeon

Longing desire prayeth always, though the tongue be silent. If thou art ever longing, thou art ever praying.

Augustine

Perhaps little praying is worse than no praying. Little praying is a kind of make-believe, a salve for the conscience, a farce and a delusion.

E.M. Bounds

Great grief prays with great earnestness.

Samuel Chadwick

Grant that I may not pray alone with the mouth; help me that I may pray from the depths of my heart.

Martin Luther

Look, as a painted man is no man, and as painted fire is no fire, so a cold prayer is no prayer.

Thomas Brooks

As a painted man is no man, and as a painted fire is no fire, so a cold prayer is no prayer.

Thomas Brooks

Have you only repeated many a form of prayer, while the breathing desire, the living words, have not come from your lips?
　　　　　　　　　C.H. Spurgeon

In prayer it is better to have heart without words, than words without heart.
　　　　　　　　　John Bunyan

What is love if it be not fiery? What are prayers if the heart be not ablaze?
　　　　　　　　　Samuel Chadwick

Cold prayers ask for a denial!
　　　　　　　　　C.H. Spurgeon

Pain produces passion which leads to prayer which leads to intimacy with God.
　　　　　　　　　Rick Warren

The sovereign God cannot be manipulated, for He knows the hearts of all who pray to Him.
　　　　　　　　　R.C. Sproul

Prayer in its highest form is agonizing soul sweat.
　　　　　　　　　Leonard Ravenhill

To pray diligently is more than half the task.
　　　　　　　　　Martin Luther

Do the angels veil their faces before You, and shall I be content to prattle through a form with no soul and no heart?
　　　　　　　　　C.H. Spurgeon

The school of prayer has its conditions and demands. It is a forbidden place to all but those of set purpose and resolute heart.
　　　　　　　　　Samuel Chadwick

That which is not God can never satiate the heart exclusively created for God's presence.
　　　　　　　　　A.W. Tozer

Hurried prayers and muttered Litanies can never produce souls mighty in prayer.
　　　　　　　　　Samuel Chadwick

Prayers should be brief, frequent, and intense.
　　　　　　　　　Martin Luther

I am Thy servant to do Thy will, and that will is sweeter to me than position or riches or fame, and I choose it above all things on Earth or in Heaven.
　　　　　　　　　A.W. Tozer

Prayer, to the patriarchs and prophets, was more than the recital of well-known and well-worn phrases-it was the outpouring of the heart.
　　　　　　　　　Herbert Lockyer

Passion is the best motivation for discipline.
　　　　　　　　　Bill Johnson

The prayer preceding all prayers is May it be the real I who speaks. May it be the real Thou which I speak to.
　　　　　　　　　C.S. Lewis

Wishing will never be a substitute for prayer.
> Ed Cole

Cold prayers, like cold suitors, are seldom effective in their aims.
> Elisabeth Elliot

Passive prayer is no more than a worry or complaint session with God.
> Bill Johnson

Many pray with their lips for that for which their hearts have no desire.
> Jonathan Edwards

The recovery of passion begins with the recovery of my true self as the beloved.
> Brennan Manning

When we pray, we must remember who we are and whom we are addressing.
> R.C. Sproul

When we are passionate about God, we can trust our passions.
> Erwin McManus

Real prayer comes from falling in love.
> Brian Clark

Beloved, our weak prayer times may not move us, but they move the heart of God.
> Mike Bickle

To be loved by God is the highest relationship, the highest achievement, and the highest position in life.
> Henry Blackaby

Intensity is a law of prayer. God is found by those who seek Him with all their heart. Wrestling prayer prevails. The fervent effectual prayer of the righteous is of great force.
> Samuel Chadwick

Prayers are measured neither by time nor by number, but by intensity.
> Samuel Chadwick

If we're not careful, discouragement can slip in like a fog and chill our prayer lives.
> David Jeremiah

God hears no more than the heart speaks; and if the heart be dumb, God will certainly be dumb.
> Thomas Brooks

Pray often rather than very long at a time. It is hard to be very long in prayer, and not slacken in our affections.
> William Gurnall

You are before the Lord; let your words be few, but let your heart be fervent.
> C.H. Spurgeon

Is not the lack of urgent desire, rather than the lack of adequate time, at the root of our meager praying?
J. Oswald Sanders

The lazy man does not, will not, cannot pray, for prayer demands energy.
E.M. Bounds

It is reasonable that God should withhold a blessing, until we feel our need of it sufficiently.
William Patton

Importunity is a condition of prayer. We are to press the matter, not with vain repetitions, but with urgent repetitions. We repeat, not to count the times, but to gain the prayer. We cannot quit praying because heart and soul are in it. We pray "with all perseverance." We hang to our prayers because by them we live. We press our pleas because we must have them, or die.
E.M. Bounds

A minute with God seldom lays hold of Him.
Walter J. Chantry

We are encouraged to come freely to God but not flippantly.
John Blanchard

Too often we use petty little petitions, oratorical exercises, or the words of others rather than the cries of our inmost being. When you pray, pray!
Billy Graham

The only way to Heaven is prayer; a prayer of the heart, which everyone is capable of, and not of reasonings which are the fruits of study, or exercise of the imagination, which, in filling the mind with wandering objects, rarely settle it; instead of warming the heart with love to God, they leave it cold and languishing.
Madame Guyon

What you need is a vision from God that captures your imagination and consumes your energy.
Mark Batterson

When we pray, we are not passive observers or neutral, detached spectators. Energy is expended in the exercise of prayer.
R.C. Sproul

No erudition, no purity of diction, no width of mental outlook, no flowers of eloquence, no grace of person can atone for lack of fire. Prayer ascends by fire. Flame gives prayer access as well as wings, acceptance as well as energy. There is no incense without fire; no prayer without flame.
E.M. Bounds

Prayer is life passionately wanting, wishing, desiring God's triumph. Prayer is life striving and toiling everywhere and always for that ultimate victory.
George Campbell Morgan

When your passion begins to decline, you already start to die. You were born to burn.
Bill Johnson

Those who know God the best are the richest and most powerful in prayer. Little acquaintance with God, and strangeness and coldness to Him, make prayer a rare and feeble thing.
E.M. Bounds

Prayers counted on a rosary are easier than the prayers of a soul poured out in unrestrained speech to God.
Samuel Chadwick

Cold prayers shall never have any warm answers. God will suit His returns to our requests. Lifeless, services shall have lifeless answers. When men are dull, God will be dumb.
Thomas Brooks

We can never know God, as it is our privilege to know Him, by brief repetitions that are requests for personal favors, and nothing more.
E.M. Bounds

God's not going to deal with me according to my behavior. He's going to deal with me according to His passion for Christ in me.
Graham Cooke

Prayer is measured, not by time, but by intensity.
The Kneeling Christian

Prayers that don't move you, won't move Him.
Bill Johnson

When we ask of the Lord cooly, and not fervently, we do as it were, stop His hand, and restrain Him from giving us the very blessing we pretend that we are seeking.
C.H. Spurgeon

There is a marked absence of travail. There is much phrasing, but little pleading. Prayer has become a soliloquy instead of a passion. The powerlessness of the church needs no other explanation...To be prayerless is to be both passionless and powerless.
Samuel Chadwick

When our passion for God fails to find its expression in joy, it often finds it's expression in legalism.
Bill Johnson

Oh, those cold-hearted prayers that die on our lips! Those frozen supplications would not even move men's hearts, how should they move the heart of God?
C.H. Spurgeon

Our prayers may be very beautiful in appearance and might appear to be the very paragon of devotion, but unless there is a secret spiritual force in them, they are vain things.
C.H. Spurgeon

Whatever makes us spiritually passive also leaves us spiritually vulnerable.
Francis Frangipane

Do not pray by heart, but with the heart.
Unknown

It is necessary to rouse the heart to pray, otherwise it will become quite dry.
John of Kronstadt

Fasting is calculated to bring a note of urgency and importance into our praying, and to give force to our pleading in the court of heaven. The man who prays with fasting is giving heaven notice that he is truly in earnest.
Arthur Wallis

The simple fact is, we are too vague and, as a consequence, too indifferent in our prayers and prayer meetings. We do not seem like people asking for what they want, and waiting for what they ask. This is what destroys our prayer meetings, rendering them pithless, pointless, powerless; turning them into teaching or talking meetings, rather than deep-toned, earnest prayer meetings.
CHM

We must be earnest, otherwise we have no right to hope that the Lord will hear our prayer.
C.H. Spurgeon

The Role of Poverty

We must give up all that we are in order to possess all that He is.
Heidi Baker

No man gives anything acceptable to God until he has first given himself in love and sacrifice.
A.W. Tozer

Prayer does not consist in gifted expressions and a volubility of speech; but in a brokenness of heart.
John Mason

God will often give you more than you can handle so you can learn to depend on him rather than on yourself.
Craig Groeschel

I believe being poor in spirit is a choice-a decision-we all have to make to go lower still, fully dependent on the One who is always dependable.
Heidi Baker

God is attracted to weakness. He can't resist those who humbly and honestly admit how desperately they need Him.
Jim Cymbala

A true prayer is an inventory of needs, a catalog of necessities, an exposure of secret wounds, a revelation of hidden poverty.
C.H. Spurgeon

Prayer is a mysterious instrumentality and can, in the final analysis, be employed to full effect and with perfect success only by those who are helpless.
O. Hallesby

Natural strength is often as great a handicap as natural weakness, both must be utterly yielded to the Lord.
Hannah Hurnard

It is much easier for me to imagine a praying murderer, a praying prostitute, than a vain person praying. Nothing is so at odds with prayer as vanity.
Dietrich Bonhoeffer

The reason we must ask God for things He already intends to give us is that He wants to teach us dependence, especially our need for Himself.
Erwin Lutzer

Our infirmities are the trumpets which call us to prayer.
Jack Taylor

Prayer moves us from self-dependency to total dependency and hope in God.
Bob Hartley

When we finally get serious about prayer, the trigger is usually desperation, not duty.
David Jeremiah

Pride, unforgiveness, and false humilty in our lives can cause us to not hear God clearly.
Doug Addison

Prayer needs fasting for its full and perfect development.
Andrew Murray

Is prayer your steering wheel or your spare tire?
Corrie ten Boom

God loves an open heart, and a humble prayer.
Marcos Rubalcava

Where there is a willing heart there will be a continual crying to heaven for help.
John Mason

We make a daily declaration that God is our source by spending time with Him.
Trisha Cwir

Your weakness isn't an obstacle to prayer; it's the very context in which prayer has divine power.
J.D. Greear

Prayer is the act of seeing reality from God's point of view.
Phillip Yancey

God is greatly grieved at the lack of trust among His children. Yet He delights when we come to Him in simple, childlike confidence.
Madame Guyon

Prayer is the language of a man burdened with a sense of need.
E.M. Bounds

God listens to our weeping when the occasion itself is beyond our knowledge, but still within His love and power.
Daniel A. Poling

We can rest assured that God will never give up with us until we are totally given over to God. Then he will kill off in us anything that remains alive but which ought to be put to death.
Madame Guyon

Perhaps the greatest hindrance to our work is our own imagined strength; and in fasting we learn what poor, weak creatures we are—dependent on a meal of meat for the little strength which we are so apt to lean upon.
Hudson Taylor

When prayer has become secondary, or incidental, it has lost its power. Those who are conspicuously men of prayer are those who use prayer as they use food, or air, or light, or money.
M.E. Andross

Prayer humbles us as needy and exalts God as wealthy.
John Piper

We always pray best when we pray out of the depths—when the soul gets low enough she gets a leverage; she can then plead with God.
C.H. Spurgeon

The prayer that prevails is not the work of lips and fingertips. It is the cry of a broken heart and the travail of a stricken soul.
Samuel Chadwick

Prayer admits and voices dependence upon the only One who is the ultimate source of help and strength.
Stephen Olford

We need to see much our deep needs, our great sins, for ah! that prayer shall go highest that comes from the lowest.
C.H. Spurgeon

We all have to appear fools in the eyes of the world at some time or other. For, after all, pride is the greatest cause of unbelief and unreality in spiritual things, and looking foolish is one of the ways by which we take up the cross and crucify our pride.
Hannah Hurnard

Before we pray that God would fill us, I believe we ought to pray that He would empty us.
D.L. Moody

I have been driven many times to my knees by the overwhelming conviction that I had nowhere else to go. My own wisdom, and that of all about me, seemed insufficient for the day.
Abraham Lincoln

Sacrifice is the ecstasy of giving the best we have to the One we love the most.
Hannah Hurnard

God's plan is not just to revolutionize your prayer life, but to make your life a prayer.
John Crowder

I would love to have a more earnest prayer life! In my life, prayer is the single most difficult discipline. I love God and there's something in me that would rather do things for God than talk to God. I'm not by nature a mystical, devotional person. I like to do things. And so it's a challenge for me to have a faithful prayer life, but I know God loves me and He's not mad at me. He just wishes I would slow down and turn things over to Him. And that's what I think you achieve through prayer.
Max Lucado

Fasting is a choice for God and against the flesh.
Mahesh Chavda

Ignorance and helplessness in prayer are indeed blessed things if they cast us upon the Holy Spirit.
The Kneeling Christian

It does not need to be a formal prayer: the most stumbling and broken cry—a sigh, a whisper, anything that tells the heart's loneliness and need and penitence—can find its way to Him.
Phillip Brooks

We must cooperate with and help to bring about God's purposes which tend to strip us of all our own self-effort so that God may be enthroned in our lives. Let this be done in you; and do not allow yourself to be attached to anything, however good it may appear.
Madame Guyon

To admit the existence of a need in God is to admit incompleteness in the divine Being. Need is a creature-word and cannot be spoken of the Creator. God has a voluntary relation to everything He has made, but He has no Necessary relation to anything outside of Himself. His interest in His creatures arises from His sovereign good pleasure, not from any need those creatures can supply nor from any completeness they can bring to Him who is complete in himself.
A.W. Tozer

Prayer, in its most basic form, is the surging of the human spirit in its weakness, grasping at the Spirit of God in His strength.
Ravi Zacharias

There is nothing a natural man hates more than prayer.
Robert Murray M'Cheyne

God looks not at the oratory of your prayers, how elegant they may be; nor at the geometry of your prayers, how long they may be; nor at the arithmetic of your prayers, how many they may be; not at logic of your prayers, how methodical they may be; but the sincerity of them He looks at.
Thomas Brooks

The more helpless you are, the better you are fitted to pray, and the more answers to prayer you will experience.
O. Hallesby

The prayer-life of man lies rooted in his instinctive recognition of his dependence on some power or being greater than himself.
Albert D. Belden

Although posture is not important, I find that I am able to express my dependence better on my knees, a sign of our helplessness apart from the divine enablement.
Erwin Lutzer

If you are swept off your feet, it's time to get on your knees.
Fred Beck

Men are always quarrelling with God because He will not submit His will to their dictation.
C.H. Spurgeon

Influence at the court of heaven depends not upon birth, or brilliancy, or achievement, but upon humble and utter dependence upon the Son of the King.
The Kneeling Christian

From birth we have been learning the rules of self-reliance as we strain and struggle to achieve self-sufficiency. Prayer flies in the face of those deep-seated values.
Bill Hybels

Helplessness united with faith produces prayer, for without faith there can be no prayer.
O. Hallesby

Prayer is an acknowledgment that our need of God's help is not partial but total.
Alistair Begg

The very fact that spiritual hearing can so easily be confused with imagination is a great safeguard against spiritual pride and ought to develop in us holy cautiousness and humble dependence.
Hannah Hurnard

Trouble and prayer are closely related. Trouble often drives men to God in prayer, while prayer is but the voice of men in trouble.
E.M. Bounds

If I say, "I ought to pray," I will soon run out of motivation and quit; the flesh is too strong. I have to be driven to pray.
Jim Cymbala

We lean to our own understanding, or we bank on service and do away with prayer, and consequently by succeeding in the external we fail in the eternal, because in the eternal we succeed only by prevailing prayer.

Oswald Chambers

We are made for God alone, who can only be pleased when we turn away from ourselves to devote ourselves to Him.

Brother Lawrence

Even if no command to pray had existed, our very weakness would have suggested it.

François Fénelon

Praying from fear only puts us in a place of having to control. It makes you feel like you are the only one who can change the circumstance and brings on stress, anxiousness and striving, which gets you nowhere.

Beni Johnson

Sometimes God has His hand on our forehead, waiting for us to stop punching the air and collapse from exhaustion -surrender over commitment.

Kevin Adams

Prayer is not so much submitting our needs to God but submitting ourselves to Him. Praying is much more difficult than saying words to God.

John Blanchard

Many of the most blessed seasons of prayer I have ever known have begun with the feeling of utter deadness and prayerlessness; but in my helplessness and coldness I have cast myself upon God, and looked to Him to send His Holy Spirit to teach me to pray, and He has done it.

R.A. Torrey

The Third Petition of the Lord's Prayer is repeated daily by millions who have not the slightest intention of letting anyone's will be done but their own.

Aldous Huxley

[Prayer] gives us relief from the melancholy burden of self-absorption.

Tim Keller

A friend of mine defines prayer as a declaration of dependence.

Billy Graham

Here is the life of prayer, when in or with the Spirit, a man being made sensible of sin, and how to come to the Lord for mercy; he comes, I say, in the strength of the Spirit, and crieth Father. That one word spoken in faith is better than a thousand prayers, as men call them, written and read, in a formal, cold, lukewarm way.

John Bunyan

Most will only truly hunger for the Bread of Life when it's the only thing left in the cupboard.

Kevin Adams

The bottom line is that we give all of ourselves to obtain all of Him. There's never been a better deal.
Bill Johnson

By prayer we couple the powers of heaven to our helplessness, the powers which capture strongholds and make the impossible possible.
O. Hallesby

Every need is a call to prayer.
Watchman Nee

We have been so busy depending on our own natural strengths, our good training and our busyness for God that we are near spiritual bankruptcy.
Wesley Duewel

God creates out of nothing. Therefore, until a man is nothing God can make nothing out of him.
Martin Luther

Prayer is reaching out after the unseen; fasting is letting go of all that is seen and temporal. Fasting helps express, deepen, confirm the resolution that we are ready to sacrifice anything, even ourselves to attain what we seek for the kingdom of God.
Andrew Murray

There is nothing about which I do not pray. I go over all my life in the presence of God. All my problems are solved there.
Samuel Chadwick

Prayer brings to us blessings which we need, and which only God can give, and which prayer can alone convey to us.
Gerhard Tersteegen

Pride prevents prayer. As long as we believe the lie that we're in control of everything we fail to ask for God's help.
Rick Warren

The observation of some kind of fast is important because it shows a desperation and determination to touch the Lord.
Mahesh Chavda

The more we pray, the more we sense our need to pray. And the more we sense a need to pray, the more we want to pray.
Jim Cymbala

Prayer is weakness leaning on omnipotence.
W.S. Bowd

Fasting tells God that I am hungrier for Your world than for this one.
Bill Johnson

God doesn't need you to put yourself down for Him to look good. He has space to call out your greatness and still be greater still.
Kevin Shorter

True prayer presupposes an attitude of humble submission and adoration to the Almighty God.
R.C. Sproul

We fast to become weak before God so God's power can be strong.
Mahesh Chavda

Let none expect to have the mastery over his inward corruption in any degree, without going in weakness again and again to the Lord for strength. Nor will prayer for others, or conversing with the brethren, make up for secret prayer.
George Müller

It takes a tremendous amount of reiteration on God's part before we understand what prayer is. We do not pray at all until we are at our wits' end.
Oswald Chambers

The supernatural life that we are called to is nothing more than getting all of God that you can by giving Him all of you.
Kevin Shorter

Proud prayers may knock their heads on mercy's lintel, but they can never pass through the portal.
C.H. Spurgeon

Prayer is a silent surrendering of everything to God.
Soren Kierkegaard

Prayer helps us to utter dependence upon God and gives Him the opportunity to confirm our trust in Him and experience His grace in a way which would be absolutely impossible otherwise.
Hannah Hurnard

I believe we should pray that God will take possession of our lives totally and completely. We should pray that we will be emptied of self—self-love, self-will, self-ambition—and be placed completely at His disposal.
Billy Graham

Prayer reorients our dependence on God and He exalts the humble.
Kevin Shorter

Prayer is the disciplined refusal to act before God acts.
Eugene Peterson

I have now concentrated all my prayers into one, that I may die to self and live wholly to Him.
C.H. Spurgeon

Helplessness is the real secret and the impelling power of prayer.
O. Hallesby

Prayer is designed by God for our humbling. Prayer, real prayer, is a coming into the Presence of God, and a sense of His awful majesty produces a realization of our nothingness and unworthiness.
A.W. Pink

You pray in your distress and in your need; would that you might pray also in the fullness of your joy and in your days of abundance.
Kahlil Gibran

Fasting in the biblical sense is choosing not to partake of food because your spiritual hunger is so deep, you determination in intercession so intense, or your spiritual warfare so demanding that you have temporarily set aside even fleshly needs to give yourself to prayer and meditation.
Wesley Duewel

The Role of Perspective

Too many Christians are actors rather than believers. They are trying to act like Jesus instead of believing like Him.
Wendy Backlund

Perception is the key to power. How you see yourself in Him will provide you with the keys to victory in every situation.
Graham Cooke

Our human shortsighted view is dwarfed by God's eternal and divine vision.
Jay Harris

What causes us to think of prayer as the last option rather than the first? I can think of two reasons: feelings of independence and feelings of insignificance.
Max Lucado

Prayer is powerful, but if our prayers are aimless, meaningless, and mingled with doubt, they will be of little hope to us.
Billy Graham

God can do without the bended knee, but not without the broken heart.
Horatius Bonar

Dependency is the heartbeat of prayer.
Paul Miller

You are not made to be earth bound in your thinking.
Graham Cooke

How you position yourself before God affects the way that you pray.
Graham Cooke

I know the only way for me to see the world is to see it through his eyes.
Henri Nouwen

Most of desperation prayers are because we don't see what God sees and don't have hope in our situation.
Matt Peterson

Whatever you focus on becomes your reality, whether it is based on reality or not.
Doug Addison

Expectation changed your mindset and the language of your prayers.
Allison Brown

You need to agree with what God says about you.
Lance Wallnau

Even in prayer I am amazed at how often people will repeat to God the negative, hopeless thoughts that were inspired by listening to the enemy.
Wendy Backlund

Hope is essential for the Christian life. When we have lost hope, we have lost God's perspective.
Kevin Shorter

Pray as though everything depended on God; work as though everything depended on you.
Augustine

As we grow increasingly more aware of God, we grow simultaneously less aware of ourselves.
Francis Frangipane

Misguided understandings about prayer mess more people up spiritually than anything else out there!
Andrew Wommack

Being alone with God is a reminder of priorities. Quiet time forces busyness to find its victims elsewhere.
Bill Johnson

When I stay more conscience of need than conscience of blessing, I will tend to pray out of a hole instead of heavenly places.
Bill Johnson

Learn to look beyond your situation and see the fine hand of God at work!
Graham Cooke

Most of the time we see what we expect to see, hear what we expect to hear, and feel what we expect to feel about others.
Rick Warren

You rarely see what you are not looking for.
Bill Johnson

The root-trouble of the present distress is that the Church has more faith in the world and the flesh than in the Holy Ghost, and things will get no better till we get back to His realized presence and power.
Thomas Brooks

Prayer turns us into first-class noticers. It helps us see what God wants us to notice. The more you pray, the more you notice.
Mark Batterson

Our natural human perception can at best only lead us to the doorway of understanding and never through it.
Jack Hayford

How do you pray a prayer so filled with faith that it can move a mountain? By shifting your focus from the size of your mountain to the sufficiency of the Mountain Mover and then stepping forward in obedience.
Bill Hybels

Many people are releasing the power of death into their lives through their negativity in prayer.
Andrew Wommack

We must learn to persist in God's nature, not persevere in the problem.
Graham Cooke

Most Christians speak to God about their mountain instead of speaking to their mountain about God.
Andrew Wommack

Let this truth grip you with hope: If the promise of God concerning His coming Messiah, His own Son, was interrupted by the failure of humanity (in this case, the later generations of David's offspring) and God bridged and reconnected that 'cut-off,' then He wants us to understand this as a power-principle for prayer. Just as God navigated that failure and brought the tender plant out of the stump that had been cut off, so He is inviting you to pray and believe that He will do the same in your relationships.
Jack Hayford

There will be a crack in our spiritual foundation if we use "if it be your will" in prayer for things God already declared as His will.
Steve Backlund

Anytime we are more aware of the size of our problem than the size of the solution we are bringing we will live in reaction to the problem.
Bill Johnson

Where you allow you thoughts to go, you heart will sure to follow.
Kevin Shorter

We tend to have more faith in Adam's ability to make us a sinner than faith in Jesus' ability to make us righteous.
Wendy Backlund

Without doubt, the mightiest thought the mind can entertain is the thought of God, and the weightiest word in any language is its word for God.
A.W. Tozer

A great part of my time is spent in getting my heart in tune for prayer.
Robert Murray M'Cheyne

To pray is to let God into our lives. He knocks and seeks admittance, not only in the solemn hours of secret prayer. He knocks in the midst of your daily work, your daily struggles, your daily grind. That is when you need Him most.
O. Hallesby

Prayer removes you from the burdens of life and resets your priorities on the eternal and real.
Kevin Shorter

Contentment is the peaceful happiness that comes when we are in awe of how God feels about us.
Graham Cooke

The greatest answer to prayer is that I am brought into a perfect understanding with God, and that alters my view of actual things.
Oswald Chambers

What we say about a matter after we pray is just as important as what we say when we pray.
Steve Backlund

How can we think of Him but by a holy habit we should form of it?
Brother Lawrence

God is as much with you when you are not praying as when you are.
Reinhard Bonnke

We have to see ourselves as God sees us if we are to be everything He wants us to be.
Graham Cooke

The eyes of faith are more apt to see God's answers to prayers.
Kevin Shorter

Focusing on what God didn't do for others erodes personal trust. Focusing on what God did do for others should build trust for the same to happen to me.
Paul Rapley

Knowledge that is not married to love and spiritual awareness can become religious.
Shawn Bolz

God wants to get our prayers and expectations into unity.
Steve Backlund

[God] wants to reveal His nature to you and rewire your brain with kingdom thinking and living.
Shawn Bolz

I'm not moved by what I see, I'm not moved by what I feel, I'm moved by what I believe.
Smith Wigglesworth

Truth is what Jesus says is true; you are who God says you are.
Kevin Shorter

We are not suppose to spend our lives by being preoccupied by what we are not.
Graham Cooke

A change in perspective might be exactly what your prayer life needs.
Kelly O'Dell Stanley

What you speak has power to either interrupt or partner with God in what He is doing.
Lance Wallnau

It's amazing how much you see when you are unwilling to look anywhere else.
Bill Johnson

All earthly things with earth will pass away; Prayer grasps eternity. Then pray, always pray!
E.H. Bickersteth

Your view of God will impact everything about your life.
Bill Bright

We don't pray to get God's attention. We pray to turn our attention toward Him.
Christopher Knippers

Your problem is not your problem, your perspective is.
Steve Backlund

God is better than you think. So let's change the way we think.
Bill Johnson

Circumstances are transformed when we think differently about them.
Graham Cooke

Prayer doesn't bring God closer to me, it causes me to see how close He already is.
Elijah Waters

You aren't making God do something. You just know in your heart that He's already supplied, so you reach out and take it.
Andrew Wommack

When I do well, God approves of me. When I do badly, God accepts me.
Graham Cooke

When we know Him properly, we behold His majesty. When we know that we are His Beloved, we bask in His favor.
Graham Cooke

Many people have lost their authority in prayer because they are coming into agreement with the accuser.
Doug Addison

People on sinking ships do not complain of distractions during their prayer.
Phillip Yancey

If you don't believe it, you can't see it. If you can't see it, you can't have it.
Michael Brodeur

I entreat you, give no place to despondency. This is a dangerous temptation–a refined, not a gross temptation of the adversary. Melancholy contracts and withers the heart, and renders it unfit to receive the impressions of grace. It magnifies and gives a false colouring to objects, and thus renders your burdens too heavy to bear. God's designs regarding you, and His methods of bringing about these designs, are infinitely wise.
Madame Guyon

Allow your discernment to be the door for spiritual revelation that goes beyond your thoughts, feelings, opinions, or faith.
Shawn Bolz

When a man makes alliance with the Almighty, giants look like grasshoppers.
Vance Havner

What is your perception of God when you pray? Is He inclining His ear toward you, or do you feel as though you have to persuade Him, or trick Him, into listening? If your image of God is that He is interested and delighted in you, your whole prayer life and approach to Him will be changed. You'll love prayer!

Graham Cooke

The power of the heavenly minded is that our hearts and our minds are always in sync with who God is for us.

Graham Cooke

Bad emotions are not going to go away just by praying longer and harder or fasting. We replace them by repenting of wrong core beliefs that hinder confidence in the power of our prayers.

Wendy Backlund

Remember, your circumstances are not the problem. Your perception of your circumstances is the problem!

Graham Cooke

Prayer is a bridge from despair to hope.

Bill Hybels

Expectation liberates us from apprehension that blinds us to the majesty before us.

Allison Brown

If we are thinking low of ourselves, people will not see a friend of God – they will see a slave.

Kevin Shorter

We must pray that the kingdom of God will become visible on the earth, that the invisible will be made visible.

R.C. Sproul

Learn to walk in God's perception of who you are, because yours is not good enough.

Graham Cooke

If we had a larger vision of what God wanted to accomplish in us and through us, our petty problems would cease to exist because they would cease to be important.

Mark Batterson

Being vigilant in prayer gives you insight into things unseen. It allows you access into the spiritual realm.

John Bevere

Vision for the future gives power for the present.

Steve Backlund

When God gives us a promise, He is releasing us from logic to imagination. He wants us to see beyond the problem to the promise's fulfillment.

Graham Cooke

How to Pray

The Bible formula is that we pray to the Father, through the Son, and in the Spirit.
Warren Wiersbe

There is no way of learning to pray but by praying.
Samuel Chadwick

The Lord's Prayer may be committed to memory quickly, but it is slowly learnt by heart.
Frederick Denison Maurice

We see that the Holy Fathers made extraordinary efforts in prayer, and by their struggles they kindled the warm spirit of prayer.
St. Theophan

Prayer, genuine and victorious, is continually offered without the least physical effort or disturbance.
Dr. Handley Moule

Pray not for crutches but for wings.
Phillip Brooks

The first rule of prayer is not 'faith,' but whether the request is according to God's will.
Jim Cymbala

The most important lesson we can learn is how to pray. Prayers do not die, prayers live before God, and God's heart is set on them.
E.M. Bounds

To pray in His name is to pray in His character, as His representative sent by Him: it is to pray by His Spirit and according to His will.
The Kneeling Christian

No one can say his prayers are poor prayers when he is using the language of love.
John Maillard

Tell God all that is in your heart, as one unloads one's heart to a dear friend. People who have no secrets from each other never want subjects of conversations; they do not weigh their words because there is nothing to be kept back.
François Fénelon

Prayer includes moments of ecstasy and also dullness, mindless distraction and acute concentration, flashes of joy and bouts of irritation.
Phillip Yancey

The spirit in which we pray is much more important than the words in which our prayers are clothed.
J. Oswald Sanders

Well-developed faith results in well-defined prayers, and well-defined prayers result in a well-lived life.
Mark Batterson

We are to pray only for what God has promised, and for the communication of it unto us in that way whereby he will work it and affect it.

John Owen

The tendency nowadays is to worship prayer, stress is put on nights of prayer and the difficulty and cost of prayer. It is not prayer that is strenuous, but the overcoming of our own laziness. If we make the basis of prayer our effort and agony and nights of prayer, we mistake the basis of prayer. The basis of prayer is not what it costs us, but what it costs God to enable us to pray.

Oswald Chambers

Praying is not a lesson got by forms and rules of art, but flowing from principles of new life itself.

William Gurnall

Prayer is simple, prayer is supernatural, and to anyone not related to our Lord Jesus Christ, prayer is apt to look stupid.

Oswald Chambers

Without formal prayers, we would not know how to pray correctly at all.

St. Theophan

Right prayer sees nothing substantial or worth being concerned about except God.

John Bunyan

We have this list of expectations and tell them to God. This is what we often call prayer.

Danny Silk

Prayer opens the heart to God, and it is the means by which the soul, though empty, is filled with God.

John Bunyan

To seek after God in the right way is easier and more natural than breathing.

Madame Guyon

When I typed the prayers of the Bible into the computer, I discovered that the really effective prayer warriors gave God a reason He should answer their prayers.

T.W. Hunt

I think that some of the greatest prayer is prayer where you don't say one single word or ask for anything.

A.W. Tozer

Don't pray for an easier life. Ask for more strength. (Romans 4:20)

Rick Warren

We must pray in line with God's purposes, not our problems.

Graham Cooke

Pleading the promises of God is the whole secret of prayer, I sometimes think.

Martyn Lloyd-Jones

God doesn't have to add His power to crush what is already headed for destruction, but He is asking us to partner with redemption, transformation, and hope.
Shawn Bolz

Prayer without love has no suction. It does not draw the blessing down.
W.E. Sangster

How often have we prayed something like, O Lord, be with cousin Billy now in a special way? Have we stopped to consider what it is we're requesting? Imagine that you are a parent who is preparing to leave your children with a babysitter. Would you dream of saying, O Betsy, I ask you now that you would be with my children in a special way? No way. You would say, Betsy, the kids need to be in bed by 9 pm. They can have one snack before their baths, and please make sure they finish their homework. You can reach us at this number if there's any problem. Any questions before we go? We are very specific with our requests and instructions for our babysitters. We want them to know specifics. It should be no different with prayer.
David Jeremiah

If you want that splendid power in prayer, you must remain in loving, abiding union with the Lord Jesus Christ.
C.H. Spurgeon

When you're worrying you're not praying. Stop worrying start praying.
Lecrae

In prayer Jesus slows us down, teaches us to count how few days we have, and gifts us with wisdom.
Brennan Manning

To pray strenuously needs careful cultivation. We have to learn the most natural methods of expressing ourselves to our Father.
Oswald Chambers

Three principles of prayer: 1. Keep it honest, 2. Keep it simple, 3. Keep it up.
Nicky Gumbel

Some of our shortest prayers are our most effectual ones.
V.R. Edman

There is no need to get to a place of prayer; pray wherever you are.
Oswald Chambers

Prayer is such a great effort to most of us because we do not pray right.
O. Hallesby

If your knees are shaking, kneel on them.
Charles Allen

When we go to our meeting with God, we should go like a patient to his doctor, first to be thoroughly examined and afterwards to be treated for our ailment. Then something will happen when you pray.
O. Hallesby

When we come to the end of ourselves, we come to the beginning of God.
Billy Graham

What I have learned to do better is to try to keep my mind turned toward God and ear inclined toward God throughout the day, and I think I'm doing better at that, but I've got a long way to go.
Max Lucado

Prayer is the proper work of the heart; yet in this present state, in secret as well as in social prayer, the language of the lips is an excellent aid in this part of worship.
Issac Watts

Moses gave neither command nor regulation with regard to prayer: even the prophets say little directly of the duty of prayer; it is Christ who teaches to pray.
Andrew Murray

God has told me that I can always pray for one thing: to expand our hearts to love more.
Heidi Baker

Prayer can assume very different forms, from quiet, blessed contemplation of God, in which eye meets eye in restful meditation, to deep sighs or sudden exclamations of wonder, joy, gratitude or adoration.
O. Hallesby

If our first response is prayer, we often pray more out of fear than a place of rest.
Graham Cooke

The more deeply we grow into the psalms and the more often we pray them as our own, the more simple and rich will our prayer become.
Dietrich Bonhoeffer

Private place and plenty of time are the life of prayer.
E.M. Bounds

The Lord's Prayer is not merely the pattern prayer, it is the way Christians must pray... The Lord's Prayer is the quintessence of prayer.
Dietrich Bonhoeffer

I define intimacy as belonging to or revealing one's deepest nature to another and it is marked by close association, presence, and contact.
John Wimber

Don't know what to pray for others? Pray for them what you wish people would pray for you.
Kevin Shorter

Don't fool yourself into thinking you'll be heard by praying long periods of time.
Andrew Wommack

Praying hard is two dimensional: praying like it depends on God, and working like it depends on you.
Mark Batterson

I am convinced that when a Christian rightly prays the Lord's prayer... His praying is more than adequate.
Martin Luther

Those postures of the body which the light of nature rule of Scripture seem to dictate as most proper for prayer are standing, kneeling or prostration.... But I cannot think that sitting, or other postures of rest and laziness, ought to be indulged in solemn times of prayer, unless persons are in some respect infirm or aged.
Isaac Watts

The future is in the mouth of intentional speakers.
Steve Backlund

(There are) four obstacles to answered prayer: unbelief, willful disobedience, neglect of God's Word, and hypocrisy masked by religion.
Warren Wiersbe

I do believe in being informed about things so I can pray better.
Beni Johnson

We may pray most when we say least, and we may pray least when we say most.
Augustine

Much of the traditional teaching on prayer is impossible to implement in daily life.
Andrew Wommack

It was your Lord who put an end to long-windedness, so that you would not pray as if you wanted to teach God by your many words. Piety, not verbosity, is in order when you pray, since He knows your needs. Now someone perhaps will say: 'But if He knows our needs, why should we sate our requests even in a few words?
Augustine

Prayer is more than a wish; it is the voice of faith directed to God.
Billy Graham

Pray absolutely for those things you may pray for absolutely. Pray conditionally for those things you may pray for conditionally. For those things you can't pray for - don't.
Paul Gerhardt

Prayer needs three organs of the body that are all located on the head. The ear hears His word to us, the tongue repeats what we've heard from Him back to Him, and the eye looks expectantly for the answer.
Armin Gesswein

You must learn to relate to Him in the midst of your daily responsibilities and weekly routines because they occupy the majority of your life.
Andrew Wommack

Habits of prayer need careful cultivation.
F.B. Meyer

In order to pray like a child, you might need to unlearn the nonpersonal, nonreal praying that you've been taught.
Paul Miller

Just because you spend an hour, or more, in what you call "prayer" doesn't mean you're accomplishing anything.
Andrew Wommack

It is a tremendously hard thing to pray aright, yea, it is verily the science of all sciences.
Martin Luther

Listen for the word of the Lord going out and join in its declaration. You want success in your prayers? Partner with those words because they don't come back void.
Kevin Shorter

Many times when I am teaching on prayer, I will have people wait before God, and then in the waiting, I will have them re-ask God about a request they have been praying for. Sometimes we need the fresh wind of God on our prayers that will make them more effective.
Beni Johnson

There is an inseparable union between the Spirit, the Word and prayer.
H.W. Frost

The prayer of guidance constantly precedes and surrounds the prayer of faith.
Richard Foster

We ought to act very simply towards God, speaking frankly to Him, and asking His help in things as they occur.
Brother Lawrence

Wherever... thou shalt be, pray secretly within thyself. If thou shalt be far from a house of prayer, give not thyself trouble to seek for one, for thou thyself art a sanctuary designed for prayer. If thou shalt be in bed or any other place, pray there; thy temple is there.
Bernard of Clairvaux

Praying is the same to the new creature as crying is to the natural.
William Gurnall

Inarticulate prayer, the impulsive prayer that looks so futile, is the thing God always heeds. The habit of ejaculatory prayer ought to be the persistent habit of each one of us.
Oswald Chambers

What if the whole point of prayer is that you don't pray to get an answer but you pray with the answer.
Graham Cooke

A most beneficial exercise in secret prayer before the Father is to write things down exactly so I see exactly what I think and want to say. Only those who have tried these ways know the ineffable benefit of such strenuous times in secret.
Oswald Chambers

It is not the body's posture, but the heart's attitude that counts when we pray.
Billy Graham

Like sex, techniques of prayer are not the source of pleasure; it's in the relationship. A misplaced focus only brings about frustration and distance.
Kevin Shorter

God's promises are to be our pleas in prayer.
Matthew Henry

To find God, you must look with all your heart. To remain present to God, you must remain present to your heart. To hear his voice, you must listen with all your heart. To love him, you must love with all your heart. You cannot be the person God meant you to be, and you cannot live the life he meant you to live, unless you live from the heart.
John Eldredge

You do not have to speak to God in "religious" language about "spiritual" matters only.
James Coburn

You should, in Tertullian's phrase, with a holy conspiracy, besiege heaven.
Thomas Manton

[In prayer] the fewer words the better prayer.
Martin Luther

Anything big enough to occupy our minds is big enough to hang a prayer on.
George MacDonald

I do not pray for a lighter load, but for a stronger back.
Phillip Brooks

The man who says his prayers in the evening is a captain posting his sentries. After that, he can sleep.
Charles Baudelaire

I find He never guides us into an intolerable scramble of panting feverishness.
Thomas Kelly

I grew up believing that if I was going to pray, I had to use words. I have discovered that is only one form of prayer.
Beni Johnson

If you are so focused on the techniques of prayer, then you misplace the intended purpose.
Kevin Shorter

When we speak we give something to the unseen realm to work with.
Wendy Backlund

Just pray for a tough hide and a tender heart.
Ruth Graham Bell

Be yourself. Be natural before God. Do not pretend to emotions you do not feel. Tell Him whatever is on your heart and mind with whatever words are most natural to you. This natural expression of yourself at the outset is the guarantee that you can go on to a creative, free, and mature relationship with God.
James Coburn

True prayer is measured by weight, not by length. A single groan before God may have more fullness of prayer in it than a fine oration of great length.
C.H. Spurgeon

A prayer for self is not by any means necessarily a selfish prayer.
R.A. Torrey

Dealing in generalities is the death of prayer.
J.H. Evans

Prayer cannot truly be taught by principles and seminars and symposiums.
Jim Cymbala

Effective prayer is a quartet—the Father, the Son, the Spirit and the Christian.
John Blanchard

For the brevity of prayer can naturally lead to the frequency of prayer and more frequent prayer might lead to more fervent prayer. And that's what we want. It is of no value to pray for prayer's sake.
Frederick Bruner

As a camel kneels before his master to have him remove his burden, so kneel and let the Master take your burden.
Corrie ten Boom

Remove from prayer much speaking, not much praying.
Augustine

Though we cannot by our prayers give God any information, yet we must by our prayers give Him honor.
Matthew Henry

The Role of God's Word

Prayer grows in proportion to its grounding in God's Word.
Ben Jennings

We cannot be men of prevailing prayer unless we study God's Word to find out His will for us.
The Kneeling Christian

The Word of God is the fulcrum upon which the lever of prayer is placed, and by which things are mightily moved.
E.M. Bounds

We tend to use our experience to challenge the word of God when we are supposed to use the word of God to challenge our experience.
Wendy Backlund

After you have been meditating in the Word and praying it out to God for some time, you will gradually find how easy it is to come into His presence. You will remember other Scriptures with less difficulty. Prayer has now become easy, sweet, and delightful.
Madame Guyon

You cannot separate the Word of God and prayer, for in His Word He gives us the promises that we claim when we pray.
Warren Wiersbe

We must turn God's promises into prayer, and then they shall be turned into performance.
Ivan French

When people do not mind what God speaks to them in His Word, God doth as little mind what they say to Him in prayer.
William Gurnall

The richness of God's Word ought to determine our prayer, not the poverty of our heart.
Dietrich Bonhoeffer

Meditation on a passage of Scripture keeps me from being distracted in prayer.
Tim Keller

Prayer flows from doctrine.
John Calvin

When we know the Word, we pray the Word, and heaven echoes.
Lisa Bevere

Prayer that is loaded with God's Word is charged with life and power.
Suzette Caldwell

There is no avoiding the fact that Scripture insists God has hard-wired the universe in such a way that He works primarily through prayer.
David Jeremiah

It seems to me that the prayers of the Bible can be distilled into one. The result is a simple, easy-to-remember, pocket-sized prayer: Father, you are good. I need help. They need help. Thank you. In Jesus' name, amen. Let this prayer punctuate your day.
Max Lucado

Prayers are never meaningless. We may feel nothing, but don't measure by how you feel. Measure them by what God says in His Word.
IHOP

If we lack confidence in prayer, then we need to study God's Word until we know His promises concerning the key areas of our lives.
Steve Backlund

The first step in understanding the Bible is asking God to help us. We should read prayerfully.
Max Lucado

Prayer that is born of meditation upon the Word of God is the prayer that soars upward most easily to God's listening ears.
R.A. Torrey

The mightiest prayers are often those drenched with the Word of God.
Herbert Lockyer

As we approach God's Word, our prayer should be the words of Psalm 119:18: "Open my eyes, that I may see wondrous things from Your law." Remember, the reason for our study of the Bible is that we may become approved unto God (see 2 Tim. 2:15). There is little use to read and study the Bible if we do not obey its teachings. Do you want to be "approved unto God"? If so, you must study His Word.
Henrietta Mears

When we are praying in the Spirit, He will remind us of verses we know and give us promises to claim.
Warren Wiersbe

The Book of Psalms is the Bible's hymnbook. It will show you what it means to walk with God in prayer and praise.
Billy Graham

If we fill our minds with His Word, our inarticulate stammers will change to accomplished patterns of meaningful praise.
R.C. Sproul

If we want to read and to pray the prayers of the Bible and especially the Psalms, therefore, we must not ask first what they have to do with us, but what they have to do with Jesus Christ...It does not depend, therefore, on whether the Psalms express adequately that which we feel at a given moment in our heart. If we are to pray aright, perhaps it is quite necessary that we pray contrary to our own heart. Not what we want to pray is important, but what God wants us to pray.
Dietrich Bonhoeffer

Prayer by itself is like a diet without protein! Prayer is important to our spiritual growth—but of even greater importance is God's Word, the Bible.
Billy Graham

If you study the Bible and it doesn't lead you into an encounter with the Almighty, then you are already deceived!
Kris Vallotton

Praying God's Word connects us with His reality and makes His reality ours.
Suzette Caldwell

We learn to pray by reading the prayers in the Bible.
John Piper

God has promised joy to the world. He is waiting on kingdom carriers to drag the promise to the surface.
Alan Scott

The Bible is not an end in itself, but a means to bring men to an intimate and satisfying knowledge of God, that they may enter into Him, that they may delight in His Presence, may taste and know the inner sweetness of the very God Himself in the core and center of their hearts.
A.W. Tozer

The best way to pray is to open the Bible and pray Scripture back to the Lord, claiming His promises and asking that He strengthen and guide [us] in obeying His Word.
Billy Graham

The richness of God's Word ought to determine our prayer, not the poverty of our heart.
Dietrich Bonhoeffer

Prayer means reminding God of His promises and claiming them for ourselves.
Warren Wiersbe

Meditating on God's Word in prayer is desirable, but known by very few.
Madame Guyon

Prayer is only true when it is within the compass of God's Word.
John Bunyan

The cure of souls is Scripture directed and prayer shaped.
Eugene Peterson

A profitable prayer life is impossible without solitude, but it's also impossible without God's word.
Tim Keller

The Psalter is the great school of prayer.
Dietrich Bonhoeffer

The word of God is the food by which prayer is nourished and made strong. A life growing in its purity and devotion will be a more prayerful life.
E.M. Bounds

God's Word must be the guide of your desires and the ground of your expectations in prayer.
Matthew Henry

Prayer and Bible study are inseparably linked. Effective prayer is born out of the prompting of God's Spirit as we read His Word.
Billy Graham

Without its biblical principles being taught, prayer is unstable. Without our catching the principles by applying them to our lives, it is sterile.

Ben Jennings

The richness of the Word of God ought to determine our prayer, not the poverty of our heart.

Dietrich Bonhoeffer

Scripture enables you to enter in prayer and empowers you to have confidence before God.

Kevin Shorter

The Word of God represents all the possibilities of God as at the disposal of true prayer.

A.T. Pierson

It is the present Voice which makes the written Word all-powerful.

A.W. Tozer

So many Christians have a lackluster, ineffective prayer life because they do not incorporate the Scriptures into their prayers.

Suzette Caldwell

True prayer lays hold of God's Word and seeks to accomplish God's purposes.

Warren Wiersbe

Praying Scriptures expands your view of God and what you would naturally pray for by yourself.

Kevin Shorter

We pray well when we are immersed in scripture.

Tim Keller

Prayer is nothing but the promise reversed, or God's Word formed into an argument, and retorted by faith upon God again.

William Gurnall

Pray frequently as you read [the Bible] and you will discover a fellowship with God.

Billy Graham

The reason why our prayers so often fall flat or come out "stale" is because they have been "uprooted from the soil of the word of God.

Eugene Peterson

A mighty piece of weaponry in the battle of prayer is God's promise.

C.H. Spurgeon

Triumphant prayer is almost impossible where there is neglect of the study of the Word of God.

R.A. Torrey

No man can pray Scripturally who prays selfishly.

John Blanchard

Great pray-ers have always been great students of the Word of God.

Unknown

If we then let the words of Christ abide in us, they will stir us up in prayer.

R.A. Torrey

We cannot attain to the understanding of Scripture either by study or by the intellect. Your first duty is to begin by prayer.
Martin Luther

Furnish thyself with arguments from the promises to enforce thy prayers, and make them prevalent with God.
William Gurnall

Prayer turns theology into experience.
Tim Keller

Theology and prayer are inextricably intertwined.
Richard Bewes

To pray in the Spirit means to pray in harmony with the Word of God, which He has inspired.
J. Oswald Sanders

The Role of the Secret Place

It is by no haphazard chance that in every age men have risen early to pray. The first thing that marks decline in spiritual life is our relationship to the early morning.
Oswald Chambers

Prayer unfolds in the stillness of the soul.
Phillip Yancey

Some place must be found that shall be a trysting place with God.
Samuel Chadwick

Prayer is more than a plea, it is a place where we must spend time if we are to learn its power.
Billy Graham

Every one must have some solitary spot where he can be alone with his God.
Andrew Murray

Christ choosing solitude for private prayer, doth not only hint to us the danger of distraction and deviation of thoughts in prayer, but how necessary it is for us to choose the most convenient places we can for private prayer. Our own fickleness and Satan's restlessness call upon us to get into such places where we may freely pour out our soul into the bosom of God.
Thomas Brooks

He manifests Himself to those who pray in secret as He cannot to those who have no inner sanctuary of the soul.
Samuel Chadwick

Prayer is really a place, a place where you meet God in genuine conversation.
Billy Graham

God wills that men should pray everywhere, but the place of His glory is in the solitudes, where He hides us in the cleft of the rock, and talks with man face to face as a man talks with his friend.
Samuel Chadwick

Jesus assures us that secret prayer cannot be fruitless: its blessing will show itself in our life.
Andrew Murray

How can I lead people into the quiet place beside still waters if I am in constant motion?
Eugene Peterson

The soul which has come into intimate contact with God in the silence of the prayer chamber is never out of conscious touch with the Father; the heart is always going out to Him in loving communion, and the moment the mind is released from the task upon which it is engaged, it returns as naturally to God as the bird does to its nest.
E.M. Bounds

It is important to have a regular time for prayer, because without regularity prayer will never become a habit.
Bill Hybels

O, let the place of secret prayer become to me the most beloved spot on earth.
Andrew Murray

Everything is about my own time alone with God. Period.
Francis Chan

The secret place of prayer calls for every faculty of mind and heart.
Samuel Chadwick

All, prayer is hidden. It is behind a closed door. The best spade diggers go down into the deep ditches out of sight. There are numbers of surface workers, but few who in self-obliteration toil alone with God.
Seth Joshua

That the only reason why God asks us to spend more time in the secret place is because He misses us.
Trisha Cwir

God does not bestow His gifts on the casual of hasty comers and goers. Much with God alone is the secret of knowing Him and of influence with Him.
E.M. Bounds

The place of isolation can become the place of revelation.
Steven Furtick

The secret of all failure is our failure in secret prayer.
The Kneeling Christian

It was once said to a useful minister: Sir, if you did not plough in your closet, you would not reap in your pulpit.
Samuel Prime

The acid test of where your heart is: where does it go when you are alone? Your religion is revealed in solitude.
Tim Keller

Therefore, whether the desire for prayer is on you or not, get to your closet at the set time; shut yourself in with God; wait upon Him; seek His face; realize Him; pray.
R.F. Horton

It is impossible to carry on your life as a disciple without definite times of secret prayer.
Oswald Chambers

When the Lord returns, the hidden life and the hidden glory will become manifest.
Adolph Saphir

Public prayers are of little worth unless they are founded on or followed up by private praying.
E.M. Bounds

I take my prayer closet with me on the plane, in the car, or walking down the street. I pray always. My life is a prayer.
Kathryn Kuhlman

If we don't have a hidden life with God, our public life for God cannot bear fruit.
Henri Nouwen

Noise and crowds have a way of siphoning our energy and distracting our attention, making prayer an added chore rather than a comforting relief.
Charles Swindoll

Jesus doesn't participate in the rat race. He's into the slower rhythms of life, like abiding, delighting, and dwelling.
Lysa TerKeurst

Unless we fix certain hours in the day for prayer, it easily slips from our memory.
John Calvin

True prayer is done in secret, but this does not rule out the fellowship of prayer altogether, however clearly we may be aware of its dangers. In the last resort it is immaterial whether we pray in the open street or in the secrecy of our chambers, whether briefly or lenghtily, in the Litany of the Church, or with the sigh of one who knows not what he should pray for. True prayer does not depend either on the individual or the whole body of the faithful, but solely upon the knowledge that our Heavenly Father knows our needs.
Dietrich Bonhoeffer

The secret of praying is praying in secret.
Leonard Ravenhill

A holy life does not live in the closet, but it cannot live without the closet.
E.M. Bounds

It is impossible to conduct your life as a disciple without definite times of secret prayer.
Oswald Chambers

The best Christian is he that is the greatest monopolizer of time for private prayer.
Thomas Brooks

They who prevail in the secret place of the Most High cannot be beaten anywhere.
Samuel Chadwick

Get a place for prayer where no one imagines that that is what you are doing. Shut the door and talk to God.
Oswald Chambers

It is a great delusion to think that the times of prayer ought to differ from other times.
Brother Lawrence

Faith is being willing to test the faithfulness of God, and cannot often do that secretly and safely.
Hannah Hurnard

The study and the oratory are allies, but the inner chamber is better to be a place apart; then prayer enlightens thinking, and thinking kindles the altar fires of the heart.
Samuel Chadwick

The interior is not a stronghold to be taken by storm and violence; but a kingdom of peace, which is to be gained only by love.
Madame Guyon

No heart thrives without much secret converse with God, and nothing will make amends for the want of it.
John Berridge

God sees us in secret, therefore, let us seek His face in secret. Though heaven be God's palace, yet it is not His prison.
Thomas Brooks

Being happy in the secret place is a major key to your growth in God.
Brian Clark

Humility is the way for us to open communication with the merciful God of heaven. It is far better to pray in a private room, be unseen by man, and have the approval of God than to give a public display of prayer and have a heart full of pride.
Unknown

If you commit to start each day in prayer, you will find God waking you early because He can't wait!
Jay Harris

If you have ever prayed in the dawn you will ask yourself why you were so foolish as not to do it always: it is difficult to get into communion with God in the midst of the hurly-burly of the day.
Oswald Chambers

Great supplicants have sought the secret place of the Most High, not that they might escape the world, but that they might learn to conquer it.
Samuel Chadwick

The place of real prayer is the Christian's treasure chamber. He is there in the midst of the treasures of grace which God has given him, and it is there that God enriches him more and more; but in the secret place of the Most High where he dwells, he is rich in love, joy, peace, and all the fruits of the Spirit.
Amzi Clarence Dixon

Much secret prayer means much public power.
The Kneeling Christian

Do you wish to pray in the temple? Pray in your own heart. But begin by being God's temple, for He will listen to those who invoke Him in His temple.
Augustine

The real victory in all service is won in secret beforehand by prayer.
S.D. Gordon

God never calls us to do something we're capable of. God calls us to do things that are beyond our ability so He gets all the credit.
Mark Batterson

God, is only to be found in our inner selves, which is the holy of holies where God dwells.
Madame Guyon

To be much alone with God is the secret of knowing Him and of influence with Him.
E.M. Bounds

The real secret of prayer is secret prayer.
John Blanchard

Learn to love the cave. It's in the hidden place of prayer that God shapes your life for lasting impact.
Banning Liebscher

The divine pattern of each life is still to be seen in the secret place of the Most High God.
Samuel Chadwick

The closet is not an asylum for the indolent and worthless Christian. It is not a nursery where none but babes belong. It is the battlefield of the church, its citadel, the scene of heroic and unearthly conflicts. The closet is the base of supplies for the Christian and the church. Cut off from it there is nothing left but retreat and disaster. The energy for work, the mastery over self, the deliverance from fear, all spiritual results and graces, are much advanced by prayer. The difference between the strength, the experience, the holiness of Christians is found in the contrast of their praying.
E.M. Bounds

When you go into the secret place, you are hidden from the evils of the world.
Trisha Cwir

Prayer in secret is life finding expression in the realized Presence of God our Father.
Samuel Chadwick

Secret prayer is the spring-time of life.
> *Evan Roberts*

Above all be much in secret prayer and meditation. By this you will fetch the heavenly fire that must kindle your sacrifice: remember you cannot decline and neglect your duty to your own hurt alone, many will be losers by it as well as you.
> *Richard Baxter*

What man is alone on his knees before God, that he is, and no more.
> *Robert Murray M'Cheyne*

Every mighty move of the Spirit of God has had its source in the prayer chamber.
> *E.M. Bounds*

The place for prayer is everywhere.
> *John Blanchard*

God knows that it is better for us to be found in Him and to have our hearts be made one with Him in that secret place.
> *Trisha Cwir*

Secret prayer is the secret of prayer.
> *Reinhard Bonnke*

Without set times of prayer, the spirit of prayer will be dull and feeble. Without the continual prayerfulness, the set times will not avail.
> *Andrew Murray*

7

THE BENEFITS OF PRAYER

General Benefits

Even when our minds wander and it feels so hard to connect to Him in prayer, He still sees & hears us and loves that we came before Him.
Justin Rizzo

He who knows how to overcome with God in prayer has heaven and earth at his disposal.
C.H. Spurgeon

When you agree with Heaven, then you release its resources.
Graham Cooke

You cannot do anything more hopeful, more promising, more useful than to ask for God to move on your behalf.
Mario Murillo

Our inheritance is the Lord when we give Him ourselves (Lam. 3:24).
Kevin Shorter

Prayer should be the means by which I, at all times, receive all that I need, and, for this reason, be my daily refuge, my daily consolation, my daily joy, my source of rich and inexhaustible joy in life.
John Chrysostom

It must be to the glory of God, in full surrender to His will, in full assurance of faith, in the name of Jesus, and with a perseverance that, if need be, refuses to be denied.
Andrew Murray

All of us love miracles. We just don't like being in situations where we need one.
Mark Batterson

Your prayer for someone may or may not change them, but it always changes YOU.
Craig Groeschel

As we lift up our soul in prayer to the living God, we gain the beauty of holiness as surely as a flower becomes beautiful by living in the sunlight.
The Kneeling Christian

When pressure builds up, don't panic. Pray! Prayer is a tremendous stress reliever. It can be your safety valve.
Rick Warren

Whether we like it or not, asking is the rule of the Kingdom. If you may have everything by asking in His Name, and nothing without asking, I beg you to see how absolutely vital prayer is.
C.H. Spurgeon

A man who prays much in private will make short prayers in public.
D.L. Moody

Man's access in prayer to God opens everything and makes his impoverishment his wealth. All things are his through prayer.
E.M. Bounds

Prayer is work. The experiences of many children of God demonstrate that it accomplishes far more than does any other form of work.
Watchman Nee

Anything is a blessing which makes us pray.
C.H. Spurgeon

You will observe that the desire to commune with God is intensified by the failure of all other sources of consolation.
C.H. Spurgeon

The prayer of faith is the only power in the universe to which the Great Jehovah yields. Prayer is the sovereign Remedy.
Robert Hall

Prayer affects the plans of God.
Kevin Shorter

I have never met anyone who spent time in daily prayer, and in the study of the Word of God, and was strong in faith, who was ever discouraged for very long.
Billy Graham

When you pray to God regularly, irregular things happen on a regular basis.
Mark Batterson

If we would inquire of the Lord before we make big decisions, it would save us a lot of heartache and pain.
Joel Osteen

When at any time the passions are turbulent, a gentle retreat inwards to a present God, easily deadens and pacifies them.
Madame Guyon

The greatest thing anyone can do for God and man is pray. It is not the only thing; but it is the chief thing. The great people of the earth today are the people who pray. I do not mean those who talk about prayer; nor those who say they believe in prayer; nor yet those who can explain about prayer; but I mean those people who take time to pray.
S.D. Gordon

Prayer does not influence God? Prayer surely does influence God. It does not influence His purpose. It does influence His action.
S.D. Gordon

Walking with God down the avenue of prayer we acquire something of His likeness, and unconsciously we become witnesses to others of His beauty and His grace.
E.M. Bounds

When you pray in tongues long enough, your soul quiets down.
John Bevere

Prayer is the only entryway into genuine self-knowledge.
Tim Keller

It's our capacity for prayer that will ultimately determine our creative potential.
Mark Batterson

There is much praying that avails nothing, so far as we can judge.
Samuel Chadwick

Worry increases pressure; prayer releases peace.
Joyce Meyer

Learning to pray doesn't offer us a less busy life; it offers us a less busy heart.
Paul Miller

His goodness is beyond our ability to comprehend, but not our ability to experience. Our hearts will take us where our heads can't fit.
Bill Johnson

God has given us a secret weapon called prayer that gives us access to anywhere in the world!
Morris Cerrulo

Closet communion needs time for the revelation of God's presence. It is vain to say, 'I have too much work to do to find time.' You must find time or forfeit blessing. God knows how to save for you the time you sacredly keep for communion with Him.
A.T. Pierson

Prayer awakens your heart to the love of Christ. It reminds you that there is more to this life.
Kevin Shorter

If in the first waking moment of the day you learn to fling the door back and let God in, every public thing will be stamped with the presence of God.
Oswald Chambers

The value of a daily habit of withdrawal and hallowed seclusion is beyond exaggeration.
Samuel Chadwick

Heaven remembers the prayers you stopped praying.
Danny Silk

A moment of prayerful reflection can prevent a lifetime of bitter regret. Fervent prayers produce phenomenal results.
Woodrow Kroll

God will give us peace, but we must first give Him our worries.
Joyce Meyer

Prayer is a work to which we must commit ourselves if we are to make sense of our lives in light of eternity.
Terry Glaspey

The prayer power has never been tried to its full capacity. If we want to see mighty wonders of divine power and grace wrought in the place of weakness, failure and disappointment, let us answer God's standing challenge, Call unto me, and I will answer thee, and show thee great and mighty things which thou knowest not!'
Hudson Taylor

One thing is sure: The Lord wants us to believe most certainly that asking, seeking, and knocking cannot be in vain. Receiving an answer, finding God, and the opening of His heart and home are the certain fruits of prayer.
Andrew Murray

Prayer is the highest intelligence, the profoundest wisdom, the most vital, the most joyous, the most efficacious, the most powerful of all vocations.
E.M. Bounds

As we wait and pray, God weaves his story and creates a wonder.
Paul Miller

Prayer is of transcendent importance. Prayer is the mightiest agent to advance God's work. Praying hearts and hands only can do God's work. Prayer succeeds when all else fails.
E.M. Bounds

Whatever success I have had in bringing clean, informative entertainment to all ages, I attribute in great part to my congregational upbringing and my life-long habit of prayer. To me today at age 61 all prayer by the humbly or highly placed has one thing on common supplication for strength and inspiration to carry on the best human impulses which should bind us together for a better world in Jesus.
Walt Disney

While there are many verses telling us to seek God, none tell us to seek guidance. God will communicate His will as we develop our relationship with Him.
Graham Cooke

Love to pray. Feel often during the day the need for prayer, and take trouble to pray. Prayer enlarges the heart until it is capable of containing God's gift of Himself. Ask and seek, and your heart will grow big enough to receive Him and keep Him as your own.
Mother Teresa

It is no more true that God is a Creator of worlds, than it is that he is a Hearer of Prayer.
William Patton

Prayer does not change God, but it changes him who prays.
Soren Kierkegaard

Prayer changes the way God acts.
Wayne Grudem

To pray is to enter the treasure-house of God and to gather riches out of an inexhaustible storehouse.
C.H. Spurgeon

Praying most often doesn't get us what we want but what God wants, something quite at variance with what we conceive to be in our best interests.
Eugene Peterson

The Christian's heart must be soaked in prayer before the true spiritual fruits begin to grow.
A.W. Tozer

Prayer does not change God's will; it taps into it and enables it.
Kevin Shorter

It has nothing to do with God's heart or desire to act in our world. It's that he has made the terms. He said, 'I'll act when you ask.'
Jack Hayford

We got to pray just to make it today.
MC Hammer

Only enduring faith has access to the wonder of compound interest as it pertains to the answer.
Bill Johnson

Your praying is training for reigning with Christ.
Ben Jennings

Prayer pushes us through life's slumps, propels us over the humps and pulls us out of the dumps. Prayer is the oomph we need to get the answers we seek.
Max Lucado

Do not turn to prayer hoping to enjoy spiritual delights; rather come to prayer totally content to receive nothing or to receive great blessing from God's hand, which ever should be your heavenly Father's will for you at that time. This will enable you to live close to God in times of sadness as well as in times when you are being comforted by God.
Madame Guyon

Preaching without praying is pathetic.
Rick Warren

We pray to glorify God, but we also pray in order to receive the benefits of prayer from His hand.
R.C. Sproul

Prayer wonderfully clears the vision; steadies the nerves; defines duty; stiffens the purpose; sweetens and strengthens the spirit.
S.D. Gordon

Prayer, real prayer, is the noblest, the sublimest, the most stupendous act that any creature of God can perform.
The Kneeling Christian

Prayer will never do our work for us; what it will do is to strengthen us for work which must be done.
William Barclay

We become practical atheists when we start to believe our effort is better than God's power.
Craig Groeschel

There are things God is not planning to do but is willing to do through prayer.
Kevin Shorter

To struggle in prayer is never a waste of time and energy.
Jay Harris

Probably in the Day of Judgment it will be found that nothing is ever done by the truth, used ever so zealously, unless there is a spirit of prayer somewhere in connection with the presentation of truth.
Charles Finney

There is a cumulative effect in prayer. The focusing of many prayers on one life or on a situation can change defeat into victory.
J. Oswald Sanders

Prayer is a sacred and appointed means to obtain all the blessings that we want, whether they relate to this life or the life to come. Shall we not know how to use the means God has appointed for our own happiness?
Isaac Watts

Prayer is the key to success. Not to pray is to fail. To pray aright is never to fail.
Amzi Clarence Dixon

If you chase God, blessings will chase you.
Joyce Meyer

To pray well is the better half of study.
Martin Luther

Prayer is the answer to every problem there is.
Oswald Chambers

What can be more excellent than prayer; what is more profitable to our life; what sweeter to our souls; what more sublime, in the course of our whole life, than the practice of prayer!
Augustine

The Disciplines of the faith allow us to place ourselves before God so that He can transform us.
Richard Foster

Draw nigh to God, that you may live a happy and useful life.
D.A. Carson

Voice your position in God and you will be surrounded by all the resources of God in the time of trial.
Smith Wigglesworth

When a man's mouth is thus opened, God's ears are never closed. When the penitent is talking the Savior is listening.
W. Graham Scroggie

The prophetic will show up in all the key times of your life, if you are open.
Shawn Bolz

When I pray coincidences happen, and when I do not, they don't.
William Temple

We can be tired, weary and emotionally distraught, but after spending time alone with God, we find that He injects into our bodies energy, power and strength.
Charles Stanley

Prayer covers the whole of man's life. There is no thought, feeling, yearning, or desire, however low, trifling, or vulgar we may deem it, which if it affects our real interest or happiness, we may not lay before God and be sure of sympathy.
Henry Ward Beecher

Prayer is the one hand with which we grasp the Invisible; fasting the other, with which we let loose and cast away the visible.
Andrew Murray

The fear of diligently praying for blessing may be the most acceptable selfish attitude in the church. Tragically it's called humility.
Bill Johnson

Prayerless decisions lead to tragic loses.
Ben Jennings

We know not what prayer cannot do!
C.H. Spurgeon

The spirit of prayer is more precious than treasures of gold and silver.
John Bunyon

By prayer, the ability is secured to feel the law of love, to speak according to the law of love, and to do everything in harmony with the law of love.
E.M. Bounds

If we are not in touch with being beloved in Christ, we cannot love others as God desires.
Graham Cooke

I think a starting place is to recognize that if we don't pray, it's not going to happen.
Jack Hayford

When you pray, you shape the environment before you step into it.
Lance Wallnau

Our prayers may be awkward. Our attempts may be feeble. But since the power of prayer is in the one who hears it and not in the one who says it, our prayers do make a difference.
Max Lucado

It is not wrong to pray in the early morning, but it is wrong to have the motive that it should be known.
Oswald Chambers

As the spirit of prayer goes up, so His kingdom goes down.
William Gurnall

God performs acts of power in response to prayer that he would not otherwise do. If this is not true, then the Bible is filled with countless inaccuracies and fairy tales.
Jim Cymbala

Praying is planting. Each prayer is like a seed that gets planted in the ground. It disappears for a season, but it eventually bears fruit that blesses future generations. In fact, our prayers bear fruit forever.
Mark Batterson

Put prayers in the bank, so you can make withdraws in the future.
Bishop Tudor

Prayer incites the angels, restrains darkness, and releases nations into their destiny.
Kris Vallotton

By praying, we can both release God's blessing in greater measure and cut off the work of the enemy.
IHOP

The possibilities of prayer are found in its allying itself with the purposes of God, for God's purposes and man's praying are the combination of all potent and omnipotent forces.
E.M. Bounds

Prayer is far-reaching in its influence and worldwide in its effects. It affects all men, affects them everywhere, and affects them in all things. It touches man's interest in time and eternity. It lays hold upon God and moves Him to interfere in the affairs of earth. It moves the angels to minister to men in this life. It restrains and defeats the devil in his schemes to ruin man. Prayer goes everywhere and lays its hand upon everything.
E.M. Bounds

A man who is intimate with God will never be intimidated by men.
Leonard Ravenhill

When we confess that we never get answers to our prayers, we are condemning not God, or His promises, or the power of prayer, but ourselves.
The Kneeling Christian

There is nothing more important than prayer; therefore, our greatest attention and most diligent attention must attend it.
St. Theophan

Time spent in prayer is never wasted.
François Fénelon

Prayer is the key, and faith both turns the key and opens the door, and claims the blessing.
The Kneeling Christian

Prayer is the key which unlocks the door of God's treasure-house.
The Kneeling Christian

Prayer is appointed to convey The blessing God designs to give.
Unknown

Prayer and poetry are the closest of kin. In poetry we say it; in prayer we become what we say.
Eugene Peterson

God has ordained the Disciplines of the spiritual life as the means by which we place ourselves where He can bless us.
Richard Foster

Prayer guards hearts and minds and causes God to bring peace out of chaos.
Beth Moore

Prayer heightens our awareness and gives us a sixth sense that enables us to perceive spiritual realities.
Mark Batterson

No one can pray and worry at the same time.
Max Lucado

Prayer is the root, the fountain, the mother of a thousand blessings.
John Chrysostom

Prayer is a golden key that, kept bright by constant use, will unlock the treasures of earth and heaven.
Henrietta Mears

A much praying minister will receive an entrance into God's will he would otherwise know nothing of.
Andrew Murray

Prayer gives vision in the secret place, intelligence in work, sense in judgment, courage in temptation, tenacity in adversity, and joyous assurance in the will of God.
Samuel Chadwick

Often we do not realize the value of spending time with God when we are not praying for needs.
Wendy Backlund

We can do nothing without prayer. All things can be done by Importunate prayer. It surmounts or removes all obstacles, overcomes every resisting force and gains its ends in the face of invincible hindrances.
E.M. Bounds

Prayer and imagination are directly proportional: the more you pray the bigger your imagination becomes because the Holy Spirit supersizes it with God-sized dreams.
Mark Batterson

Four things let us ever keep in mind: God hears prayer, God heeds prayer, God answers prayer, and God delivers by prayer.
E.M. Bounds

Our prayer is what God hears, not merely the words we utter; God hears our thoughts, the desires of our hearts.
Unknown

Many doctors today prescribe yoga as a helpful stress reliever but would not consider prescribing prayer to the One who calms our fears and anxieties.
Billy Graham

The very idea of effectual prayer is that it affects its objects.
Charles Finney

We need to learn to know Him so well that we feel safe when we have left our difficulties with Him. To know in that way is a prerequisite of all true prayer.
O. Hallesby

The very act of prayer is a blessing.
C.H. Spurgeon

Prayer enlarges the heart until it is capable of containing God's gift of himself.
Mother Teresa

The world has yet to see a Christlike, victorious, fruitful believer who was not a person of considerable prayer.
Jim Cymbala

Nothing can so quickly cancel the frictions of life as prayer.
William McElroy

God's power in your life is determined by whether you pray in just special times or all the time. Prayerlessness limits God.
Rick Warren

Prayer changes us and therein lies its glory and it's purpose.
Hannah Hurnard

Units of prayer combined, like drops of water, make an ocean which defies resistance.
E.M. Bounds

Prayer is our most formidable weapon, the thing which makes all else we do efficient.
E.M. Bounds

God's power flows primarily to people who pray.
Bill Hybels

As a sound may dislodge an avalanche, so the prayer of faith sets in motion the power of God.
Mrs. Charles E. Cowman

God is offering revelational insight based upon a pursuit of Him in prayer.
Jack Hayford

We shall have our Mount of Transfiguration when prayer has its rightful place in our lives.
The Kneeling Christian

People say they can't "pray" but its the easiest thing to do because its impossible to be rejected.
Brian Clark

God has appointed prayer as his way of dispensing, and our way of obtaining all promised good.
J.B. Johnson

Prayer catapults us onto the frontier of the spiritual life.
Richard Foster

It is only through grace that any of us could dare to hope that we could become more like Christ.
Brennan Manning

The real and obvious test of a genuine work of God is the prevalence of the Spirit of Prayer.
E.M. Bounds

O let the excellency and high value of this gift of prayer engage our earnestness and endeavours in proportion to its superior dignity. Let us covet the best of gifts with the warmest desire, and pray for it with ardent supplications. (1 Cor. 12:31).
Isaac Watts

Prayer does not change the purpose of God. But prayer does change the action of God.
Chuck Smith

If you're praying about it God's working on it.
Rick Warren

When you get a word from God, it will take the place of 10 counseling sessions.
Shawn Bolz

Prayer is simply the key to everything we need to do and be in life.
Tim Keller

Prayer is the most unexplored area of the Christian life.
Leonard Ravenhill

God shapes the world by prayer. The more praying there is in the world the better the world will be, the mightier the forces against evil...
E.M. Bounds

God's mercy visits every house where night and morning prayers are made, but where these are neglected, sin is incurred.
C.H. Spurgeon

The greatest moments in a Christian's life come through prayer.
Henry Blackaby

Prayer humbles us, stretches us, shapes us, encourages us, challenges us, deepens us, and leads us along the pathway of spiritual growth.
Dr. Ray Prichard

Prayer to the Father cannot be vain; He will reward you openly.
Andrew Murray

Prayer is doubts destroyer, ruin's remedy, the antidote to all anxieties.
C.H. Spurgeon

The life of the individual believer, his personal salvation, and personal Christian graces have their being, bloom, and fruitage in prayer.
E.M. Bounds

The contemplation of the unseen, the attempt to think in terms of the eternal, and the honest endeavor of the soul to enter in communion with God, in themselves, redeem life from all that is fitful, fretful and futile.
Samuel Chadwick

Pray, and let God worry.
Martin Luther

Nothing is beyond the reach of prayer except that which was out of the will of God.
J. Oswald Sanders

In all states of dilemma or of difficulty, prayer is an available source. The ship of prayer may sail through all temptations, doubts and fears, straight up to the throne of God; and though she may be outward bound with only griefs, and groans, and sighs, she shall return freighted with a wealth of blessings!
C.H. Spurgeon

Praying makes your Christian life supernatural; God gets His work done through your praying.
Ben Jennings

We gladly admit we may receive gifts in prayer, but we never forget that the highest kind is never the making of requests.
A.W. Tozer

The abundant life is impossible without prayer.
Kevin Shorter

All good is born in prayer, and all good springs from it.
C.H. Spurgeon

Prayer is the midwife of mercy, that helps to bring it forth.
Matthew Henry

Prayer is the only adequate way to multiply our efforts fast enough to reap the harvest God desires.
Wesley Duewel

Prayer girds human weakness with divine strength, turns human folly into heavenly wisdom, and gives to troubled mortals the peace of God. We know not what prayer can do.
C.H. Spurgeon

Expose our kids to miracles. Expose them to what we are going through so they can see how God comes through.
Kris Vallotton

God has made gravity a law in one realm, he has made prayer a law in a higher realm, and it is even greater folly to ignore the latter than the former.
William Patton

How vast are the possibilities of prayer! How wide its reach! It lays its hand on Almighty God and moves Him to do what He would not do if prayer was not offered.
E.M. Bounds

All I know is that when I pray, coincidences happen; and when I don't pray, they don't happen.
Dan Hayes

When prayers are strongest, mercies are nearest.
Edward Reynolds

Prayer is the mechanism whereby God ideas are conceived and captured.
Mark Batterson

My prayer is that the way you live your life makes zero sense to unbelievers and encourages fellow Christians to step out in faith.
Francis Chan

Faith, and hope, and patience and all the strong, beautiful, vital forces of piety are withered and dead in a prayerless life. The life of the individual believer, his personal salvation, and personal Christian graces have their being, bloom, and fruitage in prayer.
E.M. Bounds

God, in the mystery of prayer, has entrusted us with a force that can move the Heavenly world and can bring its power to earth.
Andrew Murray

Sometimes it takes a long time before you see that fruit in your life from spending time with God. But I'm telling you, it is fruitful.
Trisha Cwir

No, prayer doesn't change God, but not to make our requests known in joyful trust does deprive Him of the joy of granting our requests, and it does deprive us of the joy of experiencing His loving, intimate interest in every detail of our lives.
Hannah Hurnard

The great antidote to anxiety is to come to God in prayer. We are to pray about everything. Nothing is too big for Him to handle, and nothing is too small to escape His attention.
Jerry Bridges

It can easily be shown that all want of success, and all failure in the spiritual life and in Christian work, is due to defective or insufficient prayer.
The Kneeling Christian

God never changes His purpose, but He often does purpose a change.
John Owen

The Answers of Prayer

Complacency and ignorance tolerate unanswered prayers.
Bill Johnson

God has promised to answer prayer. It is not that He is unwilling, for the fact is, He is more willing to give than we are to receive. But the trouble is, we are not ready.
Oswald Chambers

Be specific in what you are asking for from God. Most people don't know when God answers a prayer because they are praying very general prayers.
Mark Batterson

God says no to our prayers when they would remove us from our purpose.
Bill Johnson

Most Christians do not give God a chance to show His delight in granting His children's petitions; for their requests are so vague and indefinite.
The Kneeling Christian

Oftentimes you don't know how God is going to answer your prayer. That is what makes prayer so exciting.
Kevin Shorter

God does not delay to hear our prayers because He has no mind to give; but that, by enlarging our desires, He may give us the more largely.
Anselm of Canterbury

When you pray you go to God then look for the answer.
Beni Johnson

Have you, when in prayer, ever had the witness borne in upon you that your request was granted?
The Kneeling Christian

I live in the spirit of prayer; I pray as I walk, when I lie down and when I rise, and the answers are always coming.
George Müller

The Bible says that God is anxious to answer our prayers, that He's eager to do so, that He really wants to grant our requests.
David Jeremiah

If you aren't careful, the will of God can become a cop-out if things don't turn out the way you want.
Mark Batterson

I continue to dream and pray about a revival of holiness in our day that moves forth in mission and creates authentic community in which each person can be unleashed through the empowerment of the Spirit to fulfill God's creational intentions.
John Wesley

Answers to prayer, however, do not depend upon our feelings, but upon the trustworthiness of the Promiser.
The Kneeling Christian

Continue in prayer, and though the blessing tarry, it must come; in God's own time it must appear to you.
C.H. Spurgeon

There is nothing that we are enduring that Jesus does not understand, and He waits for us to go to our Heavenly Father in prayer. If we will be obedient and if we are diligent, our prayers will be answered, our problems will diminish, our fears will dissipate, light will come upon us, the darkness of despair will be dispersed, and we will be close to the Lord.
Robert D. Hales

I've prayed many prayers when no answer came, I've waited patient and long; But answers have come to enough of my prayers, To make me keep praying on.
George Allen

The world around us will recognize us as disciples of Jesus when they see our prayers being answered.
Colin Urquart

Sometimes I think... I just prayed... and God just LISTENED to me... and He just ANSWERED me! Is there anything more amazing, anything greater than that?!?
Francis Chan

God delights to answer prayer; and He has given us His word that He will answer.
The Kneeling Christian

Time spent on the knees in prayer will do more to remedy heart strain and nerve worry than anything else.
George David Stewart

Asking with shameless persistence, the importunity that will not be denied, returns with the answer in hand.
Unknown

When the fire of prayer goes out, the barrenness of busyness takes over.
George Carry

God answers the prayer we ought to have made rather than the prayer we did make.
J.I. Packer

When life knocks you to your knees, and it will, why, get up! If it knocks you to your knees again, as it will, well, isn't that the best position from which to pray?
Ethel Barrymore

What God gives in answer to our prayers will always be the thing we most urgently need, and it will always be sufficient.
Elisabeth Elliot

We are so egoistically engrossed about God's giving of the answer that we forget His gift of the prayer itself.
P.T. Forsyth

God answers only the requests which He inspires.
Ralph A. Herring

Long after you and I are gone, God will still be at work—and many of the things we prayed for will finally come to pass.
Billy Graham

You are worthy because God says you are worthy; therefore there is no good thing that God will withhold from you.
Kevin Shorter

We are surprise when our prayers are answered; Jesus' disciples were surprised when their prayers were not answered.
Bill Johnson

Remember God's previous answers to prayer to have faith for the ones you're waiting on.
Kevin Shorter

It is through our praying and His answering that He strengthens our relationship with Him.
Mike Bickle

Asking God to test our faith is stepping onto a mine field. But the explosions only injure things we don't need: pride, fear, unforgiveness.
Kevin Adams

Faithful servants have a way of knowing answered prayer when they see it, and a way of not giving up when they don't.
Max Lucado

God says to us, "Pray, because I have all kinds of things for you; and when you ask, you will receive."
Jim Cymbala

When we pray what's on God's heart, He answers in ways that blow our minds.
Alan Scott

I firmly believe God continues to answer the prayers of His people even after He has taken them to heaven. Never forget that God isn't bound by time the way we are. We see only the present moment; God sees everything. We see only part of what He is doing; He sees it all.
Billy Graham

More things are wrought by prayer than this world dreams of.
Alfred Lloyd Tennyson

God means every prayer to have an answer; and not a single real prayer can fail of its effect in heaven.
The Kneeling Christian

The answer to prayer is assured not only by the promises of God, but by God's relation to us as a Father.
E.M. Bounds

God will either give you what you ask, or something far better.
Robert Murray M'Cheyne

Some consider it selfish to receive answers to their prayers, but Jesus never affirmed a passive attitude of indifference about receiving.
IHOP

God's way of answering the Christian's prayer for more patience, experience, hope, and love often is to put him into the furnace of affliction.
Richard Cecil

If you have a delayed answer [to prayer], it is gaining interest.
Bill Johnson

Do you know why the mighty God of the universe chooses to answer prayer? It is because His children ask.
Richard Foster

Our prayers are answered when they are consistent with our purpose.
Bill Johnson

To pray without expectation is to misunderstand the whole concept of prayer and relationship with God.
A.W. Tozer

You have no idea how many times God wants to say "yes" to you in your life!
Graham Cooke

Do believers or unbelievers ever say of us, We know your prayers are answered?
The Kneeling Christian

When you ask for something in prayer, you have to start speaking about it as if it already exists.
Myles Munroe

Many are not willing to pray for God's miracles for fear of getting people's hopes up only for God not to show up.
Kevin Shorter

Keep on praying until the Spirit stops you or the Father answers you. Just about the time you feel like quitting, God will give the answer.
Warren Wiersbe

Real faith not only believes that God can, but that He does answer prayer.
The Kneeling Christian

God does nothing except in response to believing prayer.
John Wesley

God's answers are wiser than our prayers.
Unknown

We have one crystal clear reason apart from the blessed happiness of this way of life. It is this: prayer is the core of our day. Take prayer out, and the day would collapse, would be pithless, a straw blown in the wind. But how can you pray--really pray, I mean--with one against who you have a grudge or whom you have been discussing critically with another? Try it. You will find it cannot be done.
Amy Carmichael

It is not well for a man to pray cream and live skim milk.
Henry Ward Beecher

Many Christians don't pray for God's miracles because they fear raising people's hopes only for God not to show up.
Kevin Shorter

Asking is man's part. Giving is God's part. The praying belongs to us. The answer belongs to God.
Gerhard Tersteegen

God delays in answering our prayers because men would pluck their mercies green; God would have them ripe.
Unknown

God answers prayer for the same reason He saves people, goodness shown in grace.
A.W. Tozer

The only time my prayers are never answered is on the golf course.
Billy Graham

I have lived to thank God that not all my prayers have been answered.
Jean Ingelow

Without committal to the wisdom of God, prayer would be a very dangerous weapon in proportion as it was effective.
P.T. Forsyth

If our prayers are not answered — always answered, but not necessarily granted — the fault must be entirely in ourselves, and not in God.
The Kneeling Christian

We are not designed to coexist with unfulfilled prayers.
Bill Johnson

Nothing satisfies the heart of the Christian like seeing so-called impossibilities bow their knees to the name of Jesus.
Bill Johnson

Pray as if God wants to answer your prayers.
Kevin Shorter

The angel fetched Peter out of the prison, but it was prayer fetched the angel.
Thomas Watson

I make sure that, when I am brooding over something, I continually look for an answer because I know that God always answers my prayers. I expect it.
Beni Johnson

Heaven is full of answers to prayers for which no one ever bothered to ask.
Billy Graham

If our petitions are in accordance with His will, and if we seek His glory in the asking, the answers will come in ways that will astonish us and fill our hearts with songs of thanksgiving.
J.K. Maclean

The greatest tragedy in life are the prayers that go unanswered simply because they go unasked.
Mark Batterson

God shapes the world by prayer. The prayers of God's saints are the capitol stock of heaven by which God carries on His great work upon the earth.
E.M. Bounds

If God wants us to pray without ceasing, it is because He wants to answer without ceasing!
Armin Gesswein

God will come to the one who cries first.
Smith Wigglesworth

God wants you to have true peace by praying about everything.
Matt Slick

On our part there should be the childlike simplicity of faith, the confidence that our prayer does bring down a blessing.
Andrew Murray

Prayer is never complete until God has answered.
Woodrow Kroll

It is as natural to Him to answer prayer as it is for us to ask.
The Kneeling Christian

Sincere prayers are never lost. Energy, time, love, and longing can be endowments that will never be wasted or go unrewarded.
Wesley Duewel

Ponder for a moment what great crises would face you if tomorrow all your prayers were answered.
Frances Roberts

Prevailing, or effectual prayer, is that prayer which attains the blessing that it seeks. It effectually moves God.
Charles Finney

God answers prayer on the ground of Redemption and on no other ground.
Oswald Chambers

God has not always answered my prayers. If he had, I would have married the wrong man—several times!
Ruth Graham Bell

No answer to prayer is an indication of our merit; every answer to prayer is an indication of God's mercy.
John Blanchard

God always hears prayer. He cannot make it obvious, but He hears every time we move our lips.
Reinhard Bonnke

God shapes the world by prayer. Prayers are deathless. The lips that uttered them may be closed to death, the heart that felt them may have ceased to beat, but the prayers live before God, and God's heart is set on them and prayers outlive the lives of those who uttered them; they outlive a generation, outlive an age, outlive a world.
E.M. Bounds

The effects of prayer may be conveniently divided into the results of prayer upon the person praying and the results of prayer upon the world.
Albert D. Belden

I never prayed sincerely and earnestly for anything but it came at some time; no matter at how distant a day, somehow, in some shape, probably the least I would have devised, it came.
Adoniram Judson

Jesus never mentioned unanswered prayer. He had the unlimited certainty of knowing that prayer is always answered.
Samuel Chadwick

If the request is wrong, God says, No. If the timing is wrong, God says, Slow. If you are wrong, God says, Grow. But if the request is right, the timing is right and you are right, God says, Go!
Bill Hybels

When an answer I did not expect comes to a prayer which I believed I truly meant, I shrink back from it; if the burden my Lord asks me to bear be not the burden of my heart's choice, and I fret inwardly and do not welcome His will, then I know nothing of Calvary love.
Amy Carmichael

Some unanswered prayers are only because God doesn't want to do something for us. He wants to do something through us.
Bill Johnson

There come times in our lives when we in our desperation and pain run to God and dial our 911 prayers. Sometimes we're hysterical. Sometimes we don't know the words to speak. But God hears. He knows our number and He knows our name and He knows our circumstance. That help is already on the way; God has already begun to bring the remedy to us.
Leith Anderson

There are more tears shed over answered prayers than over unanswered prayers.
Mother Teresa

Faith brings an answer. Enduring faith brings the answer with character.
Bill Johnson

Every unanswered prayer is a clarion call to search the heart to see what is wrong there; for the promise is unmistakable in its clearness: If ye shall ask anything in My name, that will I do.
The Kneeling Christian

Possible reason God delays an answer: because He knows we need to be with Him far more than we need the things we ask of Him.
Ben Patterson

The most natural dynamic for a Christian is answered prayer.
Bill Johnson

I don't pray because it makes sense to pray. I pray because my life doesn't make sense without prayer.
Noah Benshea

As white snowflakes fall quietly and thickly on a winter day, answers to prayer will settle down upon you at every step you take, even to your dying day. The story of your life will be the story of prayer and answers to prayer.
O. Hallesby

When all our prayers are either vague or universal in scope, it is difficult for us to experience the exhilaration that goes with clear and obvious answers to prayer.
R.C. Sproul

Prayer is always in danger of degenerating into a glorified gold rush. How to get things from God occupies most [books].
A.W. Tozer

Our prayers work even when they are short, when they are weak, and they are poorly worded.
Mike Bickle

God always has the right to veto a request that undermines our purpose.
Bill Johnson

A child of God ought to expect answers to prayer.
The Kneeling Christian

His answer may not be what we expected, or when we expected it, but God often provides much more abundantly than we could think or ask.
Wesley Duewel

Converting our unceasing thinking into unceasing prayer moves us from a self-centered monologue to a God-centered dialogue.
Henri Nouwen

If God had granted all the silly prayers I've made in my life, where would I be now?
C.S. Lewis

Each prayer is a time capsule. You never know when or where or how God is going to answer it, but He will answer it.
Mark Batterson

The promises to hear prayer are not made to the mere form, but to the appropriate spirit.
William Patton

God desires to glorify His name by answering prayer.
E.M. Bounds

It is a crime for us to pray and think nothing will happen.
Bill Johnson

God has your best interest in mind when he answers no to your prayers.
John Maxwell

There has never been an instance yet of a man really seeking spiritual blessings from God without his receiving them.
C.H. Spurgeon

If you spend several hours in prayer daily, you will see great things.
John Nelson

When we don't get answers to prayer we start measuring our success by the discipline of prayer.
Kris Vallotton

You were not designed for unanswered prayer; that's why there is no instruction about them.
Bill Johnson

It will be a wonderful moment for some of us when we stand before God and find that the prayers we clamoured for in early days and imagined were never answered, have been answered in the most amazing way, and that God's silence has been the sign of the answer. If we always want to be able to point to something and say, This is the way God answered my prayer, God cannot trust us yet with His silence.
Oswald Chambers

By being thankful you are more prone to see the fulfillment of the requests you have made to God, which encourages more prayer.
Kevin Shorter

God answers prayer in the best way—not just sometimes, but every time... Do we expect God to answer prayer?
Samuel Chadwick

The disciples were so surprised their prayers were not answered they took Jesus aside to find out why.
Bill Johnson

Our Lord tells us an indisputable fact: all through the ages, true asking has been followed by receiving.
C.H. Spurgeon

The hardest part of the prayer of faith is waiting.
Jim Cymbala

God sometimes answers our prayers by giving to us what we would have asked for had we known what He knows.
Tim Keller

The man who has his mouth full of arguments in prayer shall soon have his mouth full of benedictions in answer to prayer.
C.H. Spurgeon

Never make the blunder of trying to forecast the way God is going to answer your prayer.
Oswald Chambers

All my discoveries have been made in answer to prayer.
Sir Isaac Newton

6 Way God answers prayer: Yes; No; Not yet, You be the answer, Trust Me, and Are you kidding me?
Rick Warren

Let us pray until all our prayers are answered prayers and that is our expectation of our prayers.
Kevin Shorter

Prayer adds an element of surprise to your life that is more fun than a surprise party or surprise gift or surprise romance. In fact, prayer turns life into a party, into a gift, into a romance.
Mark Batterson

I live in the spirit of prayer. I pray as I walk and when I lie down and when I arise. And the answers are always coming.
George Müller

Children expect their parents to answer them. Illegitimate children don't expect God to answer.
Kevin Shorter

There is a general kind of praying which fails for lack of precision. It is as if a regiment of soldiers should all fire off their guns anywhere. Possibly somebody would be killed, but the majority of the enemy would be missed.
C.H. Spurgeon

The story of every great Christian achievement is the history of answered prayer.
E.M. Bounds

The Prayer of Intercession

If I am unwilling to pray with a heart of passion for sinners who indulge in the perverse, the shameful and the corrupt and who do it with glee, will my passion be driven by my anger or by my sense of God's broken heart for such warping of one of His own creation, for such satanic bondage in a being He longs to know the beauty of His original purpose?
Jack Hayford

There is no power like that of prevailing prayer, of Abraham pleading for Sodom, Jacob wrestling in the stillness of the night, Moses standing in the breach, Hannah intoxicated with sorrow, David heartbroken with remorse and grief, Jesus in sweat of blood. Add to this list from the records of the church your personal observation and experience, and always there is the cost of passion unto blood. Such prayer prevails. It turns ordinary mortals into men of power. It brings power. It brings fire. It brings rain. It brings life. It brings God.
Samuel Chadwick

God has no greater controversy with His people today than this, that with boundless promises to believing prayer, there are so few who actually give themselves unto intercession.
A.T. Pierson

When you keep calling out people's gold, they will start working on their dirt in order for the gold to become more evident.
Wendy Backlund

The real business of your life as a saved soul is intercessory prayer.
Oswald Chambers

Many times that is what we are doing when we intercede. We are brooding over something, causing life to come.
Beni Johnson

Intercessors should be the happiest people on the planet because they know the plans of God. God is in a good mood, and He wants to give good gifts to His children.
Beni Johnson

The more you intercede, the more intimate will be your walk with Christ and the stronger you will become by the Spirit's power.
Wesley Duewel

If we cease to love, we will fail to pray. Love is the fuel behind all intercession.
Francis Frangipane

Paul lived to intercede for others. So should every true Sunday School teacher, Christian friend, father, mother, brother or sister remember others in their prayers without ceasing. Have you a prayer list? Do you talk with the Lord about your friends?
Henrietta Mears

If you are having difficulty loving or relating to an individual, take him to God. Bother the Lord with this person. Don't you be bothered with him - leave him at the throne.
Charles Swindoll

The power of the Church truly to bless rests on intercession—asking and receiving heavenly gifts to carry to men.
E.M. Bounds

There must be closet praying! It is in the closet that we establish the beautiful habit of spontaneous praying on every occasion. When we are fresh out of the closet we are quick to pray about every turn of events. Unceasing prayer is God's avenue for His children to react to all happenings.
Clyde Martin

When God reveals something to the intercessors, it is meant for prayer, not to bring judgement.
Doug Addison

Prevailing prayer is almost always for the sake of others.
Wesley Duewel

When we discern that people are not going on spiritually and allow the discernment to turn to criticism, we block our way to God. God never gives us discernment in order that we may criticize, but that we may intercede.
Oswald Chambers

I prayed to dispel my fear, until suddenly, and I do not know how the idea came to me, I began to pray for others. I prayed for everyone who came into my thoughts - - people with whom I had traveled, those who had been in prison with me, my school friends of years ago. I do not know how long I continued my prayer, but this I do know - - my fear was gone! Interceding for others had released me!
Corrie ten Boom

Those you know the least may need your prayers the most. Don't let the fact that you don't know someone keep you from praying for them.
Billy Graham

The sublime and holy inspiration of pleasing God should ever move us to prayer for all men.
E.M. Bounds

God urges us to bring our concerns to Him—not just petitions about our own needs, but also intercessions for others.
Billy Graham

God never gives us discernment in order that we may criticize, but that we may intercede.
Oswald Chambers

If you come out of an intense prayer time more depressed than when you went, you weren't interceding, you were complaining.
Bill Johnson

Intercession is truly universal work for the Christian. No place is closed to intercessory prayer. No continent - no nation - no organization - no city - no office. There is no power on earth that can keep intercession out.
Richard Halverson

You cannot pray for someone and hate them at the same time.
Billy Graham

Prayer, desperate prayer, seems so simple, but it's a step rarely taken by those in family conflict.
Erwin Lutzer

The cry of the poor must either be heard by us, or it will ascend up against us into the Lord of the Sabaoth.
F.D. Maurice

When we're told to pray for those who've hurt us, I'm convinced our prayers are as much for ourselves as they are for the offender.
Craig Groeschel

It is not only our duty to pray for others, but also to desire the prayers of others for ourselves.
William Gurnall

The men in the pew given to praying for the pastor are like poles which hold up the wires along which the electric current runs. They are not the power, neither are they the specific agents in making the Word of the Lord effective. But they hold up the wires upon which the divine power runs to the hearts of men. They make conditions favorable for the preaching of the Gospel.
E.M. Bounds

People may refuse our love or reject our message, but they are defenseless against our prayers.
Rick Warren

Include your children in the ministry. Invite them to pray for others.
Kris Vallotton

It is of great significance if there is a person who truly prays in a family. Prayer attracts God's Grace and all the members of the family feel it, even those whose hearts have grown cold.
Thaddeus of Vitovnica

We will only advance in our evangelistic work as fast and as far as we advance on our knees.
Alan Redpath

It is doubtful that anyone is saved apart from the believing prayers of some saint.
J. Oswald Sanders

Arrogance isn't thinking too much of ourselves but thinking too little of others.
Bill Johnson

We do not pray for people as "things," but as "persons" whom we love.
Richard Foster

It is a solemn thing to find oneself drawn out in prayer which knows no relief till the soul it is burdened with is born. It is no less solemn afterwards, until Christ is formed in them.
Amy Carmichael

As you move closer to one another, you are actually diving into the heart of God.
Kevin Shorter

Here is a key point for us to embrace as we persevere in prayer for our loved ones: Jesus wants to minister through us.
Jack Hayford

It is impossible to pray for someone without loving him, and impossible to go on praying for him without discovering that our love for him grows and matures.
John Stott

It is possible to move men, through God, by prayer alone.
Hudson Taylor

What if our role in intercession is not to get God to do something but to get people to believe He wants to do something.
Kevin Shorter

The priest pleads the needs of the people to the Lord. The prophet pleads the interests of God before the people. The prophetic intercessor does both.
James Goll

Pray for all men, for Christlessness is terrible.
Reinhard Bonnke

Persecution, whether it is physical, social, or mental, is one of the worst types of pain, but those who persecute us are to be the objects of our prayers.
Billy Graham

Prayer meets with obstacles, which must be prayed away. That is what men mean when they talk about praying through.
The Kneeling Christian

We may be always praying but not seeing results. We may think intercession and prayer are about us and how much we press in or how much time we spend praying, but what we don't realize is that intercession is about who we are.
Allison Shorter

Be careful before leaving someone in a sorrowing situation. Say a word of prayer with them and share even a brief word of encouragement from the Scriptures.
Billy Graham

All vital praying makes a drain on a man's vitality. True intercession is a sacrifice, a bleeding sacrifice.
J.H. Jowett

To make intercession for men is the most powerful and practical way in which we can express our love for them.
John Calvin

God has called us to pray for each other, not prey on each other.
Francis Frangipane

Prayer is crucial in evangelism: Only God can change the heart of someone who is in rebellion against Him. No matter how logical our arguments or how fervent our appeals, our words will accomplish nothing unless God's Spirit prepares the way.
Billy Graham

All of us would be wiser if we would resolve never to put people down, except on our prayer lists.
D.A. Carson

To stand before men on behalf of God is one thing. To stand before God on behalf of men is something entirely different.
Leonard Ravenhill

Prevailing prayer requires a tender, compassionate heart, a deep solicitude for the glory of God and the good of His people. Nehemiah wept and mourned.
Arthur Wallis

Intercession is the noblest work God entrusts to us humans.
T.W. Hunt

We have been called to heal wounds, to unite what has fallen apart, and to bring home those who have lost their way.
Francis of Assisi

Intercession is putting yourself in God's place; it is having His mind and His perspective.
Oswald Chambers

The greater your cares, the more genuine your prayers.
Max Lucado

May God open our eyes to see what the holy ministry of intercession is, to which, as His royal priesthood, we have been set apart. May He give us a large and strong heart to believe what mighty influence our prayers can exert. And may all fear as to our being able to fulfill our vocation vanish as we see Jesus, living ever to pray, living in us to pray, and standing surety for our prayer life.
Andrew Murray

Intercession means that we rouse ourselves up to get the mind of Christ about the one for whom we pray.
Oswald Chambers

All the mighty interceding of the ages that has ever shaken the kingdom of darkness has been based upon the promises of God.
Arthur Wallis

The steadfast prayer of the wounded intercessor holds great sway upon the heart of God.
Francis Frangipane

Our goal is not merely to get people saved but to fully experience all God has for them.
Kevin Shorter

With the wrong identity, intercession can also look like control or manipulation. We pray out of our flesh and what we want to see happen, not what God wants to see happen.
Allison Shorter

You cannot truly intercede through prayer if you do not believe in the reality of redemption.
Oswald Chambers

What would your prayers look like if you believed that the cross really was the measure of God's compassion for someone?
J.D. Greear

Jesus is our ultimate intercessor before God, so one way to be more like Jesus is to grow in intercession.
Allison Shorter

We must hear, know, and obey the will of God before we pray it into the lives of others.
Richard Foster

A day without morning and evening prayers and personal intercessions is actually a day without meaning or importance.
Dietrich Bonhoeffer

Notice, we never pray for folks we gossip about, and we never gossip about the folk for whom we pray! For prayer is a great detergent.
Leonard Ravenhill

The awesome demands of ministering to someone who is hurting can only be met by an active and believing prayer life.
John Wimber

Our prayer must not be self-centered. It must arise not only because we feel our own need as a burden we must lay upon God, but also because we are so bound up in love for our fellow men that we feel their need as acutely as our own.
John Calvin

As I close my eyes in prayer, let me see the faces of those who need to know You, beloved Savior.
Billy Graham

This is the goal of prophecy: to connect people to the empowering nature of God so they can become like him and display his marvelous nature to all the earth.
Shawn Bolz

The prophetic is one of the greatest gifts of love we have.
Shawn Bolz

Christ has opened the school of prayer specially to train intercessors for the great work of bringing down, by their faith and prayer, the blessings of His work and love on the world around.
Andrew Murray

Talking to men for God is a great thing, but talking to God for men is greater still.
E.M. Bounds

There is nothing to be valued more highly than to have people praying for us; God links up his power in answer to their prayers.
Oswald Chambers

The heartbeat of intercession is servanthood.
Dick Eastman

The Church has not yet touched the fringe of the possibilities of intercessory prayer. Her largest victories will be witnessed when individual Christians everywhere come to recognize their priesthood unto God and day by day give themselves unto prayer.
John R. Mott

Some of the ways we intercede are to speak up for another as an advocate, speak into a conflict that needs resolution, and stand up for the downtrodden and silenced.
Lisa Bevere

Where there is no vision of eternity, there is no prayer for the perishing.
David Smithers

Allow the love God placed in our hearts penetrate the hearts of others.
Kevin Shorter

An intercessor means one who is in such vital contact with God and with his fellowmen that he is like a live wire closing the gap between the saving power of God and the sinful men who have been cut off from that power.
Hannah Hurnard

Our prayers have the power to release dreams, visions, and angelic encounters in the lives of those we are praying for.
Matthew Prewett

Through His Spirit, the Spirit of prayer, our life may be one of continual prayer. The Spirit of prayer will help you become an intercessor, asking great things of God for those around you.
Andrew Murray

The diligent prayer of a righteous people will ultimately determine the destiny of our children.
Kris Vallotton

Learn to move man, through God, by prayer alone.
Hudson Taylor

In times of extraordinary change God has always called people to pray. Are you one of them today?
Jane Williams

In intercession our King upon the throne finds His highest glory; in it we shall find our highest glory too.
Andrew Murray

Intercession is cooperation with the Holy Spirit in his work to convict the world concerning sin, and righteousness, and judgment (John 16:8).
Lars Widerberg

If you find yourself growing angry at someone, pray for him—anger cannot live in an atmosphere of prayer.
William McElroy

Let the Holy Spirit shine a searchlight in your own heart and cleanse anything that restricts the power and liberty of your intercessory role in the family. I know that I am neutralized for effective prayer to the degree that negativity characterizes my attitude toward anyone for whom I pray.
Jack Hayford

Time spent in prayer will yield more than that given to work. Prayer alone gives work its worth and its success. Prayer opens the way for God Himself to do His work in us and through us. Let our chief work as God's messengers be intercession; in it we secure the presence and power of God to go with us.

Andrew Murray

A loving spirit is a condition of believing prayer. We cannot be wrong with man and right with God. The spirit of prayer is essentially the spirit of love. Intercession is simply love at prayer.

The Kneeling Christian

As people who stand in the gap for individuals, situations and nations, we need to see them the way God does and let go of our personal opinions and ideas about things.

Allison Shorter

Until the Holy Spirit changes our thinking about identity, intercession can also look like gossip.

Allison Shorter

When we are double-minded, we can end up praying multiple-choice prayers. If a man is sick, we may pray for 1.) his miraculous healing, 2.) for God to use the illness to instruct him, and 3.) to comfort him as he dies, all at the same time. Which one do we want God to answer? How do we know if He did answer when we give Him so many options? One of them has to work eventually. So what is God saying? Is He planning to heal this person? Or is it his time to meet God in heaven? Until we hear from God, praying can feel like a waste of time, mostly because we don't know what to pray. However, if we know we've heard from God, we can pray, intercede, and be at peace. We've done our job, and now He will do His.

Allison Shorter

Let's stop scaring people into the kingdom. There is no room for fear in a kingdom ruled by love.

Kevin Shorter

Nothing delights Him more than to find those whom He can take with Him into the Father's presence, whom He can clothe with power to pray down God's blessing on those around them, whom He can train to be His fellow-workers in the intercession by which the kingdom is to be revealed on earth.

Andrew Murray

Praying for those we love is not a substitute for their need to hear God's Word of truth—the Gospel. But many of those we find resisting already know it, and for them the 'pushiness' of a relative deepens resistance. On the other hand—as you abide in continual prayer—the truth that they may most need at the present is a sense of your acceptance of them, even as they understand that acceptance is not approval of sinful behavior. While it is painful to see a loved one persist in sin, especially if it is self-destructive, God's Spirit has spoken or is speaking to them about their need to turn to Him. Our prayer for them is pivotal in this regard. But it is also our job to leave God's part for Him to achieve, as only He can.
Jack Hayford

Don't put people down unless it's on your prayer list.
Stan Michalski

An imperfect world is "job security" for an intercessor.
Francis Frangipane

We must talk to God about men before we talk to men about God.
Bill Bright

The missionary leaves by taking ship or plane; the intercessor leaves by shutting the door of his closet.
Ivan French

Intercessory prayer for one who is sinning prevails, God says so. The will of the man prayed for does not come into question at all, he is connected with God by prayer, and prayer on the basis of the Redemption sets the connection working and God gives life.
Oswald Chambers

Prayer must carry on our work as much as preaching; he preacheth not heartily to his people that will not pray for them.
Richard Baxter

You never meet someone who was not created in the image and likeness of God.
Phil Drysdale

The more you pray, the more you will find to pray about, and the more you'll be led to pray for others.
Stormie O'Martian

When it comes to prayer and intercession, words are important but not necessary.
Beni Johnson

Scripture calls us to pray for many things: for all saints; for all men; for kings and all rulers; for all who are in adversity; for the sending forth of laborers; for those who labor in the gospel; for all converts; for believers who have fallen into sin; for one another in our immediate circles.
Andrew Murray

In the fine and difficult art of prayer, intercession is undoubtedly the most difficult of accomplishment. As far as my understanding of these things goes, intercessory prayer is the finest and most exacting kind of work that it is possible for men to perform.
O. Hallesby

Intercessory prayer is the purifying bath into which the individual and the fellowship must enter every day.
Dietrich Bonhoeffer

[God] says to pray for our enemies. How many of us have ever spent time praying for our enemies?
Billy Graham

We do not glorify God by providing His needs, but by praying that He would provide ours—and trusting Him to answer.
John Piper

Intercessory prayer might be defined as loving our neighbor on our knees.
Charles Brent

You can't shift other people's atmospheres if you can't shift your own.
Wendy Backlund

We are fit for the work of God only when we have wept over it, prayed about it, and then we are enabled by Him to tackle the job that needs to be done.
Alan Redpath

There are things that are going to happen and things that God would be willing to do if we would only ask.
Kevin Shorter

Pray for 'all men.' We usually pray more for things than we do for men. Our prayers should be thrown across their pathway as they rush in their downward course to a lost eternity.
E.M. Bounds

Prophetic intercession is our conspiring (breathing together) with God, breathing violently into situations through prayer in order to bring forth life.
James Goll

There is no better way to serve others than to pray for them. There is nothing about which I do not pray. I go over all my life in the presence of God. All my problems are solved there.
Samuel Chadwick

How we feel about ourselves will strongly affect how we feel about others.
Steve Backlund

An intercessor stands in the gap for a person or a group of people.
Allison Shorter

The world doesn't need our sadness; they need our joy.
Beni Johnson

Our role as intercessors is not only for you and me to enjoy "quiet and peaceable" lives, but also for "all men to be saved."

Jack Hayford

That we may pray for others is the deepest mystery and the crowning glory of prayer.

Samuel Chadwick

There is nothing that makes us love a man so much as praying for him.

William Law

Rest is something that we receive, so we must be willing to allow rest to displace the opposite - worry, fear and anxiety.

Graham Cooke

Men may spurn our appeals, reject our message, oppose our arguments, despise our persons, but they are helpless against our prayers.

Sidlow Baxter

Rich is the person who has a praying friend.

Janice Hughes

Learning to Pray by Praying

Painstaking care, much thought, practice and labour are required to be a skillful tradesman in praying.

E.M. Bounds

I can write about prayer and you can read about prayer, but sooner or later you have to fall to your knees and just plain pray.

Bill Hybels

Praying solves the problems of prayer.

Samuel Chadwick

I used to think the Lord's Prayer was a short prayer; but as I live longer, and see more of life, I begin to believe there is no such thing as getting through it. If a man, in praying that prayer, were to be stopped by every word until he had thoroughly prayed it, it would take him a lifetime.

Henry Ward Beecher

True prayer cannot be imitated nor can it be learned from someone else.

A.W. Tozer

Meditating on the nature and dignity of prayer can cause saying at least one thing to God: Lord, teach us to pray!

Karl Rahner

No man has found how far he can go with God because there is in the mysterious depths of God neither limit nor end.

A.W. Tozer

Men of God, whose prayers are recorded for us in the Bible, never read a book on prayer, never went to a seminar on prayer, never heard a sermon on prayer. They just prayed.
Ruth Graham Bell

If prayer is the greatest achievement on earth, we may be sure it will call for a discipline that corresponds to its power.
Samuel Chadwick

If it is a fact that I must pray, and shall pray when cornered by circumstances, then the better I pray the better for me—let me master the practice while there is leisure and time, remembering that here as elsewhere only practice makes perfect.
Albert D. Belden

People who don't believe that prayer matters, or that prayer works, are people who simply don't pray.
R.C. Sproul

Prayer constantly enlarges our horizon and our person. It draws us out of the narrow limits within which our habits, our past, and our whole personage confine us.
Paul Tournier

The more you pray the more you will pray for God' will.
Mark Batterson

The subject of prayer is inexhaustible and, I believe, we will be continually learning.
Germaine Copeland

Prayer is not learned in a classroom but in the closet.
E.M. Bounds

In these days there is no time to pray; but without time, and a lot of it, we shall never learn to pray.
Samuel Chadwick

We do not know much about prayer, but surely this need not prevent us from praying!
The Kneeling Christian

Like all good things, prayer requires some discipline.
Phillip Yancey

Prayer is both a privilege and a duty, and any duty can become laborious.
R.C. Sproul

The main lesson about prayer is just this: Do it! Do it! Do it! You want to be taught to pray. My answer is pray and never faint, and then you shall never fail.
John Laidlaw

In prayer, be teachable at the feet of Jesus.
Jay Harris

Praying together is like riding a bike. You can read how to do it or have someone tell you; but until you try it yourself, you'll never learn how to do it.
Evelyn Christianson

You will never be able to pray everywhere all the time, until you have learned to pray somewhere, some of the time.
Mark Water

Prayer may not get us what we want, but it will teach us to want what we need.
Vance Havner

The only way to pray is to pray, and the way to pray well is to pray much.
Henri Nouwen

Prayer is a trade to be learned. We must be apprentices and serve our time at it.
E.M. Bounds

All you need to do to learn to pray is to pray.
Wesley Duewel

As a leader, you want to be the hungriest one for growth in the group.
Steve Backlund

Religion only celebrates perfect; family celebrates process.
Wendy Backlund

The key to prayer is simply praying.
A.W. Tozer

There is no way to learn to pray but by praying.
Samuel Chadwick

Prayer itself is an art which only the Holy Ghost can teach us. He is the giver of all prayer. Pray for prayer - pray till you can pray.
C.H. Spurgeon

Pray until you can pray; pray to be helped to pray and do not give up praying because you cannot pray. For it is when you think you cannot pray that is when you are praying.
C.H. Spurgeon

Prayer is a fine, delicate instrument. To use it right is a great art, a holy art. There is perhaps no greater art than the art of prayer. Yet the least gifted, the uneducated and the poor can cultivate the holy art of prayer.
O. Hallesby

Playing around is one thing; following an established regimen is quite another. It's true with exercise equipment and it is true with prayer.
Bill Hybels

The Psalter is the prayer book of Jesus Christ in the truest sense of the word. He prayed the Psalter and now it has become his prayer for all time... we understand how the Psalter can be prayer to God and yet God's own Word, precisely because here we encounter the praying Christ... because those who pray the psalms are joining in with the prayer of Jesus Christ, their prayer reaches the ears of God. Christ has become their intercessor...
Dietrich Bonhoeffer

Do not pray for tasks equal to your powers. Pray for powers equal to your tasks.
Phillip Brooks

If we want to learn how to pray, then we must pray - and continue to pray.
R.C. Sproul

Our growth in prayer may be to us the test of our growth in all other respects.
C.H. Spurgeon

Good praying is more easily caught than taught.
D.A. Carson

All progress in prayer is an answer to prayer—our own or another's.
P.T. Forsyth

Intentionally give God the time to teach you to pray.
Jay Harris

As we grow in our prayer lives, we develop a strong inward push for more of God.
Kevin Shorter

If you don't pray often, you won't gain a love for praying. Prayer is work, and therefore it is not very appealing to our natural sensibilities. But the simple rule for prayer is this: Begin praying and your taste for prayer will increase. The more you pray, the more you will acquire the desire for prayer, the energy for prayer, and the sense of purpose in prayer.
Leslie Ludy

It was liberating to me to understand that prayer involved a learning process. I was set free to question, to experiment, even to fail, for I knew I was learning.
Richard Foster

An uneducated but disciplined believer may have a greater prayer life than a theologian who thinks and talks a lot about prayer.
Unknown

Is it not true that the folk who are most oppressed by the problems of prayer are the people who have least praying experience?
Albert D. Belden

If you can't pray as you want to, pray as you can. God knows what you mean.
Vance Havner

The Importance of Praying Big

When God is about to do a mighty new thing He always sets His people praying.
Jonathan Edwards

You can't be who you are now to fulfill the faith journey God is leading you on.
Kevin Shorter

Prayer flies where the eagle never flew.
Thomas Guthrie

Only he who can see the invisible can do the impossible.
Frank L. Gaines

You know your mind is renewed when the impossible seems logical.
Bill Johnson

When our requests are such as honor God, we may ask as largely as we will. The more daring the request, the more glory accrues to God when the answer comes.
A.W. Tozer

If your memories are greater than your dreams, then you're already dying.
Kris Vallotton

Confidence comes from God who has the ability to answer.
Elmer Towns

God wants us to be so convinced that we can do what He does that we don't get discouraged when we fail.
Wendy Backlund

Every problem is an opportunity to see how big my God is.
Steve Backlund

If we have the audacity to ask, God has the ability to perform.
Steven Furtick

Prayer is a wonderful power placed by Almighty God in the hands of His saints, which may be used to accomplish great purposes and to achieve unusual results. The only limits to prayer are the promises of God and His ability to fulfill those promises.
E.M. Bounds

God invites us to pray in such a way that it scares what is scared within us!
Lisa Bevere

God desires all believers to be so familiar with His love that our approach toward Him is bold.
Andrew Wommack

God wants us to push the limits of what we can ask or imagine.
Steven Furtick

Do you really think the Lord is going to get annoyed because you believe Him too much?
Graham Cooke

If you are not praying the type of prayers that scare you, your prayers are certainly not frightening our enemy.
Lisa Bevere

God is for you. If you don't believe that, then you'll pray small timid prayers; if you do believe it, then you'll pray big audacious prayers.
Mark Batterson

If we start understanding the principles of the kingdom, we will start taking risks.
Heidi Baker

Do not pray for easy lives. Pray to be stronger men! Do not pray for tasks equal to your powers. Pray for powers equal to your tasks.
Phillip Brooks

Because I believe in God's goodness, I owe it to Him to dream big.
Bill Johnson

The omnipotent God we pray to cannot have degrees of difficulty.
Unknown

We miss the grandeur because we lack audacity. If you will voice God at any time, you will find that He will be greater than any power that is round about you.
Smith Wigglesworth

God wants us to pray in such a way that we have to immediately remind ourselves of God's infinite greatness so that we don't freak out.
Steven Furtick

God is looking for those with whom He can do the impossible - what a pity that we plan only the things that we can do by ourselves.
A.W. Tozer

Wouldn't you like to know how it feels to see God accomplish the impossible right in front of your eyes?
Steven Furtick

The stronger our view of the Father, the stronger our prayer life will be.
Wes Hall

In the wilderness they were sustained by the miracles; in the promised land they were advanced by the miracles.
Bill Johnson

Never let an "impossible" problem intimidate you. Let it MOTIVATE you - to trust more, pray more, expect more from God.
Rick Warren

There comes a time when you have to leave all that is familiar and go on into the unknown with God.
John Eldredge

If we never pray audacious, courageous prayers, how can He answer them?
Francis Chan

God is not offended when we ask for more - only when we settle for less.
Alan Scott

Accomplishing the impossible is all about seeing the invisible.
Steven Furtick

God expects you to expect Him to be able to answer your requests.
Steven Furtick

It's abnormal for Christians not to have an appetite for the impossible!
Bill Johnson

Don't be afraid of praying something that isn't God's will. If it not God's will he won't answer it, but being afraid of praying something that isn't God's will keeps people from praying bold prayers.
Mark Batterson

The major problem in the Church is that we have limited an unlimited God through our lack of knowledge and experience in prayer and through our unbelief.
Morris Cerrulo

Prayer knows no boundaries because God is unlimited in power!
Morris Cerrulo

There is a holy audacity in Christian life and faith which is not inconsistent with the profoundest humility.
A.B. Simpson

Beware in your prayer, above everything, of limiting God, not only by unbelief, but by fancying that you know what He can do.
Andrew Murray

Praying scary prayers means surrendering control and letting go of our idea of "better" in exchange for God's best for us.
Lisa Bevere

If you live cautiously, your friends will call you wise. You just won't move many mountains.
Bill Johnson

God is still honoring those who pray with audacity and tenacity.
Mark Batterson

The bigger the dream the harder you will have to pray.
Mark Batterson

Live in such a way that unless God shows up what you're attempting to do is bound to fail. This is the nature of the Gospel.
Bill Johnson

The creative spirit is the easiest access to the prophetic.
Shawn Bolz

The measure of God's abilities will always surpass the measure of our audacity. No prayer is too big for our God.
Steven Furtick

Your imagination wasn't created so the enemy could have a playground but so you could have a place to cultivate your faith.
Wendy Backlund

Praying scary prayers means asking for the impossible and believing it could happen.
Lisa Bevere

God is looking for big believers who believe big things about small circumstances.
Steve Backlund

Large asking and large expectation on our part honor God.
A.L. Stone

Prayer lets God do what He does best. Take a pebble and kill a Goliath. Take the common, make it spectacular! Pray and see what He can do.
Max Lucado

God's looking for people through whom He can do the impossible; what a pity we plan only things we can do ourselves.
A.W. Tozer

Expectation positions us to see miracles, big and small.
Allison Brown

Preaching must necessarily be limited, but who can put a limit to the possibilities and power of prayer?
Ivan French

When God's love is accompanied by you faith, expect miracles.
Ranal Currie

God appreciates it when his people pray in a way that's actually worthy of the God they're praying to.
Steven Furtick

I fancy we may sometimes be deterred from small prayers by a sense of our own dignity rather than of God's.
C.S. Lewis

A LADY came to the great preacher of the last century G. Campbell Morgan and she said, "I only take the big things to God. I don't take the little things to God." G. Campbell Morgan looked at her and said, "Lady, anything you take to God is little." That is precisely the case. You can bring everything to God because anything you bring to God is little to Him, even if it is big to you.
Tony Evans

This is our Lord's will... that our prayer and our trust be, alike, large.
Julian of Norwich

When you pray dangerous prayers, your life is no longer safe... boring or small!
Liva Bevere

If you're not uncomfortable in your faith, you are not doing it right.
Jen Toledo

If you aren't believing God for big things, you probably aren't praying regularly or intensively enough.
Mark Batterson

God is ready to give more quickly, and to give more than you ask; yea, He offers His treasures if we only take them.
Martin Luther

Pray the largest prayers. You cannot think a prayer so large that God, in answering it, will not wish you had made it larger. Pray not for crutches but for wings.
Phillip Brooks

In prayer, ask for what only God can do.
Jay Harris

Will we settle for the status quo, or will we reach out for what God can supernaturally do through us?
Jim Cymbala

Nothing lies beyond the reach of prayer except that which lies outside the will of God.
Phillip Brooks

If you're not daring to believe God for the impossible, you're sleeping through some of the best parts of your Christian life.
Steven Furtick

Never tell a young person that something cannot be done. God may have been waiting for centuries for somebody ignorant enough of the impossible to do that thing.
Dr. John Andrew Holmes

Let us pray Wesley's prayer, "Lord, make me an extraordinary Christian."
Henrietta Mears

Pray the kind of prayers that scare what's scared inside of you!
Lisa Bevere

If your prayers aren't impossible to you, they are insulting to God.
Mark Batterson

The prayer of faith is a prayer willing to believe and prevail for God's answer in a situation that is utterly impossible.
Wesley Duewel

Most Christians don't pray scary prayers, they pray scared prayers.
Lisa Bevere

If the size of your vision for your life isn't intimidating to you, there's a good chance it's insulting to God.
Steven Furtick

Prayer can do anything that God can do, and as God can do everything, prayer is omnipotent.
R.A. Torrey

I don't want to play with marbles ... when God told me to move mountains!
Reinhard Bonnke

If you don't get some blank stares from people, you're not dreaming big enough.
Steven Furtick

Anyone can do the possible. Add courage and zeal, some may do the phenomenal. But only Christians are obliged to do the impossible.
A.W. Tozer

What sets lion chasers apart isn't the outcome. It's the courage to chase God-sized dreams.
Mark Batterson

We dare not limit God in our asking, nor in his answering.
John Blanchard

True prayer is rooted in the promises and covenants of God, in his past achievements, in his ability to do immeasurably more than all we ask or imagine.
Bob Cotton

If I truly believe God is good, then I must dream big.
Bill Johnson

You're never too old to overcome your fear and do something amazing for Jesus.
Jason Upton

Pray in a way that makes room for God's answer to astound you.
Lisa Bevere

Why do so many Christians pray such tiny prayers when their God is so big?
Watchman Nee

The Importance of Praying with Power

Nothing is hopeless to prayer because nothing is hopeless to God.
E.M. Bounds

The possibilities of prayer are vast! Prayer moves God to do His work in new and greater ways.
Shirley Dobson

And because you know that 'the effective prayer of a righteous man can accomplish much' (James 5:16b NASB), you can be sure that you will prevail. You just prayed prayers that were inspired by the Spirit. And who is more righteous than the Holy Spirit?
James Goll

Your weak times of prayer are still effective.
Kevin Shorter

Prayer succeeds when all else fails.
E.M. Bounds

Do not work so hard for Christ that you have no strength to pray, for prayer requires strength.
Hudson Taylor

The man on his knees has a leverage underneath the mountain which can cast it into the sea, if necessary, and can force all earth and heaven to recognize the power there is in 'His name.'
M.E. Andross

There is a kind of omnipresence and omnipotence in prayer. Nothing is too difficult or out of reach.
Kevin Shorter

Does prayer indeed move the Hand that moves the world?
The Kneeling Christian

We must begin to believe that God, in the mystery of prayer, has entrusted us with a force that can move the Heavenly world, and can bring its power down to earth.
Andrew Murray

Prayer is the secret of power.
Evan Roberts

Fear-based repentance makes us hate ourselves. Joy-based repentance makes us hate the sin.
Tim Keller

One of the reasons for our sense of futility in prayer is that we have lost our power to imagine.
Oswald Chambers

There is no distance or time in the spirit realm. The moment your prayer "hits it" accurately, the natural is moved.
Lance Wallnau

Prayer is never the least we can do; it is always the most!
A.W. Tozer

Believing prayer never asks more than is promised.
William S. Plumer

Prayer changes the atmosphere. You have the relationship with God to change the culture around you.
Lance Wallnau

In order to be effective, prayer has to be the first thing we do, not the last.
Eugene Peterson

Prayers have no boundaries. They can leap miles and continents and be translated instantly into any language.
Billy Graham

I had rather stand against the cannons of the wicked than against the prayers of the righteous.
Thomas Lye

They are not leaders because of brilliancy. ...but because, by the power of prayer, they could command the power of God.
E.M. Bounds

Our only true power is the power of prayer. When we pray, God moves from heaven. When we pray, things happen that would not otherwise happen. By prayer all things are possible.
Dr. Ray Prichard

Prayer can do whatever God can do.
Rick Warren

Believing supplications are forecasts of the future.
C.H. Spurgeon

If you are strangers to prayer you are strangers to power.
Billy Sunday

If we spent more time preparing to pray and getting our hearts right before God, our prayers would be more effective.
Warren Wiersbe

As our confidence increases, we are becoming more bold because we are becoming fully aligned with God's heart.
Graham Cooke

A servant of the Lord stands bodily before men, but mentally he is knocking at the gates of heaven with prayer.
John Climacus

There's no defense against prayer.
Adam Shepski

Your prayers are more powerful than you give them credit for.
Bill Johnson

Ask in a way that eliminates doubt.
Graham Cooke

Every miracle has a genealogy. If you trace those miracles all the way back to their origin, you'll find a prayer.
Mark Batterson

Prayer is a creature's strength, his very breathe and being.
C.H. Spurgeon

Has your relationship with God changed the way you live your life?
Francis Chan

When we learn to come to God with an intensity of desire that wrings the soul, then shall we know a power in prayer that most of us do not know now.
R.A. Torrey

Prayer is the canon set at the gate of heaven to burst open its gates.
Puritan saying

I'm certain that the disciples clearly saw the inseparable relationship between the power Jesus manifested and the hours He spent in solitude, conversing with His Father.
R.C. Sproul

A prayerless Christian is like a bus driver trying alone to push his bus out of a rut because he doesn't know Clark Kent is on board.
John Piper

Lifeless prayer is no more prayer than a picture of a man is a man.
Richard Watson

We pour out millions of words and never notice that the prayers are not answered.
A.W. Tozer

If you may have everything by asking in His name, and nothing without asking, I beg you to see how absolutely vital prayer is.
C.H. Spurgeon

Prayer turns ordinary mortals into men of power. It brings power. It brings fire. It brings rain. It brings life. It brings God.

Samuel Chadwick

Prayer is God's ordained way to bring His miracle power to bear in human need.

Wesley Duewel

I determined to learn to pray so that my experience confirmed to the words of Jesus rather than try to make his words conform to my impoverished experience.

Richard Foster

Thinking everything that happens will work out for good weakens our hope, and makes us depend on "I hope this works" praying, rather than confidence in prayer as God intends.

Steve Backlund

8

WHY WE SHOULD PRAY

Personal Reasons

Go where your best prayers take you.
Frederick Buechner

The battle of prayer is against two things in the earthlies: wandering thoughts, and lack of intimacy with God's character as revealed in His word. Neither can be cured at once, but they can be cured by discipline.
Oswald Chambers

He that is being prepared for glory is always hungry after the largest measure of grace.
C.H. Spurgeon

Prayer is inextricably linked to the whole of life, not separate from it.
Roy Searle

Whether prayer changes our situation or not, one thing is certain: Prayer will change us!
Billy Graham

Our prayers lay the track down which God's power can come. Like a mighty locomotive, his power is irresistible, but it cannot reach us without rails.
Watchman Nee

Pray alone. Let prayer be the key of the morning and the bolt at night. The best way to fight against sin is to fight it on our knees.
Philip Henry

Prayer is God's appointed means for appropriating the blessings that are ours in Christ Jesus.
D.A. Carson

Our lack of prayer causes us to forfeit His blessings, divine intervention, and provision He would have given had we prayed.
Morris Cerrulo

The more you PRAY the more you DREAM and the more you DREAM the more you HAVE TO PRAY.
Mark Batterson

Our trust in ourselves and in our talents makes us structurally independent of God... Praying seems nice but unnecessary.
Paul Miller

All the promises of God are "yes and amen." They are "yes" because they are true and "amen" because we must agree with them in prayer.
Mike Bickle

Jesus never taught His disciples how to preach, only how to pray.
Andrew Murray

As a man prays, so is he.
A.W. Tozer

To hear God speak to your heart, to understand His Word, to evaluate circumstances and to make certain that these three are in agreement, prayer is essential. Pray with the sincere desire that the Lord answer in accordance with His will.
Henrietta Mears

The reason why others succeed is because they have gained their victory on their knees long before the battle came.
R.A. Torrey

You can do more than pray, after you have prayed, but you cannot do more than pray until you have prayed.
John Bunyon

I am so busy now that if I did not spend two or three hours each day in prayer, I would not get through the day.
Martin Luther

We would never produce the full range of biblical prayer if we were initiating prayer according to our own inner needs and psychology.
Tim Keller

I must secure more time for private devotions. I have been living far too public for me. The shortening of devotions starves the soul, it grows lean and faint. I have been keeping too late hours.
William Wilberforce

O believing brethren! What an instrument is this which God hath put into your hands! Prayer moves Him that moves the universe.
Robert Murray M'Cheyne

Public prayer ought to be the overflow of one's private praying.
D.A. Carson

The entire day receives order and discipline when it acquires unity. This unity must be sought and found in morning prayer. The morning prayer determines the day.
Dietrich Bonhoeffer

To be little with God is to be little for God.
E.M. Bounds

Prayer is the means by which we get everything in our lives out in the open before God.
David Jeremiah

As we pray, the power of God enters the situation and begins to transform the situation. And in the middle of that, we are being transformed.
Jack Hayford

Prayer makes a godly man, and puts within him the mind of Christ, the mind of humility, of self-surrender, of service, of pity, and of prayer. If we really pray, we will become more like God, or else we will quit praying.
E.M. Bounds

We are never so high as when we are on our knees.
The Kneeling Christian

The important thing about prayer is not simply getting an answer, but being the kind of person whom God can trust with an answer.
Warren Wiersbe

Public praying is a pedagogical opportunity.
D.A. Carson

Even the most devout seem to think they must storm heaven with loud outcries and mighty bellowings or their prayers are of no avail.
A.W. Tozer

We are not here to prove God answers prayer, but to be living trophies of God's grace.
Oswald Chambers

He who will not pray until, on good grounds, he is sure that he has all right affections and graces, will go to hell before his prayer begins.
Samuel Prime

There is power through prayer. For many Christians, prayer is nothing special, just something we're supposed to do - go to church, tithe, read the Bible, pray. But prayer should be so much more than an item on our "to do" lists.
E.M. Bounds

A man's influence in the world can be gauged not by his eloquence, or his zeal, or his orthodox, or his energy, but by his prayers.
The Kneeling Christian

Prayer imparts the power to walk and not faint.
Oswald Chambers

No man can do a great and enduring work for God who is not a man of prayer, and no man can be a man of prayer who does not give much time to praying.
E.M. Bounds

To be a Christian without prayer is no more possible than to be alive without breathing.
Martin Luther

Wise is he in the day of trouble who knows his true source of strength and who fails not to pray.
E.M. Bounds

We can learn more in an hour praying, when praying indeed, than from many hours of rigorous study.
E.M. Bounds

The subject is beset with problems, but there are no problems of prayer to the man who prays!
Samuel Chadwick

Pray this: let me live the life You intended for me.
Kevin Shorter

Prayer is for every moment of our lives, not just for times of suffering or joy.
Billy Graham

If we would do much for God, we must ask much of God: we must be men of prayer.
Payson

We will not grow in prayer unless we plan to pray.
D.A. Carson

To be too busy with God's work to commune with God is the highway to backsliding.
E.M. Bounds

Most of modern man's troubles stem from too much time on his hands and not enough on his knees.
Ivern Boyett

The irony is that while God doesn't need us but still wants us, we desperately need God but don't really want Him most of the time.
Francis Chan

I am perfectly confident that the man who does not spend hours alone with God will never know the anointing of the Holy Spirit. The world must be left outside until God alone fills the vision.
Oswald Chambers

It would revolutionize the lives of most men if they were shut in with God in some secret place for half an hour a day.
Samuel Chadwick

Prayer is the way the life of God is nourished.
Oswald Chambers

No man can progress in grace if he forsakes prayer.
C.H. Spurgeon

Whatever is your best time in the day, give that to communion with God.
Hudson Taylor

He who fails to pray does not cheat God. He cheats himself.
George Failing

What the church needs today is not more machinery or better, not new organizations or more novel methods, but men whom the Holy Ghost can use— men of prayer, men mighty in prayer.
E.M. Bounds

You have enough time to do everything God wants you to do.
Craig Groeschel

The secret of much mischief to our souls, and to the souls of others, lies in the way that we stint, and starve, and scamp our prayers by hurrying over them.
Alexander Whyte

The faithful discipline of prayer reveals to you that you are the blessed one and gives you the power to bless others.
Henri Nouwen

No man - I don't care how colossal his intellect - No man is greater than his prayer life.
Leonard Ravenhill

The loftier the building the deeper the foundation must be.
Thomas a Kempis

A full measure of the Word and prayer each day gives a healthy and powerful life.
Andrew Murray

Our spirituality and our fruitfulness are always in proportion to the reality of our prayers.
The Kneeling Christian

No insistence in the Scripture is more pressing than that we must pray... How clear it is, when the Bible is consulted, that the almighty God is brought directly into the things of this world by the prayers of His people.
E.M. Bounds

We hear it said that a man will suffer in his life if he does not pray; I question it. What will suffer is the life of the Son of God within him, which is nourished not by food but by prayer... Prayer is the way the life of God is nourished.
Oswald Chambers

You stand tall when you kneel to pray.
John Blanchard

If there are any tears shed in heaven, they will be over the fact that we prayed so little.
Billy Graham

If prayer isn't necessary to accomplish your vision then you aren't thinking big enough!
Craig Groeschel

Prayer gives us an accurate knowledge of ourselves.
Tim Keller

Prayer becomes religious when we try to use it for what God never intended.
Andrew Wommack

Trouble is one of God's great servants because it reminds us how much we continually need the Lord.
Jim Cymbala

Prayer is not an option but a necessity.
Billy Graham

To give prayer the secondary place is to make God secondary in life's affairs. A holy mouth is made by praying.
E.M. Bounds

Prayer should be an adventure.
Beni Johnson

Prayer changes you first. Before changing your situation or others, God wants to work in you.
Rick Warren

Prayer should not be regarded as a duty which must be performed, but rather as a privilege to be enjoyed, a rare delight that is always revealing some new beauty.
E.M. Bounds

Prayer is the antidote for the disease of self-confidence.
John Piper

That saint who advances on his knees never retreats.
Jim Elliot

We must take time to pray, for GOD works in answer to prayer, and GOD at work is our greatest need.
Amzi Clarence Dixon

To not grow in His likeness is to not enjoy his fullness. When this happens, a haunting voice continues to ask, 'What could I have become in him if I would have been a man of prayer?' To grow in His likeness is to enjoy His fullness. When this happens, the priorities of the world begin to fade away.
Richard Foster

If the Son of God needed to pray before He undertook His work, how much more should we pray. Perhaps if we lack success in life, it is because we fail at this point. We have not because we ask not.
Henrietta Mears

Negligence in prayer withers the inner man.
Watchman Nee

He who has learned to pray has learned the greatest secret of a holy and happy life.
William Law

He who does not pray when the sun shines knows not how to pray when the clouds arise.
William Edward Biederwolf

The greatest and best talent that God gives to any man or woman in this world is the talent of prayer.
Alexander Whyte

That man is the most immortal who has done the most and the best praying. They are God heroes, God's saints, God's servants, God's vicegerents.
E.M. Bounds

Many times I have been driven to prayer. When I was in Bible school I didn't know what to do with my life. I used to walk the streets... and pray, sometimes for hours at a time. In His timing, God answered those prayers, and since then prayer has been an essential part of my life.
Billy Graham

People use [prayer] to soothe their consciences, feeling like they've done something to manipulate and motivate God to move on their behalf.
Andrew Wommack

Begin the day with the Word of God and prayer, and get first of all into harmony with Him.
Hudson Taylor

The men who have done the most for God in this world have been early on their knees. He who fritters away the early morning, its opportunity and freshness, in other pursuits than seeking God will make poor headway seeking Him the rest of the day. If God is not first in our thoughts and efforts in the morning, He will be in the last place the remainder of the day.
E.M. Bounds

We were created to live a life of prayer.
Billy Graham

He has never studied God who has not had his intellect broadened, strengthened, clarified & uplifted by prayer.
E.M. Bounds

Those persons who know the deep peace of God, the unfathomable peace that passeth all understanding, are always men and women of much prayer.
R.A. Torrey

Sustain us with that hope and encouragement that our prayer is not in vain when we pray 'Thy Kingdom Come!'
Peter Marshall

Our growth in grace and power depends largely upon our individual, personal prayer life. Yet public worship is nonetheless important and necessary.
Constance Garrett

God is not first in our thoughts and efforts in the morning, He will be in the last place the remainder of the day.
E.M. Bounds

If the Christian does not allow prayer to drive sin out of his life, sin will drive prayer out of his life. Like light and darkness, the two cannot dwell together.
M.E. Andross

Prayer is effective when it empowers us to bring changes that reflect the Kingdom.
Brian Clark

You are only one prayer away from a dream fulfilled, a promise kept, or a miracle performed.
Mark Batterson

He that loveth little prayeth little, he that loveth much prayeth much.
Augustine

Nothing has more greatly shaped the experiences and events of my life than prayer: personal prayer, public prayer gatherings, pointed and focused prayer, passionate prayer, and power-filled, Spirit-energized prayer!
Jack Hayford

Desire toward God and you will have desires from God and He will meet you on the line of those desires when you reach out in simple faith.
Smith Wigglesworth

The most dangerous prayer you can pray is just 2 words: "Use me!"
Rick Warren

All we have to do is to remain faithful to God and wholly attentive to his will, and everything that is necessary will be given to us.
Madame Guyon

Prayer is the most important thing in my life. If I should neglect prayer for a single day, I should lose a great deal of the fire of faith.
Martin Luther

External Motivation

Let's keep our chins up and our knees down—we're on the victory side!
Alan Redpath

So the preacher of the gospel asks your prayers: and it is a part of the duties arising out of the relationship between Christian men that those who are taught should pray for those who teach God's Word.
C.H. Spurgeon

At the judgement seat the most embarrassing thing the believer will face will be the smallness of his praying.
Leonard Ravenhill

If you do not pray, God will probably lay you aside from your ministry, as He did me, to teach you to pray.
Robert Murray M'Cheyne

One's spiritual life will never rise above the practice of one's private prayer life.
Richard Burr

All God's giants have been weak men, who did great things for God, because they believed that God would be with them.
Hudson Taylor

When we pray for others the Spirit of God works in the unconscious domain of their being that we know nothing about, and the one we are praying for knows nothing about, but after the passing of time the conscious life of the one prayed for begins to show signs of unrest and disquiet. We may have spoken until we are worn out, but have never come anywhere near, and we have given up in despair. But if we have been praying, we find on meeting them one day that there is the beginning of a softening in an inquiry and a desire to know something. It is that kind of intercession that does most

damage to Satan's kingdom. It is so slight, so feeble in its initial stages that if reason is not wedded to the light of the Holy Spirit, we will never obey it, and yet it is that kind of intercession that the New Testament places most emphasis on.
>> *Oswald Chambers*

A changed world begins with us... and a changed us begins when we pray.
>> *Eugene Peterson*

Everything we do in the Christian life is easier than prayer.
>> *David Martyn Lloyd-Jones*

Leaders must be released from the idea that they must be great prayer warriors before they can begin to call others to prayer.
>> *David Bryant*

In every truly successful ministry prayer is an evident and controlling force.
>> *E.M. Bounds*

The sanctity of prayer is needed to impregnate business. We need the spirit of Sunday carried over to Monday and continued until Saturday. But this cannot be done by prayerless men, but by men of prayer.
>> *E.M. Bounds*

The prayer is up to us; the answer is up to God.
>> *Woodrow Kroll*

Temptations which accompany the working day will be conquered on the basis of the morning breakthrough to God. Decisions, demanded by work, become easier and simpler where they are made not in the fear of men, but only in the sight of God. He wants to give us today the power which we need for our work.
>> *Dietrich Bonhoeffer*

FOR MANY of us, prayer is like a AAA card. It's there if you need it, but you really don't plan to use it very much—unless you're in an emergency.
>> *Tony Evans*

We are to pray in times of adversity, lest we become faithless and unbelieving. We are to pray in times of prosperity, lest we become boastful and proud. We are to pray in times of danger, lest we become fearful and doubting. We need to pray in times of security, lest we become self-sufficient.
>> *Billy Graham*

The prayer-meeting furnishes a very accurate discriminating test of character. The live Christian loves its enjoyments, the spiritually dead have no delights there.
>> *J.B. Johnson*

May we be known for building them up in prayer rather than tearing them down with our words.
>> *John Bevere*

A church is never more like the New Testament church than when it is praying.
J.B. Johnson

An ounce of believing prayer is worth a ton of edifying talk.
John Cowan

Any church may have a mighty man of God for its pastor, if it is willing to the price and that price is not a big salary but great praying.
R.A. Torrey

A family without prayer is like a house without a roof, open and exposed to all the storms of heaven.
Thomas Brooks

Ministers who do not spend two hours a day in prayer are not worth a dime a dozen - degrees or no degrees.
Leonard Ravenhill

We have all been uniquely created to experience God's Presence and Kingdom and release it wherever we go.
Allison Shorter

Let me have as much of heaven, even now, as I can have.
C.H. Spurgeon

If the church wants a better pastor, it only needs to pray for the one it has.
Kevin Shorter

We can change the course of events if we go to our knees in believing prayer. Someone has said, "Prayer is the highest use to which speech can be put."
Billy Graham

Prayer is buried, and lost and Heaven weeps. If all prayed the wicked would flee from our midst or to the refuge.
Evan Roberts

Pray hardest when it is hardest to pray. Prayer is a powerful thing, for God has bound and tied Himself thereto.
Martin Luther

The true church lives and moves and has its being in prayer.
Leonard Ravenhill

Prayer is the surest secret of success in any married life.
Henrietta Mears

Do we really think we can experience integration of heart and mind and spirit with an erratic prayer life?
Richard Foster

Communion with God is essential before we can have real communion with our fellow-man.
The Kneeling Christian

The Christian will find his parentheses for prayer even in the busiest hours of life.
Richard Cecil

Our Lord never referred to unanswered prayer; He taught that prayers are always answered.
Oswald Chambers

Prayer for Church unity will not bring that unity; but that which stirs, and founds, and wings prayer will.
P.T. Forsyth

No man should stand before an audience who has not first stood before God.
A.W. Tozer

Pray for wisdom to behave wisely in time of trial. When you are wronged and insulted, ask God how you shall act. "If any of you lacks wisdom, he should ask God, who gives generously to all without finding fault, and it will be given to him" (James 1:5). What a sad lack! What a mess such a lack can lead us into. Does James say, "If you lack wisdom, sit down and think or study"? No, he says the wisdom we need is from above.
Henrietta Mears

We owe the world around us answers to prayer.
Bill Johnson

God will not do for me what I can do for myself. Prayer must never be regarded as a labor-saving device.
William Barclay

This should be the motto of every follower of Jesus Christ. Never stop praying no matter now dark and hopeless it may seem.
Billy Graham

Prayer must carry on our work, as well as preaching. He does not preach heartily to his people who does not pray for them.
Richard Baxter

I'm convinced that the man who has learned to meditate upon the Lord will be able to run on his feet and walk in his spirit. Although he may be hurried by his vocation, that's not the issue. The issue is how fast his spirit is going. To slow it down takes a period of time.
Charles Stanley

Prayer is the first thing, the second thing, the third thing necessary to a minister. Pray, then my dear brother; pray, pray, pray.
Edward Payson

Until we know we are freely loved, giving love away in prayer or intercession or with our teams can be difficult. It can come off with an edge of condemnation and taint our prayers and purity of heart.
Allison Shorter

Days of trouble must be days of prayer.
Matthew Henry

When problems get Christians praying they do more good than harm.
John Blanchard

One prayer can change the course of history.
Mark Batterson

Why waste energy criticizing what's wrong when our prayers can change it!
Francis Frangipane

With God's saints in all ages: nights of prayer with God have been followed by days of power with men.
The Kneeling Christian

Prayer is the best response to hatred.
C.H. Spurgeon

Don't go into the study to prepare a sermon -- that's nonsense. Go into your study to God and get so fiery that your tongue is like a burning coal and you have got to speak.
C.T. Studd

A man who kneels before God will stand before men.
Leonard Ravenhill

Anything, and I mean anything, becomes a blessing if it drives us to prayer.
Jim Cymbala

See to it that we pray more than we preach and we will never preach ourselves out.
A.W. Tozer

The greatest thing we can do for God or for man is to pray.
The Kneeling Christian

The men upon whose shoulders rested the initial responsibility of Christianizing the world came to Jesus with one supreme request. They did not say, "Lord, teach us to preach"; "Lord, teach us to do miracles"; or "Lord, teach us to be wise"... but they said, "Lord, teach us to pray."
Billy Graham

I would rather teach one man to pray than ten men to preach.
C.H. Spurgeon

The history of every ministry is written in its prayer-life.
Mario Murillo

A prayerless Christian is a powerless Christian.
Billy Graham

Men must be in earnest when they kneel at God's footstool. Too often we get faint-hearted and quit praying at the point where we ought to begin. We let go at the very point where we should hold on strongest.
E.M. Bounds

If prayer seems to you a diversion from productivity, remember God does more in five seconds than we can in five hours.
John Piper

A survey reported that the majority of the seminaries [in the United States] had no classes on prayer. That really shouldn't surprise us when we consider how many local churches offer classes on gardening and the "Art of Conversation" instead of the study of God's Word and prayer.
Billy Graham

Great pastors know it's more important to pray for your people than preach to them.
Rick Warren

There cannot be an answer until there is a prayer.
Woodrow Kroll

Give yourselves to prayer and the ministry of the Word. If you do not pray, God will probably lay you aside from your ministry, as He did me, to teach you to pray.
Robert Murray M'Cheyne

May God break my heart so completely that the whole world falls in.
Mother Teresa

Heavenly citizenship and heavenly homesickness are in prayer. Prayer is an appeal from the lowness, from the emptiness, from the need of earth, to the highness, the fullness and to the all-sufficiency of heaven.
E.M. Bounds

Non-praying is lawlessness, discord, anarchy.
E.M. Bounds

When we miss out on prayer we cause disappointment to Christ, defeat to ourselves and delight to the devil.
John Blanchard

The fact that so many prayers are found in the New Testament Epistles calls attention to an important aspect of ministerial duty.
A.W. Pink

The men who have guided the destiny of the United States have found the strength for their tasks by going to their knees. This private unity of public men and their God is an enduring source of reassurance for the people of America.
Lyndon B. Johnson

Pray if thou canst with hope, but ever pray, Though hope be weak or sick with long delay; Pray in the darkness if there be no light.
E.M. Bounds

Praying gives sense, brings wisdom, and broadens and strengthens the mind. The prayer closet is a perfect schoolteacher and schoolhouse for the preacher. Thought is not only brightened and clarified in prayer, but thought is born in prayer.
E.M. Bounds

Sometimes our prayers are like the boy who asked his parent for help to solve his math problems while he played video games.
Phillip Yancey

Even the straws under my knees shout to distract me from prayer.
Augustine

How dare we work for Christ without being much on our knees?
The Kneeling Christian

Beware of placing the emphasis on what prayer costs us; it cost God everything to make it possible for us to pray.
Oswald Chambers

To attempt any work for God without prayer is as futile as trying to launch a space probe with a peashooter.
John Blanchard

I feel it is far better to begin with God, to see His face first, to get my soul near Him before it is near another. In general it is best to have at least one hour alone with God before engaging in anything else.
E.M. Bounds

It is through prayer that God wishes to have His will brought to pass.
Henrietta Mears

Why do we need to pray? Because the Christian life is a journey, and we need God's strength and guidance along the way.
Billy Graham

Power does not travel through words; it travels through relationships!
Morris Cerrulo

He that is never on his knees on earth, shall never stand upon his feet in heaven.
C.H. Spurgeon

Prevailing prayer is the most divine ministry you will ever have.
Wesley Duewel

Prayer need not be a burdensome duty. It is meant to be a joyful and creative privilege.
Hannah Hurnard

It was claimed for Augustus Caesar that he found Rome a city of wood, and left it a city of marble. The pastor who succeeds in changing his people from a prayerless to a prayerful people has done a greater work than did Augustus. And after all, this is the prime work of the preacher.
E.M. Bounds

I know that the Lord is always on the side of the right. But it is my constant anxiety and prayer that I and this nation should be on the Lord's side.
Abraham Lincoln

Men who are reluctant about prayer do not belong in places of leadership in the church.
Ivan French

Remember there is always access to God through prayer in Christ. We may speak not just three times a day, but whenever the need arises. The Lord Jesus invites us to pray.
Henrietta Mears

True prayer is a way of life, not just for use in cases of emergency. Make it a habit, and when the need arises you will be in practice.
Billy Graham

To pray with bitterness toward fellowmen nullifies hours on our knees.
Dick Eastman

Against the persecution of a tyrant the godly have no remedy but prayer.
John Calvin

Obligation

Draw nigh to God, so that you may dread the grave as little as your bed.
D.A. Carson

We have to realize that prayer is foolish from the commonsense point of view.
Oswald Chambers

Let Thy wonderful revelation of a Father's tenderness free all young Christians from every thought of secret prayer as a duty or a burden, and lead them to regard it as the highest privilege of their life, a joy and a blessing.
Andrew Murray

Other duties become pressing and absorbing and crowd out prayer. 'Choked to death' would be the coroner's verdict in many cases of dead praying if an inquest could be secured on this dire, spiritual calamity.
E.M. Bounds

Even pagan savages cry out to someone or something to aid them in times of danger and disaster and distress. How much more should we that know the true God.
Unknown

Do not have your concert first, and then tune your instrument afterwards. Begin the day with the Word of God and prayer, and get first of all into harmony with Him.
Hudson Taylor

You cannot afford to be too busy to pray.
Billy Graham

As prayer meetings fail in a congregation, so will the ministrations of the pastor become unfruitful, the preaching of the word fail to convert sinners and promote holiness in the professors of religion.
J.B. Johnson

Focusing on the personal prayer life only would be equivalent to trying to fly a plane on one wing.
John Franklin

Never wait for fitter time or place to talk to Him. To wait till you go to church or to your room is to make Him wait. He will listen as you walk.
George MacDonald

Prayer is to the Christian what breath is to life, yet no duty of the Christian is so neglected.
R.C. Sproul

Let the day have a blessed baptism by giving your first waking thoughts into the bosom of God. The first hour of the morning is the rudder of the day.
Henry Ward Beecher

Neglecting prayer is not a weakness; it is a sinful choice.
Ben Jennings

God's command to pray without ceasing is founded on the necessity we have of his grace to preserve the life of God in the soul, which can no more subsist one moment without it, than the body can without air.
John Wesley

The hinges on the door to our prayer closets have grown rusty due to underuse.
Max Lucado

A prayerless man is a careless man.
William W. Tiptaft

Prayer is the divine equalizer. Some preach, other teach, a few sing publically, but all can pray.
Dick Eastman

There is a need in the soul of the believer that can be satisfied only when we move from being a spectator to a participator in prayer.
Unknown

There is no other activity in life so important as that of prayer. Every other activity depends upon prayer for its best efficiency.
M.E. Andross

Prayer is the inner bath of love into which the soul plunges itself.
St. John Mary Vianney

The great people of the earth today are the people who pray! I do not mean those who talk about prayer; nor those who say they believe in prayer; nor those who explain prayer; but I mean those who actually take the time to pray.
S.D. Gordon

The most important thing a born again Christian can do is to pray.
Chuck Smith

There are many problems about prayer, but they lie outside the fact and experience of prayer, and apart from praying there is no solution to them.
Samuel Chadwick

To pray as God would have us pray is the greatest achievement of earth. Such a life costs. It takes time.
Samuel Chadwick

We repeat, not to count the times, but to gain the prayer.
E.M. Bounds

If man is man and God is God, to live without prayer is not merely an awful thing, it is an infinitely foolish thing.
Phillip Brooks

Time spent alone with God is not wasted. It changes us; it changes our surroundings; and every Christian who would live the life that counts, and who would have power for service must take time to pray.
M.E. Andross

The Church gives more time, thought, and money to recreation and sport than to prayer.
Samuel Chadwick

If I should neglect prayer but a single day, I should lose a great deal of the fire of faith.
Martin Luther

Who can measure the influence of an hour a day spent alone with God?
Samuel Chadwick

Nothing brings such leanness into a man's soul as lack of prayer.
C.H. Spurgeon

The great souls who became mighty in prayer and rejoiced to spend three and four hours a day alone with God were once beginners.
Samuel Chadwick

The greatest need of most of us regarding prayer is not the clearing up of its logical problems, but its efficient practice.
Albert D. Belden

For some of us, prayer is like putting four quarters in a Coke machine, pushing the button, and not getting a Coke. We push the button again and again, waiting for our Coke, which never comes. Finally, kicking the machine, we just wave our hand and walk away. Many of us have given up on prayer because while it is something we know we are supposed to do, we feel it just doesn't work.
Tony Evans

Running to God should be your first response not your last resort.
Lisa Bevere

We are too busy to pray, and so we are too busy to have power. We have a great deal of activity, but we accomplish little; many services but few conversions; much machinery but few results.
R.A. Torrey

God has left many things dependent upon man's thinking and working, why should He not leave some things dependent upon man's praying?
The Kneeling Christian

It is only in times of great and grievous dullness that the believer regards prayer as a duty, and not as a privilege.
Adolph Saphir

To begin the day with prayer is but a formality unless it go on in prayer, unless for the rest of it we pray in deed what we began in word.
P.T. Forsyth

There is nothing that tells the truth about us as Christians so much as our prayer life.
David Martyn Lloyd-Jones

If I fail to spend two hours in prayer each morning, the devil gets the victory through the day. I have so much business I cannot get on without spending three hours daily in prayer.
Martin Luther

The sin of prayerlessness is a proof... that the life of God in the soul is in deadly sickness and weakness.
Andrew Murray

Your god may be your little Christian habit - the habit of prayer or Bible reading at certain times of day. Watch how your Father will upset your schedule if you begin to worship your habit instead of what the habit symbolizes. We say, "I can't do that right now; this is my time alone with God." No, this is your time alone with your habit.
Oswald Chambers

Always respond to every impulse to pray. The impulse to pray may come when you are reading or when you are battling with a text. I would make an absolute law of this – always obey such an impulse.
Martyn Lloyd-Jones

True praying has the largest results for good. Poor praying the least. We cannot do too much of real praying. We cannot do too little of the sham. If we would learn the wondrous power of prayer, we must not give a fragment here and there - A little talk with Jesus, as the tiny saintlets sing - but we must demand and hold with an iron grasp the best hours of the day for God and prayer, or there will be no praying worth the name.
E.M. Bounds

You can delegate many things, but prayer is not one of them.
A.W. Tozer

Learning about prayer can be positively harmful because it increases our responsibility and intensifies our guilt if we fail to pray.
Ivan French

Don't pray when you feel like it. Have an appointment with the Lord and keep it. A man is powerful on his knees.
Corrie ten Boom

Accustom yourself gradually to carry Prayer into all your daily occupation - speak, act, work in peace, as if you were in prayer, as indeed you ought to be.
François Fénelon

We give lip service to prayer far more than we give our lips to the service of prayer.
Sue Curran

God's children should pray. They should cry day and night to Him. God hears every one of your cries in the busy hour of the daytime and in the lonely watches of the night.
Robert Murray M'Cheyne

There is more you can do after you pray, but there is nothing you can do until you pray.
Adoniram Judson

If it's big enough to worry about, pray about it instead. Don't suppress or repress it. Confess it to Him. Worry is worthless.
Rick Warren

Disciples pray because their Master does.
Reinhard Bonnke

If we really loved our blessed Savior, should we not oftener seek communion with Him in prayer?
The Kneeling Christian

Why do we piously favour prayer in general and devilishly resist it in particular?
Ray Stedman

I seriously doubt that there would be many divorces among Christians if they took the time to kneel in prayer once a day and prayed for each other.
Ruth Graham Bell

Prayer is the acid test of devotion.
Samuel Chadwick

There is no easier sin to commit than the sin of prayerlessness. It is a sin against God and against Man.
Wesley Duewel

As is the business of tailors to make clothes and cobblers to make shoes, so it is the business of Christians to pray.
Martin Luther

Work, work, from morning until late at night. In fact, I have so much to do that I shall have to spend the first three hours in prayer.
Martin Luther

The spiritual leader should outpace the rest of the church, above all, in prayer.
Oswald Sanders

You that manifest a concern about religion, why don't you pray?
Martin Luther

Prayer can never be in excess.
C.H. Spurgeon

It would seem as if the biggest thing in God's universe is a man who prays. There is only one thing more amazing, and that is-that man, knowing this, should not pray.
Samuel Chadwick

Either we pray or we faint.
Ray Stedman

You can do more than pray after you have prayed; but you can never do more than pray until you have prayed.
A.J. Gordon

No form of Christian service is both so universally open to all and so high in Christ's priority for all Christians as prevailing prayer.
Wesley Duewel

Heaven is too busy to listen to half-hearted prayers or to respond to pop-calls.
E.M. Bounds

The Christian is not always praying; but within his bosom is a heaven-kindled love-- fires of desire, fervent longings--which make him always ready to pray, and often engage him in prayer.
Thomas Guthrie

One of the most glaring discrepancies in the Christian faith today is between the size of our God and the size of our prayers.
Steven Furtick

Things that could have taken place on yesterday didn't, because those that had the opportunity didn't take the opportunity to pray.
Rondale Terry

Let's fulfill our outward duties, while inwardly absorbed by Him who alone is worthy of all our love.
François Fénelon

Love is kindled in a flame, and ardency is its life. Flame is the air which true Christian experience breathes. It feeds on fire; it can withstand anything rather than a feeble flame; but when the surrounding atmosphere is frigid or lukewarm, it dies, chilled and starved to its vitals. True prayer must be aflame.
E.M. Bounds

No learning can make up for the failure to pray. No earnestness, no diligence, no study, no gifts will supply its lack.
E.M. Bounds

I should as soon expect life in a dead man as spiritual life in a prayerless soul!
The Kneeling Christian

Prayer worth calling prayer, prayer that God will call true prayer and will treat as true prayer takes far more time by the clock, than one man in a thousand thinks.
Alexander Whyte

What wings are to a bird, and sails to a ship, so is prayer to the soul.
Corrie ten Boom

If you want to see how popular the church is, attend Sunday morning worship. If you want to see how popular the pastor is, attend Sunday evening. If you want to see how popular God is, attend the prayer meeting.
Armin Gesswein

Pray when you feel like it. Pray when you don't feel like it. Pray until you feel like it.
Stephen Olford

It takes us long to learn that prayer is more important than organization, more powerful than armies, more influential than wealth, and mightier than all learning.
     Samuel Chadwick

Make time to pray. The great freight and passenger trains are never too busy to stop for fuel. No matter how congested the yards may be, no matter how crowded the schedules are, no matter how many things demand the attention of the trainmen, those trains always stop for fuel.
     M.E. Andross

Nothing can replace a daily time spent alone with God in prayer. We can also be in an attitude of prayer throughout the day—sitting in a car or at our desks, working in the kitchen, even talking with someone on the phone.
     Billy Graham

It is significant that the schools teach everything about preaching except the important part, praying.
     A.W. Tozer

Private, personal prayer is one of the last great bastions of legalism.
     Paul Miller

Be not afraid to pray; to pray is right.
     E.M. Bounds

If your faith does not make you pray, have nothing to do with it: get rid of it, and God help thee to begin again.
     C.H. Spurgeon

How many periods of five, ten, or fifteen minutes that could be devoted to prayer do we waste or leave unemployed in the course of a day?
     J. Oswald Sanders

We are obliged to pray if we are citizens of God's Kingdom... The gospel cannot live, fight, or conquer without prayer—prayer unceasing, instant, and ardent.
     E.M. Bounds

No reasoned philosophy of prayer ever taught a soul to pray.
     Samuel Chadwick

I have so much to do that I spend several hours in prayer before I am able to do it.
     John Wesley

As it is the business of tailors to make clothes and of cobblers to mend shoes, so it is the business of Christians to pray.
     Martin Luther

You may as soon find a living man that does not breathe, as a living Christian that does not pray. For this shall every one that is godly pray. If prayerless, then graceless.
     Matthew Henry

Prayer is the most important privilege of a Christian.
> *Henrietta Mears*

Failing to pray reflects idolatry—a trust in substitutes for God.
> *Ben Jennings*

To pray as a duty and as if obliging God by our prayer, is quite ridiculous, and is certain indication of a backslidden heart.
> *Charles Finney*

We have to take time from other things that are valuable in order to understand how necessary prayer is.
> *Oswald Chambers*

Has not that which is heaven's greatest boon to man (prayer), become to us a dry dead duty?
> *C.H. Spurgeon*

The principle exercise which the children of god have is to pray. For in this way they give true proof of their faith.
> *John Calvin*

Many Christians are so spiritually frail, sickly, and lacking in spiritual vitality that they cannot stick to prayer for more than a few minutes at a time.
> *Wesley Duewel*

Prayerlessness is an insult to God. Every prayerless day is a statement by a helpless individual, 'I do not need God today.'
> *Ben Jennings*

Our disinclination to pray is our most painful experience; it is so irrational and unaccountable.
> *Adolph Saphir*

In reality, the denial of prayer is a denial of God Himself.
> *E.M. Bounds*

You know the value of prayer: it is precious beyond all price. Never, never neglect it.
> *Sir Thomas Buxton*

One of the first things He commands is that there shall be a place of prayer.
> *Samuel Chadwick*

If you can't pray a door open, don't pry it open.
> *Lyell Rader*

The only way to completely fail in prayer is to fail to pray!
> *Sue Curran*

I know of no better thermometer to your spiritual temperature than this, the measure of the intensity of your prayer.
> *C.H. Spurgeon*

The most amazing feature of that life as it is looked back upon will be its prayerlessness.
> *The Kneeling Christian*

So important a factor is prayer in Christian experience, that the history of a man's progress in the Divine life is just the history of his progress in the knowledge and in the use of prayer.
William Edward Biederwolf

As well could you expect a plant to grow without air and water as to expect your heart to grow without prayer and faith.
C.H. Spurgeon

It ought to be possible to give God one hour of twenty-four all to Himself.
Samuel Chadwick

Since [prayer] is a holy exercise both for the humbling of men and for their confession of humility, why should we use it less than the ancients did?
John Calvin

Prayer should be a lifestyle not just an emergency call.
Paula White

He that lives a prayerless life, lives without God in the world.
Jonathan Edwards

A vacant chamber of prayer means that a believer has gone out of business religiously.
E.M. Bounds

The very act of prayer honors God and gives glory to God, for it confesses that God is who He is.
Charles Kingsley

Anything large enough for a wish to light upon is large enough to hang a prayer on.
George MacDonald

One might pray and not be a Christian, but one cannot be a Christian and not pray.
R.C. Sproul

The remedy's before you: Pray.
Joseph Hart

Nothing whatever can atone for the neglect of praying.
E.M. Bounds

Never tell me of a humble heart where I see a stubborn knee.
Thomas Adams

The cause of Christ does not need less working, but more praying.
Henrietta Mears

We cannot justify our relative prayerlessness by saying that those who are peculiarly effective are more gifted than we.
D.A. Carson

Of all the duties enjoined by Christianity none is more essential and yet more neglected than prayer.
François Fénelon

Never say you will pray about a thing; pray about it.
Oswald Chambers

We ought to see the face of God every morning before we see the face of man.

      D.L. Moody

A graceless man will be a prayerless man.

      J.B. Johnson

In times of declension we are inclined to place the need of prayer instead of penitent approach to God in the forefront.

      Oswald Chambers

As impossible as it is for us to take a breath in the morning large enough to last us until noon, so impossible is it to pray in the morning in such a way as to last us until noon.

      O. Hallesby

I would rather have prayer without words then words without prayer.

      E.M. Bounds

If frequent prayer, and, at times, long hours of prayer, were necessary for our Savior, are they less necessary for us?

      The Kneeling Christian

Prayer to us is not practical, it is stupid, and until we do see that prayer is stupid, that is, stupid from the ordinary, natural, common sense point of view, we will never pray.

      Oswald Chambers

Every prayerless day is a statement by a helpless individual, I do not need God today.

      Ben Jennings

Does the Bible ever say anywhere from Genesis to Revelation, 'My house shall be called a house of preaching'? Does it ever say, 'My house shall be called a house of music'? Of course not. The Bible does say, 'My house shall be called a house of prayer for all nations'. Preaching, music, the reading of the Word - these things are fine; I believe in and practice all of them. But they must never override prayer as the defining mark of God's dwelling. The honest truth is that I have seen God do more in people's lives during ten minutes of real prayer than in ten of my sermons.

      Jim Cymbala

If we are to depend on prayer during tough times, we should be people of prayer before the crisis hits.

      Billy Graham

Work as if you were to live a hundred years, pray as if you were to die tomorrow.

      Benjamin Franklin

Prayer, in every care and anxiety and need of life, with thanksgiving, is the means God has appointed for our obtaining freedom from all anxiety, and the peace of God which passeth all understanding.

      R.A. Torrey

Our greatest victories are won on our knees and with empty stomachs.
Julio C. Ruibal

One has said that while prayer is the day's best beginning it must not be like the handsome title-page of a worthless book.
P.T. Forsyth

Too busy; O forgive, Dear Lord, that I should ever be, too much engrossed in earthly tasks, to spend an hour with thee.
A.B. Christiansen

Oh, how strenuous is life! I know a little of it. Men ought always to pray, and not to faint. How fierce the battle! I know something of the conflict, but I ought not to faint, because I can pray.
George Campbell Morgan

Prayer is acceptable in any situation.
Kevin Shorter

Prayerlessness is disobedience, for God's command is that men ought always to pray and not faint. To be prayerless is to fail God, for He says, Ask of me.
Leonard Ravenhill

Prayer should never be a source of discouragement for us.
Kevin Shorter

Be resolute in prayer. Make any sacrifice to maintain it. Consider that time is short and that business and company must not be allowed to rob thee of thy God.
Adoniram Judson

It is well said that neglected prayer is the birth-place of all evil.
C.H. Spurgeon

You can use your time to no better advantage than to pray whenever you have a moment, either alone, or with others, while at work, at rest, or walking down the street! Anywhere!!
O. Hallesby

He who runs from God in the morning will scarcely find Him the rest of the day.
John Bunyon

I ought to pray before seeing any one...Christ arose before day and went into a solitary place. David says: 'Early will I seek thee'...I feel it is far better to begin with God-to see His face first, to get my soul near Him before it is near another.
Robert Murray M'Cheyne

We need more Christians for whom prayer is the first resort, not the last.
John Blanchard

Prayer is the most sacred occupation a person could engage in.
A.W. Tozer

There is no greater test to spirituality than prayer. The man who tries to pray quickly discovers just where he stands in God's sight.
The Kneeling Christian

Many are so preoccupied with work that they allow little time for prayer.
Watchman Nee

All who have walked with God have viewed prayer as the main business of their lives.
Delma Jackson

The greatest tragedy of life is not unanswered prayer but unoffered prayer.
F.B. Meyer

Prayerlessness is sin.
Harold Lindsell

For many of us, prayer is like the National Anthem before a football game. It gets the game started, but simply has no connection with what's happening on the field. It's a courtesy.
Tony Evans

Once you realize how much God loves you, you will never neglect spending time with Him because it will become your life and fuel for life.
Kevin Shorter

Don't forget to pray today because God did not forget to wake you up this morning.
Oswald Chambers

Prayer of the heart comes when one makes an effort; to those who do not strive, it will not come.
St. Theophan

The spirit is willing, but the flesh has to get out of bed in the morning.
David Jeremiah

A spiritual life without prayer is like the Gospel without Christ.
Henri Nouwen

When I experience the power of God, why do I do anything other than pray?
Francis Chan

Stop making prayer your backup plan.
Lisa Bevere

Our Lord employed His time strategically, and in selecting His priorities, He always set aside abundant time for prayer.
Unknown

The neglect of prayer is a major cause of stagnation in the Christian life.
R.C. Sproul

Pray because Christ died to give us access to the Father. Pray because God is worthy of our praise. Pray because we need His forgiveness, cleansing, guidance, and protection. Pray because others need our prayers.
Billy Graham

One should never initiate anything that he cannot saturate with prayer.
S.D. Gordon

Prayer is so major we dare not minor on it any longer.
Armin Gesswein

The church must stop praying like a widow and start praying like a bride.
Graham Cooke

Now PRAYER is a duty founded on natural religion; the very heathens never neglected it, though many Christian heathens amongst us do.
George Whitefield

If your day is hemmed in with prayer, it is less likely to come unraveled.
Unknown

Souls without prayer are like people whose limbs are paralyzed; they possess but can't control them.
Mother Teresa

Prayer is the greatest use of my words.
Rick Warren

The little estimate we put on prayer is evidence from the little time we give to it.
E.M. Bounds

Preaching, music, the reading of the Word--these things are fine--but they must never override prayer as the defining mark of God's dwelling.
Jim Cymbala

Little praying is a kind of make believe, a salve for the conscience, a farce and a delusion.
E.M. Bounds

We carry checks on the bank of heaven and never cash them at the window of prayer.
Vance Havner

When Christ ascended into heaven all He left behind was a prayer meeting. The early Church didn't have a prayer meeting; the early Church was the prayer meeting. In fact, in the early Church every Christian was a prayer-meeting Christian.
Armin Gesswein

Nothing you can do will benefit you more than prayer.
Paul Y. Cho

If you are sick, fast and pray; if the language is hard to learn, fast and pray; if the people will not hear you, fast and pray, if you have nothing to eat, fast and pray.
Frederick Franson

The fruit of silence is prayer. The fruit of prayer is faith. The fruit of faith is love. The fruit of love is service. The fruit of service is peace.
Mother Teresa

For more than thirty-five years. I have had much intercourse with dying saints and sinners of various ages and conditions. In all that time I have not heard one express regret that he had spent too much time in prayer; I have heard many mourn that they had so seldom visited a throne of grace.

William S. Plumer

Living high, living good, living long. Take a minute, bust a prayer and you're good to go.

MC Hammer

The greatest argument for the priority of prayer is the fact that our Lord was a Man of prayer.

Warren Wiersbe

No man realising God's love will begrudge time for prayer or let business or pleasure take precedence of his sacred trust with love.

Albert D. Belden

We are slaves to our gadgets, puppets of our power, and prisoners of our security. The theme of our generation is: "Get more, know more, and do more," instead of "Pray more, be more, and serve more."

Billy Graham

We have not yet learned that we are more powerful on our knees than behind the most powerful weapons that can be developed.

Billy Graham

Prayer Meetings

Learn to be vicarious in public prayer. Allow two rivers to come through you: the river of God, and the river of human interests. Beware of the danger of preaching in prayer, of being doctrinal.

Oswald Chambers

The prayer meeting is a special means of developing and cultivating Christian graces, and of promoting individual and social edification.

J.B. Johnson

When I pray, I do not come before God as an isolated individual, but as a member of a family, a community of saints.

R.C. Sproul

What we cannot obtain by solitary prayer we may by social... because where our individual strength fails, there union and concord are effectual.

John Chrysostom

It is to our shame that, in our era, church services do not focus more on actually seeking God.

Francis Frangipane

The prayer meeting is the rallying point where the power of faith in the church concentrates, and takes hold on the arm that moves the world.
J.B. Johnson

The church upon its knees would bring heaven upon the earth.
E.M. Bounds

A congregation without a prayer meeting is essentially defective in its organization, and so must be limited in its efficiency.
Andrew Murray

There is unusual power in united prayer.
Wesley Duewel

The prayer meeting is the pulse of the church.
J.B. Johnson

The measure of believing, continued prayer will be the measure of the Spirit's working in the Church. Direct, definite, determined prayer is what we need.
Andrew Murray

Let the fires go out in the boiler room of the church and the place will still look smart and clean, but it will be cold. The Prayer Room is the boiler room for its spiritual life.
Leonard Ravenhill

Taking time to agree with others in prayer will help cut through confusion.
Doug Addison

What does it say about our churches today that God birthed the church in a prayer meeting, and prayer meetings today are almost extinct?
Jim Cymbala

If you were to ask me the greatest discovery I have made regarding the truth of the church, I would have to say it is this: When Jesus built the church, He built a praying congregation! To put it even more plainly: When Jesus built the church He built a prayer meeting.
Armin Gesswein

I came to realize the absolute necessity of praying with one's fellow worker over every detail.
Hannah Hurnard

The prayer meeting is a divine ordinance, founded in man's social nature.
J.B. Johnson

The spirit of prayer, and the love and practice of the prayer meeting, will so give organic strength to the church as to make her terrible as an army with banners.
J.B. Johnson

When you pray about every detail regularly with other people, however different you may be, you cannot help loving the people you pray with.
Hannah Hurnard

I realize more than ever that this ministry has been a team effort. Without the help of our prayer partners, our financial supporters, our staff, and our board of directors— this ministry and all of our dreams to spread the Good News of God's love throughout the world would not have been possible.

Billy Graham

Both Scripture and experience unite to indicate that there is cumulative power in unified praying.

Unknown

The New Testament prayer meeting reveals the master plan of Jesus. The last thing Jesus did on earth was to build that prayer meeting, and it is the only thing He left behind on planet Earth when He ascended to heaven.

Fred Hartley

There is tremendous power when God's people mobilize in prayer.

John Bevere

There is a power in conferring and covenanting, on the part of kindred spirits, to come before God, and plead together some special promise.

J.B. Johnson

A prayer-meeting is an index to the state of religion in a Church.

Charles Finney

Where a people prays, there is the church; and where the church is; there is never loneliness.

Dietrich Bonhoeffer

God wants each of us to mature to the point where we can enjoy just hanging out with Him. He desires our fellowship when there's nothing being said and nothing specific happening other than being together and loving each other.

Andrew Wommack

We must repent of our prayerlessness. We must make prayer our priority. Even our churches today have gotten away from prayer meetings.

Billy Graham

We feel sure that the weakness in the spiritual life of many churches is to be traced to an inefficient prayer-meeting, or the absence of meetings for prayer. Can we not make the weekly prayer-meeting a live thing and a living force?

The Kneeling Christian

But if one neglects his closet, then all evil comes of it.

C.H. Spurgeon

When you want to work for God start a committee. When you want to work with God start a prayer group.

Corrie ten Boom

Spiritual Warfare

Serving God doesn't mean we'll no longer have difficulties. We're still on the battlefield, but we don't have to fight alone.
Joyce Meyer

To strive in prayer means in the final analysis to take up the battle against all the inner and outward hindrances which would dissociate us from the Spirit of prayer.
O. Hallesby

There is no harder shield for the devil to pierce with temptation than singing with prayer.
Henry Ward Beecher

We tend to use prayer as a last resort, but God wants it to be our first line of defense.
Oswald Chambers

There is nothing the devil dreads so much as prayer?
The Kneeling Christian

The most intimidating thing to the devil is your intimacy with God.
Graham Cooke

If you only pray when you feel like it, Satan will make sure you never feel like it.
Rick Warren

Don't let the enemy push you into a battle you are not ready for. Keep your focus on Jesus, and natural obstacles will arise because of that.
Graham Cooke

The enemy tries to get us to fight him on the turf called fear.
Wendy Backlund

Complaining is to the devil what praise is to God.
Bill Johnson

Hope does not allow the enemy any place to lie to us. It allows no deception. It refuses a negative.
Graham Cooke

We have to understand that the devil does not play fair. He will take a very anointed time and twist it and turn it, and you will find yourself in a state of depression because you carried sorrow for too long. In short, something birthed by the Spirit can become fleshly if we are not careful.
Beni Johnson

The Prince of the power of the air seems to bend all the force of his attack against the spirit of prayer.
Andrew Bonar

If spiritual warfare is hard, I haven't received God's complete plan of attack.
Kevin Shorter

Nothing pleases satan more than to persuade people that he doesn't exist.
R.C. Sproul

Satan can't keep God from answering our prayers, but he will keep us from asking.
Adrian Rogers

Satan laughs at our toiling, mocks at our wisdom, but trembles when we pray.
The Kneeling Christian

The best cure for discouragement or qualms is another daring plunge of faith.
C.T. Studd

All the evil influences which seek to prevent our approach to God do not deserve to be compared with the attractive power of God.
Adolph Saphir

We are not to live in reaction to the devil. We are to live in response to God.
Bill Johnson

Do not be surprised to find hypocrites in every congregation of God's children. Satan comes to do mischief to saints. He distracts our attention. He sets us to criticizing. He sows dissension in the congregation. He excites the pride of preachers and singers, of givers and those who publicly pray. He chills our spirit and freezes our prayers.
Henrietta Mears

The sight of any trouble strikes terror into the heart of those who do not have faith, but those who trust Him say, "Here comes my food!"
Watchman Nee

Much of our praying is just asking God to bless some folks that are ill and to keep us plugging along. But prayer is not merely prattle: it is warfare.
Alan Redpath

Whenever I am conscious of Satan's presence, I try to follow the formula once offered by a little girl: "When Satan knocks, I just send Christ to the door."
Billy Graham

Prayer plumes the wings of God's young eaglets so that they may learn to mount above the clouds. Prayer brings inner strength to God's warriors and sends them forth to spiritual battle with their muscles firm and their armor in place.
C.H. Spurgeon

When a Christian shuns fellowship with other Christians, the devil smiles. When he stops studying the Bible, the devil laughs. When he stops praying, the devil shouts for joy.
Corrie ten Boom

We cannot know what prayer is for unless we know that life is war.
John Piper

Prayer is the master strategy that God gives for the defeat and rout of Satan.
Wesley Duewel

The greatest blow sent Satan-ward is made by weeping warriors of prayer.
Dick Eastman

We worship at the feet of the Savior and dance on the head of the serpent.
Kevin Shorter

Fasting, as it relates to prayer, is the spiritual atomic bomb that the Lord has given us against the enemy.
Bill Bright

Satan works constantly to steal your peace because he knows that if he does, you can't hear from God.
Kim Flanagan

Prayer is repeating the victor's name (Jesus) into the ears of Satan and insisting on his retreat.
S.D. Gordon

To say prayers in a decent, delicate way is not heavy work. But to pray really, to pray till hell feels the ponderous stroke, to pray till the iron gates of difficulty are opened, till the mountains of obstacles are removed, till the mists are exhaled and the clouds are lifted, and the sunshine of a cloudless day brightens-this is hard work, but it is God's work, and man's best labor.
E.M. Bounds

The prayers of God's saints strengthen the unborn generation against the desolating waves of sin and evil.
E.M. Bounds

God likes to see His people shut up to this, that there is no hope but in prayer. Herein lies the Church's power against the world.
Andrew Bonar

Where ever the church fails to pray, the enemy is happy to move in.
Bill Johnson

Your intimacy with God is the key source of your intimidation towards the enemy.
Graham Cooke

The devil knows if he can capture your thought life he has won a mighty victory over you.
Smith Wigglesworth

God answers prayer. For every deadline He will throw you a lifeline. Keep believing and be blessed!
Reinhard Bonnke

Prayer is the Christian's greatest weapon.
Billy Graham

The intensity of the enemy's threats is a reflection of his fear. Don't cower... pray!
Lisa Bevere

By intercessory prayer we can hold off Satan from other lives and give the Holy Ghost a chance with them. No wonder Jesus put such tremendous emphasis on prayer.
Oswald Chambers

Satan has been defeated and disarmed, and he needs us to believe his lies so we can carry him into our situations.
Wendy Backlund

A powerful and necessary weapon in the prayer warfare is thinking, sharp, discerning thinking. 1 Peter 4:7. This attitude is a manifestation of the kingdom of God in the midst of turmoil.
Lars Widerberg

The devil will tremble when you pray.
Billy Graham

I realize that many Christians have not been praying because they have not accepted the reality of war in which we find ourselves.
Francis Frangipane

If the devil can get the church to withdraw from prayer by believing reasonable excuses, the church is under his dominion.
E.M. Bounds

The 1990's will be a decade where we must focus on prayer as the main thrust to accomplish God's will and purpose on earth. The forces against us have never been greater and this is the only way we can release God's power to become victorious.
John Maxwell

The devil tells us that laughter in a church meeting is from the devil.
Steve Backlund

The one concern of the devil is to keep Christians from praying. He fears nothing from prayerless studies, prayerless work and prayerless religion. He laughs at our toil, mocks at our wisdom, but trembles when we pray.
Samuel Chadwick

Do not let the devil rob you of the unique quality God has breathed into you.
A.W. Tozer

If you don't want the Devil to hit you, hit him first, and hit him with all your might, so that he may be too crippled to hit back.
C.T. Studd

Satan's chief way of hindering us is to try to fill our minds with the thought of our needs, so that they shall not be occupied with thoughts of God, our loving Father, to Whom we pray.
The Kneeling Christian

Depend upon it, if you are bent on prayer, the devil will not leave you alone. He will molest you, tantalize you, block you, and will surely find some hindrances, big or little or both. And we sometimes fail because we are ignorant of his devices... I do not think he minds our praying about things if we leave it at that. What he minds, and opposes steadily, is the prayer that prays on until it is prayed through, assured of the answer.
Mary Warburton Booth

I fear the prayers of John Knox more than all the assembled armies of Europe.
Mary, Queen of Scots

All the darkness in the world cannot extinguish the light of a single candle.
Francis of Assisi

When the devil sees a man or woman who really believes in prayer, who knows how to pray, and who really does pray, and, above all, when he sees a whole church on its face before God in prayer, he trembles as much as he ever did, for he knows that his day in that church or community is at an end.
R.A. Torrey

God is always greater, therefore, I will worship Him in the midst of the battle.
Kevin Shorter

Prayer: a subversive activity [that] involves a more or less open act of defiance against any claim by the current regime.
Eugene Peterson

A single sunbeam is enough to drive away many shadows.
Francis of Assisi

Prayer is the most powerful weapon we have in our spiritual arsenal to stand against the world's greatest enemy, the one who presents himself as an angel of light [2 Corinthians 11:14].
Billy Graham

No one is a firmer believer in the power of prayer than the devil; not that he practices it, but he suffers from it.
Guy H. King

Prayer breaks all bars, dissolves all chains, opens all prisons, and widens all straits by which God's saints have been held.
E.M. Bounds

It is in the field of prayer that life's critical battles are lost or won. We must conquer all our circumstances there. We must first of all bring them there. We must survey them there. We must master them there.
J.H. Jowett

In prayer we bring our spiritual enemies into the Presence of God and we fight them there. Have you tried that? Or have you been satisfied to meet and fight your foes in the open spaces of the world?

J.H. Jowett

[Satan] laughs at our toil, mocks at our wisdom, but trembles when we pray.

Samuel Chadwick

Prayer is not always a quiet, joyful conversation with God. Sometimes it is a battle against the principalities arrayed against us.

Warren Wiersbe

The world needs more true praying to save it from the reign and ruin of Satan.

E.M. Bounds

How we need the Lord to enlighten our eyes that we may comprehend afresh the importance of prayer and know anew its value. Furthermore, we must recognize that had Satan not deceived us we would not be neglecting prayer so much. We should therefore watch and discover therein all the various wiles of Satan. We will not allow him to delude us any more in relaxing in prayer.

Watchman Nee

There are more battles won through prayer than by any other means.

Chuck Smith

A healthy prayer life allows you to recognize and respond to attacks from the enemy before they even happen.

John Bevere

The one concern of the devil is to keep the saints from praying.

Samuel Chadwick

I learned as never before that persistent calling upon the Lord breaks through every stronghold of the devil, for nothing is impossible with God. For Christians in these troubled times, there is simply no other way.

Jim Cymbala

Faith is a kind of immune system filtering out fears that otherwise would paralyze all activity.

Reinhard Bonnke

Prayer is a kingdom man's primary weapon of warfare. With it, he will touch Heaven and change earth.

Tony Evans

Prevailing prayer is aggressive spiritual warfare.

Unknown

If there were no devil there would be no difficulty in prayer, but it is the evil one's chief aim to make prayer impossible.

The Kneeling Christian

The peace the Savior gives is not an artificial one. It is so deep that even the devil can't disturb it.

Rees Howells

On every new level you must meet a new devil. The purpose of the devil obstacle is to give you strength and power.
Graham Cooke

Jesus is not intimidated or embarrassed by darkness. He overcame it and loved those in it.
Kevin Shorter

You have not been put on earth for the devil to torment you, you have been put on this earth to torment the devil.
Kris Vallotton

Faith replaces fear, but not without a fight.
Clayton King

The devil is not terribly frightened of our human efforts and credentials. But he knows his kingdom will be damaged when we begin to lift up our hearts to God.
Jim Cymbala

If [satan] can sink a man's mind into habit, he will prevent his heart from engaging God.
Donald Miller

Prayer enables us first inwardly to overcome the enemy and then outwardly to deal with him.
Watchman Nee

Brother, pray; in spite of Satan, pray; spend hours in prayer; rather neglect friends than not pray; rather fast and lose breakfast, dinner, tea, and supper- and sleep too- than not pray. And we must not talk about prayer, we must pray in right earnest. The Lord is near. He comes softly while the virgins slumber.
Andrew Bonar

God's greatest agency; man's greatest agency, for defeating the enemy and winning men back is intercession.
S.D. Gordon

Prevailing prayer is prayer that pushes right through all difficulties and obstacles, drives back all the opposing forces of Satan, and secures the will of God. Its purpose is to accomplish God's will on earth.
Wesley Duewel

Satan laughs at our toil, mocks at our wisdom, but trembles when we pray.
Samuel Chadwick

You can dress up church and make it look pretty. But the devil will come, and the only word he understands is prayer.
Bishop Tudor

Prayer in all regards takes a new frame of reference when we understand the war between God's Kingdom and satan's dark hordes. This battle, insofar as it involves earth, is one in which God has called us to engage, enlisting us as 'knee-soldiers' whose prayer-call for the 'incoming' of God's Kingdom will welcome a barrage of God's power to break through the darkness and bring deliverance to people we know.
Jack Hayford

The more praying there is in the world, the better the world will be; the mightier the forces against evil everywhere.
E.M. Bounds

The aim of Satanic power is to cut off communication with God. To accomplish this aim he deludes the soul with a sense of defeat, covers him with a thick cloud of darkness, depresses and oppresses the spirit, which in turn hinders prayer and leads to unbelief - thus destroying all power.
James Fraser

The greatest hindrance to effective prayer is sin. Satan's greatest goal is to keep us from our knees.
Dick Eastman

Satan trembles when he sees the weakest Christian on his knees.
William Cowper

Shout, 'Get thee behind me, Satan...' and you will have the best time on earth. Whisper it, and you won't.
Smith Wigglesworth

Before a man can bind the enemy, he must know there is nothing binding him.
Smith Wigglesworth

Jesus defeated Satan. Good > evil. Don't let evil [sin, sickness, fears] keep you from good.
Kevin Shorter

Fear activates the devil the same way faith activates God.
Nathan Morris

A praying saint performs far more havoc among the unseen forces of darkness than we have the slightest notion of.
Oswald Chambers

The prayer of the feeblest saint who lives in the Spirit and keeps right with God is a terror to Satan. The very powers of darkness are paralyzed by prayer; no spiritualistic seance can succeed in the presence of a humble praying saint. No wonder Satan tries to keep our minds fussy in active work till we cannot think in prayer.
Oswald Chambers

The devil will try to stop you from praying because prayer stops him.
Reinhard Bonnke

He who is too busy to pray will be too busy to live a holy life. Satan had rather we let the grass grow on the path to our prayer chamber than anything else.
E.M. Bounds

Pray often, for prayer is a shield to the soul, a sacrifice to God. and a scourge for Satan.
John Bunyon

Rest is a weapon against the enemy. He cannot penetrate your peace.
Graham Cooke

Faith is not the absence of fear; it is its conquest.
Reinhard Bonnke

Persistent calling upon the name of the Lord breaks through every stronghold of the devil, for nothing is impossible with God.
Jim Cymbala

Prayer is the Christian's first line of defense against demonic influence. Fervent, sincere prayer thwarts Satan's activity like nothing else.
Neil Anderson

The way you silence fear is to give attention to faith.
Bill Johnson

Our job is not to bring down the strongholds of the enemy. Our job is to bring down the Presence of God into our midst.
Graham Cooke

Satan does not care how many people read about prayer if only he can keep them from praying.
Paul E. Billheimer

Prayer releases the grip of Satan's power; prayerlessness increases it.
Alan Redpath

Revival

It is God's will through His wonderful grace, that the prayers of His saints should be one of the great principal means of carrying on the designs of Christ's kingdom in the world.
Jonathan Edwards

Prayer begets Revival, which begets more prayer.
Jim Cymbala

Nothing would turn the nation back to God so surely and so quickly as a Church that prayed and prevailed. The world will never believe in a religion in which there is no supernatural power. A rationalized faith, a socialized Church, and a moralized gospel may gain applause, but they awaken no conviction and win no converts.
Samuel Chadwick

We pray for ourselves, for the state of the world, for the peace of all things, and for the postponement of the end.
Tertullian

Our prayer for a spiritual awakening will without question be most effective if we take up the work of interceding for certain individuals in particular.
O. Hallesby

Prayer for revival will prevail when it is accompanied by radical amendment of life; not before.
A.W. Tozer

Prayer laid the tracks where the gospel was going to come.
Wellington Boone

Show me a church or a Christian organization that emphasizes prayer, and I'll show you a ministry where people are excited about Jesus Christ and are witnessing for Him.
Bill Bright

When Christians are united, and praying as they ought, God opens the windows of heaven, and pours out His blessing till there is not room to receive it (Mal. 3:10).
Charles Finney

All great soul-winners have been men of much and mighty prayer, and all great revivals have been preceded and carried out by persevering, prevailing knee-work in the closet.
Samuel Logan Brengle

Nobody worries about Christ as long as he can be kept shut up in churches. He is quite safe inside. But there is always trouble if you try and let him out.
G.A. Studdert Kennedy

Too many churches praying for revival have a "Do not disturb" sign hanging on the door.
Daniel Kolenda

The secret of reaching men is to know the secret of reaching God.
John Blanchard

Prayer is key to our effort to communicate the Gospel and win men and women to Christ.
Billy Graham

The child of the prayer movement is revival and the harvest of souls.
Matthew Prewett

Sainthood's piety is made, refined, perfected, by prayer. The gospel moves with slow and timid pace when the saints are not at their prayers early and late and long.
E.M. Bounds

Every work of God can be traced to some kneeling form.
D.L. Moody

All missionary efforts simply gather up the fruits of our praying.
David Bryant

To desire revival... and at the same time to neglect (personal) prayer and devotion is to wish one way and walk another.
A.W. Tozer

My primary goal in all things is not revival, but to bring pleasure to Christ.
Francis Frangipane

Prayer is the greatest vehicle to have a congregation united in seeing Christ's mission fulfilled.
Oni Kittle

That which begins not with prayer, seldom winds up with comfort.
John Flavel

At the heart of every revival is the spirit of prayer.
Arthur Wallis

Prayer [is] the genesis of revival. The beginning of a time of revival invariably has been marked by quickening of the ordinary prayer meetings, resulting in new vitality, more participation, more sense of the presence of the Holy Spirit, and more unction in intercession.
Erroll Hulse

The man who mobilizes the Christian church to pray will make the greatest contribution to world evangelization in history.
Andrew Murray

I believe it will only be known on the last day how much has been accomplished in overseas missions by the prayers of earnest believers at home.
James Fraser

The prayer that sparks revival begins long before the countryside seems to awaken from its slumber in sin. It starts when men fall on their knees and cry out to God. That's where true intimacy with God takes place and we begin the journey of being transformed into the image of Christ. And as men are transformed, the course of a nation can be changed.
Wellington Boone

I listened to a discussion of religious leaders on how to communicate the Gospel. Not once did I hear them mention prayer. And yet I know of scores of churches that win many converts each year by prayer alone.
Billy Graham

Persistent, prevailing, conspicuous and mastering prayer has always brought God to present.
E.M. Bounds

No great spiritual awakening has begun anywhere in the world apart from united prayer.
J. Edwin Orr

The greatest benefactor this age could have is the man who will bring the teachers and the church back to prayer.
E.M. Bounds

Revival is going to come because somebody in your generation is willing to pay the price.
Jack Hayford

When I get to China, I will have no claim on any one for anything. My claim will be alone in God and I must learn before I leave England to move men through God by prayer alone.
Hudson Taylor

To get nations back on their feet, we must first get down on our knees.
Billy Graham

The prime need of the church is not men of money nor men of brains, but men of prayer.
E.M. Bounds

Only turning God's house into a house of fervent prayer will reverse the power of evil so evident in the world today.
Jim Cymbala

A dynamic praying church must be built from the inside out, employing all four levels of prayer: the secret closet, the family altar, small group praying and finally, the congregational setting.
Richard Burr

Too many Christians are satisfied that earth is the closest they'll come to hell that they are not willing to bring more of heaven here.
Kevin Shorter

The first disciples received power but never returned to the Upper Room for another Pentecost. We do not read they had prayer retreats to recover power.
Reinhard Bonnke

What any student of scripture knows is we're already in a revival because Christ is in us.
Graham Cooke

History confirms the truth that wherever evangelical and vital religion flourish, there lives the earnest gatherings for social prayer.
J.B. Johnson

Wherever the Church is aroused and the world's wickedness arrested, somebody has been praying.
A.T. Pierson

Prayer is the key to revival, building bridges between what should be and what will be.
Kris Vallotton

Even though we may not take part audibly in the action, yet if we are there in a right spirit - there really to wait upon God, we marvelously help the tone of a meeting.
CHM

In the prayer meeting, as nowhere else, are Christian graces thus brought together with powerful reactionary and reflective force.
J.B. Johnson

We are working with God to determine the future. Certain things will happen in history if we pray rightly.

C. Peter Wagner

The Beatitudes are God's recipe for revival.

Heidi Baker

There is no way that Christians, in a private capacity, can do so much to promote the work of God and advance the kingdom of Christ as by prayer.

Jonathon Edwards

We must never get away I from the fact that when Jesus built His Church He built a prayer meeting.

Armin Gesswein

Solid, lasting missionary work is done on our knees.

James Fraser

Pentecost didn't come through a preaching service; Pentecost came to a prayer service. From Pentecost to Patmos, God never departs from the pattern.

Armin Gesswein

Apostolic preaching cannot be carried on unless there be apostolic prayer. Men of God, before anything else, are indispensable to the furtherance of the kingdom of God on earth.

E.M. Bounds

As a large fire begins with kindling of small twigs and branches, even so a large revival is preceded by the prayers of a few hidden, seemingly insignificant souls.

Gary Amirault

Prayer is your way, often the only way, to water the harvest.

Wesley Duewel

When you join with others in prayer and you are not the speaker, let your heart be kept intent and watchful to the work, that you may pray so much the better when you are the mouth of others to God.

Isaac Watts

By prayer you can bring the Holy Spirit's blessing on any Gospel effort anywhere in the world.

Wesley Duewel

Our hunger for revival must go beyond our desire for a move of God. Revival is the result of us hungering for God Himself.

Bill Johnson

Nothing tends more to cement the hearts of Christians than praying together. Never do they love one another so well as when they witness the outpouring of each other's hearts in prayer.

Charles Finney

A man can pray better because of the prayers of the past; a man can live holier because of the prayers of the past; the man of many and acceptable prayers has done the truest and greatest service to the incoming generation.

E.M. Bounds

I shall see no hope until the individual members of the church are praying for revival, perhaps meeting in one anothers' homes, meeting in groups amongst friends, meeting together in churches, meeting anywhere you like, and praying with urgency and concentration for a shedding forth of the power of God... There is no hope until we do.

Martyn Lloyd-Jones

In prayer the Church has received power to rule the world. The Church is always the little flock. But if it would stand together on its knees, it would dominate world politics—from the prayer room.

O. Hallesby

What would happen to the Church if the Lord's Prayer became a test for membership as thoroughly as the Creeds have been?

P.T. Forsyth

[To see revival] we need to pray for breakthrough in private, but then take risks in public.

Bill Johnson

The coming revival must begin with a great revival of prayer. It is in the closet, with the door shut, that the sound of abundance of rain will first be heard. An increase of secret prayer with ministers will be the sure harbinger of blessing.

Andrew Murray

No church can be said to be fulfilling its ministry to any degree if it is not laying hold of the power of God through prayer.

Ivan French

Prayer is not so much the cause of a revival as the human preparation for one.

A.W. Tozer

The evangelization of the world depends first of all upon a revival of prayer. Deeper than the need for men - aye, deep down at the bottom of our spiritless life, is the need for the forgotten secret of prevailing, world-wide prayer.

Andrew Murray

Prayer is an activity that pushes against and hinders the forces working against the will of God being manifest in our life.

Lance Wallnau

There has never been a spiritual awakening in any country or locality that did not begin in united prayer.

A.T. Pierson

History is silent about revivals that did not begin with prayer.

Edwin Orr

God's greatest movements in this world have been conditioned on, continued and fashioned by prayer. God has put Himself in these great movements just as men have prayed.

E.M. Bounds

The condition of the church may be very accurately gauged by its prayer meetings. So is the prayer meeting a grace-ometer, and from it we may judge of the amount of divine working among a people. If God be near a church, it must pray. And if He be not there, one of die first tokens of His absence will be a slothfulness in prayer!
C.H. Spurgeon

Tragically, we have failed to realize that prayer is the launch pad of all ministry and without it we short-circuit God's chosen method of work.
Richard Burr

Every preacher who does not make prayer a mighty factor in his own life and ministry is weak as a factor in God's work and is powerless to project God's cause in this world.
E.M. Bounds

The great revivals didn't start with a program or plan. They started with a core of believers bound together in passionate prayer.
Matthew Prewett

True revival lives in prayer. Prayer draws power from revival. We need only to follow the way-marks of their remarkable history to be satisfied of their inseparable unity.
J.B. Johnson

Why is there so much working and activity in the Church and yet so little result in positive conversions to God? Why so much running hither and thither and so few brought to Christ? The answer is simple: There is not enough private prayer.
Henrietta Mears

While the greatest moves of God might start with the prayer of one, they're sustained by the prayers of many.
Steven Furtick

Revivals come to those cities and communities, which have believers who have taken up the holy work of intercession.
O. Hallesby

Sometimes I'm asked to list the most important steps in preparing for an evangelistic mission, and my reply is always the same: prayer . . . prayer . . . prayer.
Billy Graham

Prayerless pulpits will produce prayerless and powerless congregations.
Wesley Duewel

Every great movement of God can be traced to a kneeling figure.
D.L. Moody

9

ADDITIONAL RESOURCES FROM PRAYER COACH

7 Tips to a Better Prayer Life

People approach prayer from different perspectives. Some people have it so planned out that they tend to miss the spontaneous encounters with God. Others don't have a plan and try to live off other people's experiences. Some pray solely for the benefits, while others desire the fullness of God but decide to stay in the shallow in so not to be too different than others. I am not trying to put you into any particular box; I'm just setting up how people can get a better prayer life.

You may prefer to either pray for yourself, follow the success of others who your admire, or make up a plan. It's good to find what works for you. Here are 7 tips that you can add to your prayer map to help you know where you want to go.

1. Pray

> *"There is no way to learn to pray but by praying." – Samuel Chadwick*

This has been said hundred of times by many Godly people, but we will never grow in prayer if we don't pray. You can't wait until you have figured it all out before you start, prayer is something you need to practice and experiment with. Prayer takes you into the presence of God and it is in His presence that you take on His likeness and change your heart. You cannot live the life God planned for you without prayer because the things He has planned require His involvement which is found in prayer.

2. Rest

> *"Our rest lies in looking to the Lord, not to ourselves." – Watchman Nee*

Prayer reminds us that everything has been accomplished through Christ's death and resurrection. The work we now do is to apply what He has done to our world. "Consider yourself dead." Rest in the presence of God, in His goodness, and in His love for you. It is out of this confidence you can work out of rest. Prayer is not earning God's favor; it enters you into the favor He already has for you.

3. God's Face

> "We don't look at problems. Whatever you look at becomes bigger. We look at God." – Pastor Spinoza

Most of our prayers become pleas for God to act because we are so focused on what we want Him to do. To enhance our prayers we need to focus on God's face, see His love for us and see His confidence in the situation. By keeping our focus on God's face the things of this world will grow strangely dim.

4. God's Voice

> "Prayer is putting oneself in the hands of God, and listening to His voice in the depth of our hearts." – Mother Teresa

Prayer is communication with God, but too often we treat it as our monologue to Him. Without taking the time to listen to God's voice, we are not valuing His input and God's role in the relationship. Allow God a chance to talk. His words will always bring you life.

5. Joy

> "Joy makes way for hope, which leads to faith that creates the atmosphere for God's miraculous answers." – Kevin Shorter

I pulled joy out of the fruit of the Spirit because too many Christians have forgotten it is required. Prayer is to be enjoyed. You get to spend time with the One who created you and loves you. You get filled with purpose and direction in life. You find joy through prayer because it is one thing that you were specifically created for. If you don't find joy in prayer, go to a trusted friend who you can talk it over with. What you will find is that there is a lie you are believing about God that is stopping up the fount of joy.

6. Ask

> "God wants us to push the limits of what we can ask or imagine." – Steven Furtick

God is our Heavenly Father and is pleased when His children ask things of Him. He will not turn us away. Sure, He longs for the relationship, but asking things from Him can enhance that relationship. Asking shows a dependence on Him, a belief that He will come through for us, and a confidence that He is more than able.

7. Thanksgiving

> "Praise and thanksgiving not only open the gates of heaven for me to approach God, but also prepare a way for God to bless me." – The Kneeling Christian

Thanksgiving is a sign that we are filled with the Spirit. It is also the avenue to get filled. To be effective in prayer we are called to give thanks in all things. Gratitude opens the heart to receive more from God. By being thankful you are also more prone to see the fulfillment of the requests you have made to God, which encourages more prayer.

I pray that these 7 tips take you into deeper levels of prayer. You may not visit each area every time you pray, but these items added to your prayer map can show you the way to experience a better prayer life. God loves you and desires you to come to Him.

5 Ways to Find God

There is a story from Jesus' childhood where his parents left him in Jerusalem (Luke 2:41-52). His parents get a day out before realizing that he was not with them, and it takes another two days to find him. After leaving him alone for three days, his mother shames him by blaming him for going missing. Jesus response was very direct: "you knew I would be about my father's business."

Here is a very interesting exchange. Substituting God for Jesus, this can be restated as following: Mary misplaces God and then blames Him for going missing. God then responds to Mary, you knew where I would be found.

Too often we get too preoccupied with our own thoughts and priorities, we don't notice when God has moved to something else or is no longer with us. When we do notice Him not there, we question where He has gone as if it was His decision for us to be separated.

A Christian without the presence of God is in a frightful place. Our life, security, and success all come from God going with us. This is why Moses told God, "if your presence doesn't go with us, don't send us from here" (Exodus 33:15). If you feel alone from God, try these five suggestions to bring you back into His presence.

1. Go look for something that only He can do.

This is something I got from Henry Blackaby's Experiencing God, and it has helped me frequently. There are things man can do and things that God can do, but God likes to do things that only He can do through me and you. As we gravitate toward activities that only God can do, He opens Himself to us to be used by Him and engaged with Him.

2. Take risks.

God is attracted to faith (Hebrews 11:6). Faith is expressed through believing in God over what we can see. When we move toward people and engage with them about God's love for them, God shows up. We can talk to them about the love of God expressed through salvation, financial provisions, release from depression, physical healings, satisfaction of dreams, etc. God cares deeply about people and when we choose faith that God is going to show up over what looks impossible, God is greatly pleased.

3. Be still and rest.

Sometimes we are too stressed to hear what God is trying to say. We need to cease from striving and wait on the Lord. Relax. Listen to some worship music or just be silent. Think about God's love for you. He adores you and will be attracted to your heart opening up to Him (James 4:8).

4. Read the Bible.

This is not meant to be a way to force God's hand, but we can allow our heart to engage and be transformed by the reading of the Scriptures. When we approach the Bible with the attitude of finding God, He can renew our minds to correct misinterpretations of God's ways. Then we are opened up to be enlightened to where God is working in our lives now.

5. Pray with friends.

We are not meant to walk this life alone. God oftentimes makes us need others to enlarge His joy. He loves the unity of His children, and He will speak to us through others because it delights Him. It is in unity that God bestows blessings (Psalm 133). It is not meant to only be us and God. Are you looking for God? He could be hiding in the presence of another.

This is not meant to be a complete list, but I hope it gives you some tracks to ride on. God wants to be found. He says if we seek Him we will find Him. At the same time, He will not prostitute Himself by giving Himself freely to those who are not wanting to commit to Him. God wants to be pursued, and He wants to be found.

4 Ways to Effectively Pray for Others

As followers of Jesus, we are called to love our neighbors as ourselves and therefore are given a heart for their betterment. We desire those we come in contact with to know God better and be successful in all they do. The tool God gives us to powerfully love them is prayer.

God allows access to His limitless power through prayer. His heart is for us to partner with Him for the advancement of heaven on earth. However, prayer is often misunderstood and set aside. Paul gives us a glimpse of how to effectively pray for others in the book of Colossians. He writes how he is always in prayer for them (1:3). He tells the church to also pray for him (4:3). And, he publicly praises Epaphras for always wrestling in prayer for the Colossians (4:12).

What are we to pray for? How are we to always be in prayer? Do we continue to read over the prayer requests? How do you pray for others? Here is a list of four ways to effectively pray for others.

1. Thank God for Them

Paul says that he always thanks God for the Colossians when he prays for them (Colossians 1:3). Nothing releases the flow of Holy Spirit over your life than being thankful. You can never go wrong with this step. Thanksgiving reminds you of your love for them. Love is the fuel for effective prayers. Allow your thankfulness lead you toward focusing on God's heart for them.

2. Listen to What God Says

Paul has specific requests He prays for the Colossians. He prays that they may live a life worthy of the Lord and may please Him in every way (Colossians 1:9-10). However, this was not his standard prayer for every church. While he may have wanted this for every church, we don't see him praying it elsewhere. In fact, to the Ephesians he prays something completely different. There he prays for the spirit of wisdom and for the eyes of the heart enlightened (Ephesians 1:17-18).

God alone knows what everyone needs. As we come into His presence through thanksgiving, ask Him what we are to pray and write down what He shows you. Even if you don't get specific prayers, there is nothing more powerful than spending time in God's presence with other people on your heart. Devote yourselves to prayer, being watchful and thankful (Colossians 4:2).

3. Consider Their Prayer Requests

The other people you want to pray for may have given you prayer requests. These requests give you a glimpse into what is going on for them. Paul asked the Colossians to pray for specific things. He wanted God to open a door for his ministry and for him to proclaim it clearly, making the most of every opportunity (Colossians 4:3-5).

Honor their requests by praying them before the Lord. Don't worry if these requests are different than what you got in your time with the Lord. Paul prayed something different for the Colossians than Epaphras. Epaphras prayed for them to stand firm in all the will of God, mature, and fully assured (Colossians 4:12). The point is not so much about getting the wording right as it is about spending time with God and bring others into His presence. God wants to connect with your heart. If you bring others to Him on your heart, He will translate that prayer into what is best for them.

4. It's Not All About You

Now that you have gotten things to pray for, you may be tempted to just pray through those requests. Remember God is the only one who knows what they need. While those requests may have been needed last week, God may have something different for you to pray today. Allow your focus to be on Him to direct your prayers. If you don't have any other specific directions, then by all means continue the last known path.

How do you pray for others? Simply by spending time with your Heavenly Father and taking those you love into His presence. If you can do this, you will know what words to pray when words are necessary. May your prayers for others see exponential increase in their effectiveness.

2 Truths to Revolutionize Your Prayers

My college roommate, Larry, loved Jesus. In fact he loved Him so much that many of my Christian friends found him a bit odd. Sometimes it felt Larry was in his own little world with just him and Jesus. We would be together than Larry would spontaneously laugh. When questioned, he would just say Jesus told him a joke. Several times he would just walk away from the group in mid-conversation. When he returned he would tell us that Jesus told him to go talk to someone. Larry either loved and had a special relationship with Jesus, or he was crazy.

As Larry's roommate, I saw a lot of him. He was definitely quirky but not at all crazy. He did have a special relationship with Jesus and his life bore that fruit. He wanted everyone to know Jesus. Within one semester's time, he had individually shared Jesus with everyone in our dorm, over 500 people.

1. Obedience is Evidence of Our Love for God.

When we love Jesus, we do things He wants us to do. It is not an effort to earn favor with God, but it is evidence of our love. "Show me your faith without deeds, and I will show you my faith by what I do" (James 2:18). Our obedience is to be an overflow of love. Jesus said, "If anyone loves Me, he will obey My teaching" (John 14:23). If we are obeying God's commands, we are positioned to abide in God's love. To say this differently, if we are intentionally not obeying God's commands, we are declaring we don't trust in God's goodness or His love for us.

How does this apply to prayer? Oftentimes we are praying for God to act when He has sent us to be the answer. The disciples saw the crowd in Bethsaida and asked Jesus to send them away so they could find food. Jesus responds for the disciples to feed the people (Luke 9:10-13). Our prayers generally ask God to heal loved ones, pull them out of bad situations, or lead them to the Gospel. Again, this is what He sent us out to do (Luke 9:1-2). We will find greater freedom in prayer if we don't ask God to move as much as we ask how He wants us to step forward in faith.

2. Revelation is Evidence of God's Love for Us.

The second point that gives freedom to prayers is knowing that God reveals things to those He loves. Many of us think it is hard to hear from God. Either He no longer speaks or He only speaks on special occasions to special people. The Bible tells us that the evidence of God's love is Him revealing to you Himself and what He does (John 5:20). Out of love He opens His heart to us that we may become more intimate with Him. He wants to reveal to those He loves what He plans, what He thinks, and what He enjoys.

He shares secrets, jokes, music, poetry, friends, etc. He intends to be a real friend, not some distant God. If you love Jesus, you will be loved by the Father, and Jesus will also love you and show Himself to you (John 14:21). If you have said yes to Jesus and opened your heart to Him, He sees your love and wants to start revealing more of Himself to you. You don't have to struggle to hear God speak. His desire to communicate is greater than our lack of ability to hear. We have open access to His throne. He invites us to come.

Prayer is meant to be a partnership where we exchange our hearts, ideas, desires, and our entire lives with one another. Prayer becomes exciting when we stop trying to make God act and instead listen to Him speak. He doesn't always share those earth-shattered truths that just blow you away and leave you trembling. More than often, He just tells you how much He likes you. He may share something He thinks is funny to get you to laugh.

The life of my college roommate, Larry, is not meant to be abnormal. God wants to be a close, personal confidant with you. As you start to allow these two truths to sink into your mind and actions, they will revolutionize your prayers. No longer will prayer be a struggle, but you will walk in the privilege of communication with God. Abiding in God's love will no longer be a foreign concept; it will be a foundational truth where the rest of your life will hang. Let's let our love grow and God's love to become more evident.

10

PRAYER LISTS

10 Things to Pray for Your Husband

1. Grant him more than enough income to provide for your family.
2. Give him success in all that he puts his hands to.
3. Recharge him at home more than at work or play.
4. Help him develop friendships with other men that would encourage, validate, bless, and focus him on who God says he is.
5. May he see you as his helpmate and may you be his best friend, supporter, and lover (Proverbs 5:18-19).
6. Make your image the model of beauty for him. (This is a concept I got from Gary Thomas' book, Sacred Marriage)
7. Help him to know that you believe in him, trust his decisions for the family, and are proud of what he is able to accomplish at work.
8. May both of you take every opportunity to bless each other and allow the Holy Spirit to be the one to convict of sin.
9. Allow him to truly enjoy time with Jesus and look to Him for direction and life to give to the family.
10. Open his eyes to God's plan for his life. May the plan he was created for and would stir up energy and passion in him.

10 Things to Pray for Your Wife

(from Proverbs 31)

1. Make her of noble character (v. 10).
2. Bless the work of her hands (v. 12-14).
    - Help me to always show my confidence in her (v. 11).
3. Give her compassion for the poor and needy (v. 20).
4. Lead her into what is best for the children (v. 21).
5. Help her love me, even when I don't deserve it, to encourage greatness in me (v. 23).
6. Give her confidence in You, O Lord (v. 25).
7. Let the words of her mouth be wisdom directly from You (v. 26).
    - May the children and I never cease to praise her (v. 28).
8. Put in her a healthy fear of You (v. 30) and may she experience the joy of the Lord.
9. May the work she does give You honor and give her joy (v. 31).
10. May others see Your beauty reflected in her (v. 31).

10 Things to Pray for Your Marriage

1. We willingly choose each other every day. We recommit in our hearts our covenant to each other.
2. We willingly sacrifice for each other (John 15:13). We will choose to help the other succeed in becoming the person God created them to be.
3. We will use our words to encourage and not tear down. Our communication will be bathed in love and free from anger. We will only speak well of each other to others (Ephesians 4:29).
4. Grant us every blessing You have in store within marriage for us (Ephesians 1:3).
5. We will not withhold our love from each other, whether in small every day choices or in sex. We will choose to use sex only to show our love for each other, not to force anything from our spouse (1 Corinthians 7:3-5).
6. We will delight only in our spouse in words, actions, thoughts, and fantasies (James 1:13-15).
7. We will be fully ourselves with each other – no hiding, masks, or shame. We will choose to fully be ourselves, so we can fully love each other as we are (Psalm 139:14).
8. We will keep no records of wrongs on each other. We will choose to allow mistakes in the past to be forgiven, so we can fully love our spouse in the present (1 Corinthians 3:5).
9. We will be one as in the unity between God the Father, God the Son, and God the Holy Spirit (Genesis 2:24 & John 17:22).
10. May our love be a witness to those around us for the love of Christ (Ephesians 5:25-32).

10 Things to Pray for Your Kids

1. Lord, may they never remember a time when they didn't love You or know that You love them.
2. May they become all You created them to be, growing up and developing in Your timing.
3. May they enjoy life knowing that You enjoy them.
4. May they be kind and loving toward others.
5. May they always know that we love them and believe in them.
6. May they see themselves as You see them, knowing You have great plans for their lives and have given them all they need to accomplish them.
7. May You protect them from the ways of the world that would try to pull their hearts away from You.
8. May they always believe You for great things.
9. May they easily hear You speaking to them and will go wherever You lead.
10. May they have the courage to live from their hearts.

As you pray for your kids these prayers, you may think you need to add a few for yourself. So here are 5 extra bonus prayer points:

1. Lord, may our marriage give our kids an example for what they want when they marry and a hope for what they can have with Jesus.
2. May we build into them everything they need from us to prepare them to accomplish all they were created to do.
3. May we help them build off our success and learn from our failures.
4. May we fully love You from our hearts and not ask anything from our kids that we are not willing to do as well.
5. May they see themselves as an overflow of our love for each other. May they know they are significant to us, but not crucial to our relationship with each other.

10 Things to Pray for Your Pastor

1. He will first take care of his wife and family.
    - God can get someone else to lead your church; He can't get anyone else to lead his family.
2. His primary purpose of meeting with God would be to know Him better and not only to lead the church better.
    - If the church is removed from Him, will he still love God?
3. He will lead from real experience with God and not just information he has learned.
4. He will lead the church close to God and not just devoted to the church or church activities.
5. He will be free to lead the church as he feels God lead him with respectful counsel from trusted friends and prayer partners.
    - He will know perfection is not expected but passion for Jesus is. He will also know he is not alone, nor is God only talking to him.
6. He will be protected from pride and only go after projects God has specifically laid before for him and the church.
7. Each week he will aim to lead people to Jesus.
    - This is not just an altar call, but a real, deep encounter with our God.
8. He will have a group of men around him that know him well and believe in him.
    - May he share with them his dreams, passions, struggles, and mistakes. This is not an accountability group but men who will remind him of what God says about him.
9. He will feel free to have a life outside of church — for his sanity and for the sake of his family.
10. May the power and love of God flow into every area he touches.

11

ABOUT PRAYER COACH

The Prayer Coach blog was start in 2009 with the purpose of drawing people into the heart of God. Prayer is the greatest tool God has given us for life by connecting us to our life, power, and provisions. However, most Christians point to prayer as their greatest area of weakness in their Christian life.

At the Prayer Coach blog, we believe that when we see God for who He is and how He loves us, spending time with Him in prayer would be a natural overflow. The problem arises in that we don't see God for who He is because life and misunderstandings have blurred our perception. By addressing these misconceptions, we can enter into the joy of our relationship with God. You can follow the Prayer Coach on the blog, Twitter, or Facebook.

An overflow of the writings of the Prayer Coach has been the ministry of Josiah's Covenant. The desire to show people that God wants to be intimately involved in their lives became a growing desire for a specific group of people: teenage orphan girls in China. Women without education, skills, or family are at high risk of falling into human trafficking. Josiah's Covenant has a farm in China where we actively become a family to these girls, supplement their education, and give them skills they can use to find jobs. You can find out more at JosiahsCovenant.com.

If you enjoyed this book, please consider giving a review or sharing it with your friends.

Other Books by the Prayer Coach Family:

Creative Intercession: How Simplicity, Fun, and Art Can Move the Hand of God

- This book helps reduce the journey to freedom by:
    1. Reminding you of God's heart for your life.
    2. Identifying the roots of addiction.
    3. Finding tactics to remove the addiction.
    4. Seeing addiction from God's perspective.

Breaking Free: How to Be Completely Free from any Addition

- Partnering with God doesn't have to be burdensome or make you weary. Come take a new adventure with Jesus and learn how to use everyday things like cooking, working, and hobbies to intercede for others. You will add power to your life and in the process enjoy a fun God!

Academy of Powerful Caregivers: The Motivation of a Caregiver

- As a caregiver or someone in the helps profession, you desire to make an effective change for the better. Delays, roadblocks, discouraging people steal our focus turn our genuine desire to help into just a job or service you are providing. Get your power back in your role to help others.

Church Search: How to Get Your Ministry to Show Up on Search Engines by Kevin Shorter

- Churches and ministries are missing free advertising and prospective visitors by neglecting search engine optimization for their website. Church Search will lead you through practical steps to get your ministry to show up in search engines and lead to new visitors.

DEDICATION

I dedicate this book to my girls, Rachel and Elizabeth. I am grateful to have you both in my life. May every bit of insight and experience that I have gained from compiling, thinking, and editing all of this information on prayer be a well that you can freely draw from. My prayer for the two of you is that you will never know a time that you don't know and love God.

Endnotes

There are over 500 authors quoted in this book. I have limited the background to just those authors whom we have included over 20 quotes.

- **Steve & Wendy Backlund** are leaders of Igniting Hope Ministries which is dedicated to igniting hope, joy, and personal victory through renewing the mind with Truth. * ignitinghope.com
- **Mark Batterson** is lead pastor of National Community Church in Washington, D.C and author of several books including the Circle Maker on prayer. * markbatterson.com
- **John Blanchard** is an internationally known Christian preacher, teacher, apologist and author from Britain. * johnblanchard.org
- **Shawn Bolz** and his wife are also the founders of Bolz Ministries, created to inspire and empower God's love around the world, and he wrote Translating God on helping people to hear God for themselves. * bolzministries.com
- **Dietrich Bonhoeffer** was a German pastor, theologian and anti-Nazi dissident. The Cost of Discipleship is recognized as a modern classic.
- **Reinhard Bonnke** a German-born evangelist committed to bringing Christ throughout Africa. * http://reinhardbonnke.com
- **E.M. Bounds** was an early 1900s pastor and author who wrote nine books on prayer.
- **John Calvin** was a French theologian, pastor and reformer in Switzerland during the Protestant Reformation and developed a system of theology called Calvinism.
- **Samuel Chadwick** was an early twentieth century English pastor who wrote the *Path of Prayer*.
- **Oswald Chambers** was a Scottish evangelist and teacher, best known for his work, *My Utmost for His Highest*. * utmost.org
- **Graham Cooke** is a British speaker and author with a focus seeing God as the kindest person you'll meet. * http://brilliantperspectives.com
- **Jim Cymbala** is pastor of Brooklyn Tabernacle in Brooklyn, New York and author of several books including *Fresh Wind, Fresh Fire*. * brooklyntabernacle.org
- **Wesley Duewel** was a missionary to India for 25 years and wrote several books, emphasizing prayer as the key to revival.
- **P.T. Forsyth** was a Scottish theologian and pastor who was committed to bringing grace back to theology of his time.
- **Richard Foster** is an author of the modern classic, The Celebration of Discipline and founded the renewal ministry, Renovaré. * renovare.org
- **Billy Graham** is a Christian statesman and evangelist widely considered the most influential Christian of the twentieth century. * billygraham.org
- **Jeanne "Madame" Guyon** was a French mystic from the early 1700s. She was imprisoned for her beliefs after writing, *A Short and Easy Method of Prayer*.
- **O. Hallesby** was a leading Norwegian theologian and educator writing the book, *Prayer*.
- **Jack Hayford** is the founder of King's College and Seminary in Dallas, Texas and the former senior pastor of the Church on the Way in Van Nuys, California. * jackhayford.org
- **Hannah Hurnard** was a Christian author and missionary to Palestine/Israel for 50 years. She is best known for her book, *Hinds' Feet on High Places*.

- **Bill Hybels** founded and is the senior pastor of Willow Creek Community Church in South Barrington, Illinois. He also founded the Willow Creek Association to encourage and support Christian leaders. * willowcreek.org
- **Bill & Beni Johnson** - are Charismatic speakers, authors, and senior pastors at Bethel Church in Redding, California. * bjm.org
- **Tim Keller** is the founding pastor of Redeemer Presbyterian Church in New York City, New York and has authored several books, including *Prayer: Experiencing Awe and Intimacy with God*.
- **The Kneeling Christian** is a popular book written under the name, "Unknown Christian."
- **Brother Lawrence** served in a monastery in Paris, France and is remembered for his book, *The Practice of the Presence of God*.
- **Max Lucado** is a popular Christian author with over 100 books and several on the New York Times Bestseller lists. * maxlucado.com
- **Martin Luther** was a German professor of theology and the central figure of the Protestant Reformation.
- **Andrew Murray** was a South African pastor and a champion of the South African Revival of 1860. He wrote many books including, *With Christ in the School of Prayer*.
- **Watchman Nee** was a Chinese teacher and church leader and was imprisoned during the Communist Revolution in China. * watchmannee.org
- **Leonard Ravenhill** was an English evangelist with a particular interest in church revival history.
- **R.C. Sproul** is founder of Ligonier Ministries and the international radio show, Renewing Your Mind. * ligonier.org
- **C.H. Spurgeon** was a famous British preacher, often labeled as the Prince of Preachers.
- **R.A. Torrey** was an American pastor and evangelist who preached in every country of the English-speaking world.
- **A.W. Tozer** was pastor of Southside Alliance Church in Chicago, Illinois and author of several books including, *The Pursuit of God*.
- **Kris Vallotton** is a senior leader at Bethel Church in Redding, CA and regularly trains people in the prophetic. * krisvallotton.com
- **Rick Warren** is the founder and senior pastor of Saddleback Church in Lake Forest, California. He is best known for his book, *The Purpose-Driven Life*. * pastorrick.com
- **Smith Wigglesworth** was a British evangelist known for his healing ministry. * smithwigglesworth.com
- **Andrew Wommack** is an American evangelist and teacher and has his own radio show, *Gospel Truth*. He wrote several books including, *A Better Way to Pray*. * awmi.net

www.ingramcontent.com/pod-product-compliance
Lightning Source LLC
Chambersburg PA
CBHW022100090426
42743CB00008B/661